THE LINCOLN
No One Knows

THE LINCOLN

THE
MYSTERIOUS
MAN WHO RAN
THE CIVIL WAR

No One Knows

WEBB GARRISON

RUTLEDGE HILL PRESS®
NASHVILLE, TENNESSEE
A THOMAS NELSON COMPANY

Published by Rutledge Hill Press, a Thomas Nelson Company, P.O. Box 141000, Nashville, Tennessee 37214.

Typography by D&T/Bailey, Nashville, Tennessee
Design by Harriette Bateman, Studio Six

Library of Congress Cataloging-in-Publication Data

Garrison, Webb B.
    The Lincoln no one knows : the mysterious man who ran
the Civil War / Webb Garrison.
      p. cm.
    Includes bibliographical references (p.   ) and index.
    ISBN 1-55853-847-X (pbk)
    1. Lincoln, Abraham, 1809–1865. I. Title.
E457.G26 1992
973.7'092—dc20   92–32431
                                                CIP

Printed in the United States of America
1 2 3 4 5 6 7 8 9 — 05 04 03 02 01

To Mary
as a tiny token of
lasting love and gratitude

Clean-shaven Abraham Lincoln prior to his presidency.
[AUTHOR'S COLLECTION]

CONTENTS

■

**Part Four: Unanswered Questions Lurk in the Shadow of the
     Executive Mansion**

Part Five: Nancy Hanks's Son Was a Cluster of Unsolved Riddles

PREFACE

■

Major libraries include dozens of shelves crammed with books about Abraham Lincoln. Hence it would seem that every question concerning his life, his consuming ideals, and his decision-making process could be answered with certainty.

Perhaps the sheer abundance of material is deceptive. While we know with reasonable accuracy most things he did in his public life, his motives and goals were seldom revealed. His life as a private citizen includes many enigmas and unanswered questions. While bulky, indeed, primary source materials give hardly any clear clues concerning the inner life of a man who seemed almost to pride himself upon being secretive.

This volume does not attempt to provide clear answers to questions about the "president no one knows." Rather, it seeks to raise questions to which a variety of responses may be more or less plausible. Often, no suggested solution to a mystery seems acceptable; here, you are encouraged to fashion your own.

In order to see how many big gaps there are in the Lincoln story, you are invited to examine at least part of his verbal output. When you do so, you will quickly come to realize that the same set of words, presented in different visual form, sometimes conveys different sets of connotations.

By all means, spend some time with the ninety-seven-reel microfilm Lincoln *Papers* (see Bibliography for this and other listings). If you delve into the early two-volume edition of his works issued by one of his secretaries, be sure to compare it with the later ten-volume collection edited by John G. Nicolay and John Hay. Roy P. Basler's nine-volume *Collected Works* and supplements is an essential tool in any attempt to understand the Great Emancipator, but other anthologies and collections are often suggestive and revealing.

No one knows with certainty what Abraham Lincoln, public speaker par excellence, meant when he underlined a word or a phrase. Indeed, significance of this practice may have varied from a signal ("Shout!") to a reminder ("Stop for a moment of silence" or "Lift hands to heaven").

Lincoln's manuscripts are replete with dashes, commonly used in lieu of periods to indicate ends of sentences. But to the writer, many may have signified "Emphasis," "Short pause," or "Insert a story here." At its best, translation of such material into print includes many conjectures.

His penmanship is remarkably clear and uniform. Yet, skilled as he was in the use of words, self-taught Lincoln never mastered spelling. For the sake of readability, such usages as his "verry" for "very," "pettitioners" for petitioners," "horid" for "horrid," and "melancholly" for "melancholy" have been brought into standard form. Lincoln's "New-salem" is rendered "New Salem," and his "burthens" here appears as "burdens." Also for the sake of clarity, some extraneous articles and connectives have been omitted, and quotations have occasionally been slightly edited.

All quotations from letters, telegrams, proclamations, dispatches, debates, and other speeches are from primary sources (See Bibliography). An early version of this volume, meticulously annotated, became so replete with footnotes that its physical appearance was forbidding to the audience for which it was written. Should specialists in Lincolnana browse through these pages, they should have little difficulty in locating the exact sources of all quotations.

Because of the extraordinary complexity of the life of the mysterious man from Illinois and the war he masterminded, I sought and received help with the manuscript. Thomas F. Schwartz, curator of the Henry Horner Lincoln Collection of the Illinois State Historical Society, and James M. McPherson of the Department of History, Princeton University, read all 575 pages of the manuscript with scrupulous care. They pointed out errors of fact but did not comment upon the viewpoints and conclusions expressed.

Over a period of years, I have tried to assimilate tens of thousands of pages—both as Lincoln wrote them and as editors have translated his words into printed pages. This odyssey has not produced greater understanding of the inner man, but less. I now find this most forceful of all chief executives to be much more mysterious than he seemed at the beginning of my lengthy quest. Perhaps the volume resulting from it will lead you to re-examine some of your own views concerning the enigmatic figure who dominated the Civil War from Fort Sumter to Appomattox. For good or for ill, the impact of Nancy Hank's son shaped the subsequent course of our nation—with far-reaching effects upon my life and yours.

—WEBB GARRISON

THE LINCOLN
No One Knows

PART ONE

■

*Half a Century
Punctuated
with Baffling
Questions*

A tiny log cabin with breakway chimney, dwarfed by the protective structure built to contain it, is a Kentucky tourist attraction—allegedly once the home of the Thomas Lincoln family.

1

*What Blood Ran Through
the Veins of*

THE MAN WHO REMEMBERED KNOB CREEK?

■

"FOR CERTAIN REASONS," mused Abraham Lincoln, "illegitimate children are oftentimes sturdier and brighter than those born in lawful wedlock."

Kentucky-born William H. Herndon, who was Lincoln's law partner from 1844 until his death, vividly remembered having heard that comment a number of times. About 1850 he began to think he understood why the man with whom he was so closely associated seemed to brood over this matter.

In a rare mood of talkativeness about his background, Lincoln confided to his partner that Nancy Hanks, his mother, "was the illegitimate daughter of Lucy Hanks and a well-bred Virginia farmer or planter." It was vital, he told Herndon, that this matter be kept secret.

With the two lawyers working jointly on a Menard circuit court case that required a discussion of heredity, Lincoln turned to his partner:

> "Billy, I'll tell you something, but keep it a secret while I live. My mother was a bastard, was the daughter of a nobleman so called of Virginia. My mother's mother was poor and credulous, etc., and she was shamefully taken advantage of by the man. My mother inherited his qualities and I hers.
>
> "All that I am or hope ever to be I got from my mother, God bless her. Did you never notice that bastards are generally smarter, shrewder, and more intellectual than others? Is it because it is stolen?"

William H. Herndon, Lincoln's long-time law partner who claimed to have learned secrets from him. [NICOLAY & HAY, *ABRAHAM LINCOLN*]

This is a substantial statement made to me by Lincoln just on a hot overlapping spring creek on the road to Petersburg two and a half miles west of this city about 1851.

According to Herndon, Lincoln drew significant conclusions from knowledge that his mother was born out of wedlock. His unknown grandfather, he suggested, must have been the source of his own "power of analysis, logic, mental activity, ambition, and all the qualities that distinguished him from other members and descendants of the Hanks family."

Doubtless he speculated about that unknown grandfather, but he never gave a hint concerning his guess about identity. William E. Barton made a detailed investigation of the lineage of the president whom he revered and in 1929 published a book in which he concluded that Nancy Hanks was descended from the Lees of Virginia. According to him, that meant Abraham Lincoln and Robert E. Lee were distantly related. Barton's conclusion is pure speculation; Woodrow Wilson may have been closer to the mark. Writing of his predecessor, Wilson said he "came of the most unpromising stock on the continent, the 'poor white trash' of the South."

While Lincoln's ancestry is not fully known, yet even deeper riddles center in the matter of the paternity of the man who considered his unusual gifts to be inherited from his Virginia grandfather. Herndon insisted that when his long-time partner fell victim to John Wilkes Booth, he believed *himself* to be illegitimate.

On the heels of having become the Republican nominee for the presidency, Abraham Lincoln may have decided to put ugly rumors to rest. To quash stories that he didn't know the name of his father, he corresponded with circuit clerk Samuel Haycraft of Elizabethtown, Kentucky.

Initial correspondence has been lost, but Lincoln's follow-up of May 28, 1860, has been preserved. In it he told the Kentucky official that he was the son of Thomas Lincoln and Nancy Hanks—rather than Sarah Bush Johnston (second wife of Thomas)—as Haycraft had assumed. His earliest memories, he wrote, centered upon a farm on Knob Creek in Hardin County (now Larue). His primary purpose in contacting a man he'd never seen, but whose handwriting he said he instantly recognized, was to obtain copies of the records concerning the marriage of his father and mother.

After a diligent search that seems to have extended into adjoining counties, Haycraft reported that he couldn't find the all-important documents. Ward Hill Lamon, who was intimately acquainted with Lincoln and who provided the material for an 1872 biography, considered the marriage to have been a common law agreement.

Thomas and Sarah Lincoln moved to this cabin on Goose-nest prairie near Farmington, Illinois. Abraham, who owned the land, did not visit Thomas during his terminal illness. [NICOLAY & HAY, ABRAHAM LINCOLN]

"The license and the minister's return in the case of [Thomas] Lincoln and Sarah Johnston, his second wife," according to the Lamon biography, "were easily found in the place where the law required them to be; but of Nancy Hanks's marriage there exists no evidence but that of mutual acknowledgement and cohabitation."

Uncertainty about what blood flowed through his veins may account for Lincoln's near-pathological reticence concerning his background.

David Davis, who rode the legal circuit with him long before managing his 1860 political campaign, called his friend "the most reticent, secretive man I ever saw or hope to see." Herndon added that he "never poured out his soul to any mortal creature at any time." That made him, according to his partner, "the most secretive—reticent—man that ever existed."

Charles H. Ray, owner of a controlling interest in the Chicago *Tribune*, sensed in 1858 that Lincoln would soon become nationally prominent. He requested material for a short biography and received a flat, blunt, and final refusal.

Chicago journalist John L. Scripps fared only a trifle better upon his first encounter with the up-and-coming political figure. Having expressed a strong desire for information with which to prepare a campaign biography, the writer was told by Lincoln:

"Why, Scripps, it is a great piece of folly to attempt to make anything out of me or my early life. It can all be condensed into a single sentence, and that you will find in Gray's Elegy:

'The short and simple annals of the poor.'

That's my life, and that's all you or anyone else can make out of it."

He later relented and provided for Scripps a brief autobiography destined to be published by the New York *Tribune*. Years later, the journalist remembered:

"Mr. Lincoln communicated some facts to me about his ancestry, which he did not wish published and which I have never spoken of or alluded to before. I do not think, however, that Dennis Hanks, if he knows anything about these matters, would be very likely to say any thing about them."

If anyone knew secrets, it was Dennis Hanks. Also a native of Hardin County, he is thought to have been the illegitimate son of an earlier Nancy Hanks, who was the aunt of Lincoln's mother. Ten years older than Abraham, he moved into the Lincoln cabin just north of the Ohio River in 1818. Measuring sixteen feet by eighteen feet, the cabin now commemorated at Indiana's Lincoln Boyhood Park may have had a single window. Inside, it included an overhead ledge, or loft, not far above head level.

About the time Dennis moved in, Lincoln's mother died of "milk sickness." The man destined for the presidency later said he knew

Dennis Hanks, Abraham's older cousin who bedded with him in the loft of the tiny cabin in which he is believed to have been born. [NICOLAY & HAY, *ABRAHAM LINCOLN*]

nothing of his mother's background, and of her remembered little except having carved pegs for her coffin. It was his stepmother whom he called Mother and always lauded.

Within a year of Nancy Hanks's death, the former Sarah Bush— now the widow Johnston—became Thomas Lincoln's second wife. From Kentucky she brought with her two daughters and a son: Elizabeth, Matilda, and John. With Dennis Hanks included, eight persons lived in a 288-square-foot cabin on Little Pigeon Creek, not far from Gentryville, Indiana.

Abraham and his cousin used pegs driven into the wall in order to climb into the loft where they slept—perhaps sent there to separate them from Sarah's daughters.

Herndon, who contacted every person he could find who had known the Lincoln family during Abraham's boyhood, received strange reports. Numerous correspondents told him that Thomas Lincoln—short, stout, and "tightly built and compact"—couldn't possibly have been the father of six-foot, four-inch Abraham; he was incapable of getting a child. One writer said he was a victim of mumps. Another was sure that one or both testicles had not developed properly. Charles Friend, a pioneer resident of Hardin County, insisted that Thomas Lincoln had been castrated, though he didn't know when.

Herndon considered it beyond dispute that Thomas was sterile. No one knows how many babies Sarah produced during her ten-year marriage to Dan Johnston; three of them survived and went to Indiana with their new stepfather. But after she became the wife of Lincoln at age thirty-one, she gave birth no more.

Abraham and an older sister Sarah, about whom hardly anything is known, were the children of Nancy Hanks. But to pioneer biographers intimately acquainted with the Civil War president, that didn't mean they were sired by Thomas Lincoln. Hardin County gossip, preserved as a result of Herndon's inquiries, said that Thomas returned to his cabin earlier than expected one evening. When he found his wife in bed with Abraham Enlow (or Inlow), they had a furious fight. In the course of it, Lincoln bit off the end of Enlow's nose.

Familiarity with the Enlow story, according to which he may have been the son of a miller, is one explanation for the future president's attitude toward Thomas. Soon after Abraham left home, Thomas— who didn't attend Abraham's wedding—was virtually erased from his life. When informed that Thomas was on his death bed, Abraham found it inconvenient to pay a final visit. When he died, Abraham did not go to the funeral.

Most surviving letters that passed between the two deal with financial woes of Thomas. Once, when he faced the loss of yet another parcel of land, Congressman Lincoln sent him from Washington twenty dollars plus a scolding. When he learned that Thomas and Sarah were destitute, Abraham bought 200 acres of land and gave them use of it.

Reluctantly providing biographical notes to Jesse Fell in 1859, Abraham Lincoln wrote of Thomas only that he was "a wandering laboring boy." After telling Scripps the same thing, the man who was then a candidate for the presidency, continued:

". . . [Thomas] grew up literally without education. He never did more in writing than to bunglingly sign his own name."

Hard facts are few and far between, while intriguing questions abound. Oral tradition includes nearly a dozen stories concerning Lincoln's paternity. Nearly two centuries after he was born, these tales continue to circulate in Kentucky, North Carolina, and South Carolina.

According to them, three of the most likely candidates for having fathered Abraham Lincoln are: Samuel Davis of Kentucky, father of Jefferson Davis; John C. Calhoun of South Carolina, whose nullification doctrine paved the way for secession; and prosperous teacher-merchant Abraham Enloe of western North Carolina.

For professional Lincoln scholars, all such tales were laid to rest by a little-known official of Washington County, Kentucky. About thirteen years after the death of the president, W. F. Booker made headlines throughout the nation. He announced that, as clerk of court in Springfield, he had spent months going through piles of loose documents. Finally he discovered a June 10, 1806, marriage bond signed

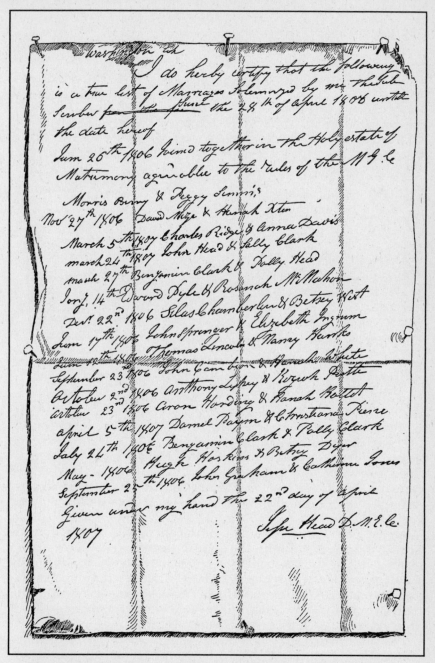

Facsimile (decorated by artist) of the "marriage return" by the Rev. Jesse Head, discovered about 1886 by W. F. Booker, clerk of Washington County, Kentucky, in a pile of loose documents and never subjected to expert scrutiny. [BARTON, THE PATERNITY OF LINCOLN]

Facsimile (decorated by artist) of the marriage bond of Thomas Lincoln. [BARTON, THE PATERNITY OF LINCOLN]

by Thomas Lincoln and by Richard Berry, guardian of Nancy Hanks.

He also reported having discovered an April 22, 1807, "marriage return" by Methodist circuit rider Jesse Head—turned in later because laws of the time did not require the records that later became standard. Head's list, not in chronological order, certified that on June 12, 1806, he performed the marriage of Thomas Lincoln and Nancy Hanks.

Booker later issued a formal certification of authenticity concerning the document from the hand of Head. Louis A. Warren and R. Gerald McMurtry later confirmed Booker's statement on the basis of having examined specimens of Jesse Head's signature. No holographic materials by Head, which could be compared with the "marriage return," are known to exist.* In the absence of contrary evidence, however, it must be considered authentic.

Abraham Lincoln never knew that records discovered by Booker existed. He may or may not have heard tales about the alleged infidelity of his mother; and although he seems to have known that his grandmother, Lucy Hanks, was illegitimate, there is no certainty that he ever learned she had been "taken up for fornication."

Whether or not he was the biological offspring of Thomas Lincoln is wholly unimportant. However, his apparent beliefs concerning his lineage seem to have been of great significance to him. Positive that he was the grandson of an unknown but prominent Virginian, he was free to imagine that ancestor to have been anyone he cared to choose.

---

*Many Lincoln scholars who fall into the traditionalist category tend to take documentation of the Thomas Lincoln marriage casually. In response to an inquiry, one of them responded, "Records were found in a courthouse, so they must be authentic."

Lacking evidence to the contrary, the marriage bond and the "return" by Jesse Head must be accepted as part of the record, but the validation of the latter document rests upon the signature alone. Diligent inquiry has uncovered no known set of holographic materials from the hand of Jesse Head with which the "marriage return" may be compared. Organizations that report they hold nothing written by him other than autographs and know of such material nowhere else include: the Lincoln Museum, Fort Wayne, Indiana; the Kentucky State Historical Society, Frankfort; Kentucky State Archives and History, Frankfort; the Filson Club, Louisville, Kentucky; and the General Commission on Archives and History of The United Methodist Church, Madison, New Jersey.

2

Did a Boyhood Injury Lead to

MINOR, BUT LASTING, DAMAGE TO THE BRAIN?

■

TYPICALLY ANIMATED, READING if he was not swapping tales with comrades, Abraham Lincoln sometimes acted a bit strangely. According to those who knew him best, he might abruptly stop what he was doing; during such an interval, he'd say nothing and do nothing. He'd simply sit and stare, appearing not even to see those with whom he'd been talking.

A boyhood accident may account for that odd pattern of behavior, largely overlooked in accounts of his life. Only his long-time partner, William H. Herndon, fully described the accident. In doing so, he reported that he had been told about the incident by Lincoln, who included a terse account in his autobiography prepared for Scripps.

Within a few months after John Wilkes Booth fired his fatal bullet, Herndon conceived the idea of writing a biography of the wartime president. He traveled throughout eastern Illinois and southern Indiana visiting places where Lincoln had lived. There he hunted up old-timers and probed their memories. Then Herndon wrote letters to every person he could find who had known his partner before he came to Springfield, Illinois.

To supplement the information he gathered firsthand, Herndon persuaded attorneys to interview persons who said they remembered Lincoln. Although most of his research was completed in about a year, he kept up a vigorous correspondence for more than twenty years, always seeking more information, additional details, and corroboration.

Herndon's account is considered to be suspect at several points, and yet scholars unite in admitting themselves to be in debt to him. For there is no other source of significant information about the early years of the stubbornly secretive mystery man who became the nation's sixteenth president.

Big, tough Ward Hill Lamon was Lincoln's bodyguard and biographer. [LIBRARY OF CONGRESS]

Writing from Springfield to Ward Hill Lamon in March 1870, Herndon told Lincoln's faithful bodyguard and would-be biographer about an incident described in full only in the long letter he wrote. According to Lincoln's own account, when he was about ten years old and living in a cabin near present-day Gentryville, Indiana, he could easily have been killed.

Slightly edited, the story was incorporated in the three-volume account of Lincoln's life that appeared in 1889. As made public there, with additional paragraph breaks added, it runs:

> No feature of his backwoods life pleased Abe so well as going to mill. It released him from a day's work in the woods, besides affording him a much desired opportunity to watch the movement of the mill's primitive and cumbersome machinery. It was on one of these trips that David Turnham accompanied him.
>
> In later years Mr. Lincoln related the following reminiscence of his experience as a miller in Indiana:
>
> One day, taking a bag of corn, he mounted the old flea-bitten gray mare and rode leisurely to Gordon's mill. Arriving some-

For a period, Lincoln's law office was on the third floor of the U.S. court building in Springfield. [1886 PHOTOGRAPH FROM AUTHOR'S COLLECTION]

what late, his turn did not come till almost sundown. In obedience to the custom requiring each man to furnish his own power, he hitched the old mare to the arm, and as the animal moved round, the machinery responded with equal speed.

Abe was mounted on the arm [or pole by which the power of the mule was transmitted to the grindstone], and at frequent intervals made use of his whip to urge the animal on to better speed. With a careless 'Get up, you old hussy,' he applied the lash at each revolution of the arm.

In the midst of the exclamation, or just as half of it had escaped through his teeth, the old jade, resenting the continued use of the goad, elevated her shoeless hoof and striking the young engineer in the forehead, sent him sprawling to the earth.

Miller Gordon hurried in, picked up the bleeding, senseless boy, whom he took for dead, and at once sent for his father. Old Thomas Lincoln came—came as soon as embodied listlessness could move—loaded the lifeless boy in a wagon and drove home [a distance of about seventeen miles].

Abe lay unconscious all night, but towards break of day the attendants noticed signs of returning consciousness. The blood beginning to flow normally, his tongue struggled to loosen itself, his frame jerked for an instant, and he awoke, blurting out the words, 'You old hussy,' or the latter half of the sentence interrupted by the mare's heel at the mill.

Mr. Lincoln considered this one of the remarkable incidents of his life. He often referred to it, and we had many discussions in our law office.

Most biographers omit this story of near-tragedy, even though it came directly from Lincoln.

Some persons who knew the future president during his Illinois years remembered that he sometimes seemed "in a world by himself." That is, he ignored his surroundings and visitors to his office while sitting quietly and staring straight ahead. A few men who had frequent contact with him described him as rejoining his friends "like one awakened from sleep" when such an interval ended. In Washington, at least one distinguished foreign observer noticed this pattern and described it. Charles A. Pineton, Marquis de Chambrun, wrote, "Suddenly, he would retire himself and close his eyes. After a few moments, he would shake off his mysterious weight and his generous and open disposition again reasserted itself." On a single evening, said the French nobleman, he counted "twenty such alternations."

Herndon tried to analyze this seldom-mentioned trait of his intimate friend and colleague and concluded:

Home of Abraham Lincoln at Springfield, Illinois. [NINETEENTH-CENTURY ENGRAVING; AUTHOR'S COLLECTION]

Mr. Lincoln was a peculiar, mysterious man [with] a *double consciousness*, a double life. The two states, never in the normal man, co-exist in equal and vigorous activities though they succeed each other quickly.

One state predominates and, while it so rules, the other state is somewhat quiescent, shadowy, yet living, a real thing. This is the sole reason why L. [Lincoln] so quickly passed from one state of consciousness to another and a different state.

In one moment he was in a state of abstraction and then quickly in another state when he was a social, talkative, and a communicative fellow.

If a similar incident were to occur today, the victim probably would be diagnosed as having suffered a brain concussion. Such a condition frequently—but not invariably—causes brain tissue to be scarred and leaves the victim with *petit mal*, a minor but incurable and often troubling condition.

Did the man whose adolescence was spent near Pigeon Creek take *petit mal* with him to Washington? Did he sometimes experience transient aphasia—inability to deal with words and memories— while grappling with key issues of the Civil War?

Not even a blood test such as is considered to be definitive with regard to Marfan syndrome will yield an answer. This much is clear, however. A heel of that mule flogged by an adolescent landed so squarely against his head that he remained unconscious for many hours. Incidents described by numerous intimates sound remarkably like attacks of transient aphasia produced by *petit mal*.

3

What Led Lincoln to Form

UNUSUAL KINDS OF RELATIONSHIPS?

■

ABRAHAM LINCOLN'S PERSONAL RELATIONSHIPS are almost as mysterious as his biological heritage. Tall and muscular— "a man's man" by every standard—he had only a handful of male intimates. As an eligible bachelor who usually found himself tongue-tied and awkward in the presence of young unmarried females, he gravitated toward married women.

About the time of his twenty-first birthday Lincoln's loftmate, Dennis Hanks, took what appears to have been a typical step for the time and the place. Unable to wait any longer, he took to his marital bed fifteen-year-old Sarah Johnston, who slept on the floor below the loft after Thomas Lincoln's second marriage. Abraham, with whom Dennis almost certainly talked freely about sex, waited until age thirty-three to make Mary Todd his bride in a "marriage of opposites" that some who knew them both regarded as a state of mutual torment.

His law partner, Herndon, dug up stories that suggested Lincoln fell desperately in love with Kentucky-born nineteen-year-old backwoods beauty Ann Rutledge. Daughter of the New Salem tavern owner with whom Lincoln boarded in 1833–34, Ann developed what was described as a fever. Soon the malady led to her death on August 25, 1835.

Relying on memories of persons who had known Ann well, Herndon became convinced that she was the one true love of Lincoln's life. To him, it was clear that the long spells of despondency his partner suffered stemmed from his memories of Ann.

Herndon's theory influenced his contemporary, Ward Hill Lamon. Later, it was adopted and given wide currency by Carl Sandburg. Without documentary evidence, Sandburg described grief-stricken Lincoln as having wandered absently in the forest and stumbling across a crude cemetery. Falling to the ground, he sprawled there with an arm across Ann's grave.

*Kentucky belle Mary Todd
became Lincoln's wife when
he was past the usual age
of marriage.* [NICOLAY & HAY,
ABRAHAM LINCOLN]

Even greater liberties were taken by Wilma Francis Minor in 1928. Writing a series of articles for the *Atlantic Monthly*, she described the Lincoln-Rutledge romance in detail. Her source material—letters claimed to have been inherited from relatives—were proved to be clumsy forgeries.

Reacting to Minor and Sandburg and not having access to documents used by Herndon, later biographers tended to discount everything Lincoln's partner wrote. Some of them took pains to point out that Ann's name does not appear in the voluminous *Collected Works of Abraham Lincoln.* They did not, however, deal with the unsolved mystery of lost and destroyed documents (see chapter 38). Noted scholar J. G. Randall dismissed out of hand all accounts of a love affair that nearly drove Lincoln insane.

John Simon, editor of the monumental *U. S. Grant Papers*, recently gained access to long-unavailable source material Herndon used in creating his three-volume biography of Lincoln. Sensing that future generations would want to know much more about Lincoln than his personal statements reveal, Herndon tried to contact everyone who had known his partner during his early years. He accumulated a massive stack of letters, but he also traveled to Petersburg, Indiana, to interview old-time residents of New Salem.

Simon makes it clear that Herndon's documents are far more important than is the biography based upon them. Surprisingly, to those whose ideas have been shaped by Randall and his followers, persons who knew both Lincoln and Rutledge considered their relationship to have been highly important.

Prior to Simon's investigation, only Albert J. Beveridge had complete access to the Herndon papers, and he never challenged accounts according to which the death of Ann left Abraham devastated. Following the lead of Simon, Douglas L. Wilson has taken a new and detailed look at accounts by persons who knew young Lincoln. A scrupulous analysis of information provided to Herndon by twenty-four informants shows that twenty-two of them believed Abraham Lincoln loved or courted the Kentucky girl. Sixteen of these persons felt that the two had "an understanding about marriage." Seventeen considered him to have been grieved at her untimely death.

Some living relatives of Rutledge rely upon family tradition and continue to believe that she was "his one true love." Their testimony is not nearly so compelling as that of twenty-four persons with whom Herndon communicated in an attempt to learn the story of his dead partner's early life. The work of Simon and Wilson goes far toward re-establishing the validity of stories about a central incident in the life of the maturing Lincoln.

Prior to his involvement with Ann, Lincoln had a relationship of sorts with another Kentucky girl. Visiting her sister, Mrs. Bennett Abell, in 1833, Mary Owens became acquainted with him. Not long

Springfield home of Ninian W. Edwards, son of the territorial governor. It was here that Mary Todd's visits to her sister led to marriage with Lincoln. [NINETEENTH-CENTURY ENGRAVING; AUTHOR'S COLLECTION]

after the death of Ann, Mrs. Abell told Lincoln that she planned to visit Mary. She promised—perhaps jokingly, perhaps seriously—that she would bring her sister back to New Salem with her if he would take her as his wife. Already noted as a storyteller and prankster, Abraham seems to have said something like, "Bring your sister back here, and I will make her Mrs. Lincoln!"

But nothing happened when Mary Owens re-entered his life in November 1836. She remained in New Salem almost eighteen months. By then, Lincoln was frequently away attending sessions of the legislature. After being instrumental in helping to have the state capital shifted from Vandalia to Springfield, he moved to the new center of government on April 15, 1837.

In a letter of May 7, 1837, the politician recently admitted to the bar warned Mary that if the two were to make a life together she would "have to be poor without the means of hiding your poverty." Three months later he rode his horse from Springfield to New Salem and seemed to have made a half-hearted marriage proposal. Back home, he wrote a strange August 16 letter in which he indicated she was at liberty to marry him if it would make her happier but that he would release her from any promises, if she wished.

No surviving letter includes a single romantic phrase.

Without evidence dating from the period, many biographers have described detailed preparations for a wedding in the home of Ninian W. Edwards, son of the territorial governor. A brief reference in one letter has been taken to mean that an engagement was abruptly broken on January 1, 1841, when the bridegroom failed to show up for the ceremony.

Nothing in the voluminous Lincoln papers even hints of a forthcoming wedding that was not held.

But the comment that looms so large may not mean what many have thought. Writing on March 27, 1842, to his longtime friend Joshua F. Speed, who had married Fanny Henning on February 15, in Kentucky, Lincoln was keenly aware that his comrade had been as hesitant to marry as he himself had been. When he learned that after Speed's February marriage his friend was far happier than he ever expected to be, Lincoln exulted.

He was not exaggerating, he wrote, when he said that "the short space it took me to read your last letter, gave me more pleasure than the total sum of all I have enjoyed since that fatal first of Jany. '41."

Sensing the emotional impact of "the fatal first," many analysts have taken it to refer to Lincoln's supposed undocumented failure to appear for his marriage to Mary Todd on January 1, 1841. This view rests partly upon a reference to unhappiness he caused Mary Todd. But the accepted interpretation overlooks two significant matters. First, the potent reference to "the fatal first" appears only in a letter directed to Speed. Second, Speed sold his store on January 1, 1841,

*Joshua Fry Speed, who
spent four years as Lincoln's
bedmate, carefully
preserved letters that are
remarkable for their
intimacy.* [NICOLAY & HAY,
ABRAHAM LINCOLN]

abruptly ending his long and intimate relationship with Lincoln.

Hence "the fatal first" reference may be to a crisis in Speed's earlier romantic relationship with Sarah Rickard—or to severance of the Lincoln/Speed intimacy, rather than to the breaking of a Lincoln/Todd engagement.

Throughout his life, the man from Springfield typically brought a letter to an end with a word or a phrase such as "Respectfully," or "Your friend, as ever." Both Mary Todd Lincoln and her distinguished son, Robert Todd Lincoln, opposed making family letters public. But four letters written by him to her during his years in Congress escaped destruction. Three of these husband-to-wife communications end simply, "Affectionately, A. Lincoln." One concludes, "Most affectionately, A. Lincoln."

Some letters to Speed conclude almost casually with a phrase such as "Your friend" or "As ever." But others conclude with far more powerful words: "Ever yours" (7/4/42) and even "Yours forever" (6/19/41, 2/13/42, 10/5/42). This departure from customary usage is made more prominent by the fact that Speed—and only Speed—often received letters signed simply "Lincoln," in lieu of the all-but-universal "A. Lincoln" of private and public correspondence.

This deviation from his normal pattern of signing letters supports views of Lincoln's contemporaries who said that during his entire life he formed an intimate friendship with only one person—Joshua Speed, who was five years his junior.

*John G. Nicolay, seated at left, was Lincoln's chief secretary.
With assistant John Hay, standing, he wrote the first lengthy
biography of Abraham Lincoln.* [LIBRARY OF CONGRESS]

If he didn't bother to take most whom he met into his inner circle
of friendship, he changed his ways when he met a person whom he
admired or liked. London-born Edward Baker, who came to Springfield in 1835 at age twenty-four, soon became a friendly political rival
of Lincoln. Baker won a contest for a seat in the House of Representatives, but by honoring an unwritten agreement by which he would
not seek re-election, he vacated a seat that was soon occupied by
Lincoln. In what may have been a dramatic gesture of gratitude, the
future president named his second son for the future U.S. senator.

His ties with two younger men were much more intimate. Bavarian-
born John G. Nicolay, age twenty-five, came to Springfield in 1857
and soon became one of Lincoln's favorites. On the heels of his

nomination for the presidency, fifty-one-year-old Lincoln chose Nicolay as his chief secretary, a post he held until April 15, 1865.

John M. Hay, a native of Salem, Indiana, met Nicolay in 1851 and formed a quick and lasting friendship. Following Nicolay to Springfield in 1858, twenty-year-old Hay became acquainted with forty-nine-year-old Lincoln. Soon after Nicolay was chosen as the chief secretary of the president-elect, Hay became a junior secretary and kept the job until Lincoln's death.

In 1980 a photograph long held by Hay's descendants was made public. Taken on November 9, 1863, it reveals a seated Lincoln with Nicolay sitting at his right and Hay standing at his left. Never before had Lincoln been photographed with members of his administration, and he bestowed upon the print an autograph that is rare, indeed—"Abraham Lincoln" instead of the usual "A. Lincoln" or even the "Lincoln" of the Speed letters.

Lincoln's bond with Elmer Ellsworth is a separate puzzle. In 1860 the twenty-two-year-old New York native began reading law in Lincoln's office. When the fifty-two-year-old president-elect set out for Washington, Ellsworth was on the train. Although Ellsworth was soon killed, in Lincoln's *Collected Works* he figures in more than twice as many documents as does Mary Todd Lincoln.

One day after his inauguration, the president asked that Ellsworth be made chief clerk in the war department. When nothing came of the request, on March 18 Lincoln named him adjutant and inspector general of militia for the United States.

Ten weeks after the dashing young soldier became the first highly publicized casualty of the war, the president requested and got a commission for Edward Ellsworth—about whom he knew nothing except that he was Elmer's cousin.

In most cases, Lincoln seemed to erect a barrier between himself and persons with whom he frequently was in contact. He and Herndon were partners for more than twenty years, but theirs was a professional relationship that never reached the stage of intimacy.

Lincoln called Illinois attorney Ward Hill Lamon "my particular friend," perhaps in gratitude that Lamon was cheerfully willing to risk his life for the president. Although Lamon served for a time as Lincoln's personal bodyguard of sorts, he never enjoyed close personal bonds such as those that bound Nicolay and Hay to Lincoln.

If Joshua Speed was in a class by himself, Nicolay, Hay, and Ellsworth were not far behind. Baker and Lamon trailed them by a wide margin. No one else came close to being an intimate of the secretive man noted for being brooding and mysterious by those who knew him.

4

What Induced Lincoln to Enter into

"A MARRIAGE OF OPPOSITES"?

■

ABRAHAM LINCOLN TOOK off his black stovepipe hat at the door. His trousers, so short that they revealed his sharp and bluish shin bones, were baggy at the knees. His collar was too large, and his waistcoat was wrinkled.

Dark hair—almost black—surmounted a high, narrow forehead above heavy eyebrows. His large gray eyes were somber above a long, blunt nose—not quite so leathery and saffron-colored as his cheeks. A single mole was visible on his right cheek not far above the corner of lips so thick and red that some who saw them thought he might have a tendency toward consumption or tuberculosis. At age thirty-three his weather-beaten face clearly revealed the rough-and-tumble frontier background of the beginning attorney who may have had as much as a year of formal schooling.

Mrs. Simeon Francis, who met him at the door of her Springfield home, had grown accustomed to his appearance, which suggested that his chest, narrow and thin, seemed to have been stretched by his towering body. Several times, she had noticed that a pronounced squint caused his left eye to jerk upward occasionally. He obviously was uncomfortable in a "boiled" shirt, and his neck—marked by a conspicuous Adam's apple—seemed too small for his collar.

Escorting him into the parlor, the wife of the editor of the local newspaper led him into the presence of a young woman he already knew. Wearing a gown cut low at the neck, with the skirt fluffed out by hoops, Mary Todd was a full twelve inches shorter than the visitor. Plump as she was short, her large blue eyes sparkled from underneath a mass of shining brown hair. Her complexion—always lovely—contrasted vividly with that of Lincoln.

A few weeks earlier, Lincoln had written a letter to which he signed a fictitious name. As published in the *Sangamon Journal*, it in-

Joshua Speed and his wife after the marriage over which both he and Lincoln agonized for weeks. [NICOLAY & HAY, *ABRAHAM LINCOLN*]

formed readers that Democrats led by state auditor James Shields were making life impossible for ordinary working folk. Lincoln expected the matter to end at this point, so he was baffled when three more "Rebecca letters" appeared in the newspaper. Shields was so outraged that he demanded the real name of the writer. Editor Francis protected the women who had written the letters by giving him Lincoln's name only—so Shields insisted upon a duel with the man who had insulted him.

It was this matter that brought Lincoln to the Francis home in September 1842. Mary Todd and he had hardly begun to exchange pleasantries in the home of a mutual acquaintance before she blurted out a confession. Except for the first, the "Rebecca letters" that threatened to lead to pistols at dawn were penned by her and her friend Julia Jayne.

Once Lincoln learned what he may have already suspected, that Mary Todd helped to produce the letters that triggered a challenge, he volunteered to claim authorship in order to protect her. Shortly afterward, he informed Shields that as the man challenged, he chose for weapons "cavalry broadswords of the largest size."

As depicted in Godey's Lady's Book, *the bride of clumsily dressed Lincoln, was at the epitome of fashion.* [AUTHOR'S COLLECTION]

When the political rivals met across the river from Alton, seconds managed to arrange an uneasy peace. No duel was fought. Temporarily the talk of Springfield, the affair probably hastened a reconciliation between Abraham Lincoln and Mary Todd, who a year earlier had been close to announcing their engagement to marry but had broken off their relationship. Soon they began seeing a great deal of one another, leading friends to speculate that in spite of objections from Mary's relatives, they were likely to make a match of it.

Born and reared in Lexington, Kentucky, Mary Todd was only seven years old when her mother died. Soon her wealthy, aristocratic father, a long-time member of the legislature and president of the Bank of Kentucky, remarried. Mary and her stepmother never got along well, so at age fourteen the girl was sent to a boarding school operated by Madame Mentello. Students were permitted to converse only in French and were forced to practice until they had mastered the polka, scottische, galop, and waltz.

Probably to get away from her stepmother, Mary visited Springfield for three months in 1837. There her sister was the wife of Ninian W. Edwards, son of the territorial governor and famous as "a fashion plate in black broadcloth, with a gold-headed cane." Mary is not known to have met Lincoln on that visit. When she returned two years later for a lengthy stay, they became acquainted and soon showed considerable interest in one another.

Elizabeth Edwards repeatedly told her sister that she and Lincoln constituted "a pair of opposites." They differed dramatically in size, background, and education. Mary was accustomed to wealth; Lincoln was dirt poor, still saddled with debts from his failed venture as a New Salem storekeeper.

When she sensed that friendship was progressing to courtship, Mary's sister began to treat Lincoln coldly. Years later, she confessed to William H. Herndon that she noticed "Lincoln could not hold a lengthy conversation with a lady—was not sufficiently educated and intelligent in the female line to do so." When he came calling, he sat and gazed at Mary, "listening, but scarcely saying a word."

Consequently, "after the first crash of things," Ninian Edwards, his wife, or the two of them "told Mary and Lincoln that they had better not ever marry. Their natures, minds, education, raising, etc., were so different, that they could not live happy as man and wife." Accomplished ballroom dancer Mary could never be satisfied with a gawky fellow who "looked like Father Neptune" when he awkwardly tried to waltz.

By the time the young woman from Lexington received that lecture, she and Lincoln were looking ahead. In a letter of December 1840, Mary told Mercy Levering that they had reached an understanding—a step just short of formal engagement.

Their relationship ended abruptly and mysteriously. Because severe depression followed the day Lincoln called "the fatal first," it has been widely assumed that he failed to show up for a wedding scheduled for January 1, 1841. Nothing in the voluminous letters of Mary Todd gives even a hint that so dramatic an episode ever took place. Perhaps they simply agreed to disagree, and parted company without fanfare.

By the time he began offering consolation and advice to Speed about his forthcoming marriage, Lincoln was so concerned that he insisted, "I want you to write me every mail." Writing on February 13, knowing that his friend's marriage would have been consummated before the letter arrived, the Springfield attorney ventured to hope that it would be "a plaster for a place that is no longer sore."

Aware that as a newly married man, Speed still found "something indescribably horrible and alarming" haunting him, Lincoln assured him that once his nerves got steady, the trouble would be over forever. A separate letter, conveying none of the high emotion revealed to her husband, was enclosed for Fanny. Two days later, Lincoln again wrote to Speed. This time, he exulted at having heard of his friend's happiness, a message, he wrote, that "gave me more pleasure than the total sum of all I have enjoyed since that fatal first day of Jany. '41."

It was still possible, Lincoln warned, that Speed's spirits might "flag down" and leave him miserable. But by July 4 Lincoln had arrived at the conclusion that Almighty God made him "one of the instruments of bringing your Fanny and you together." This time he was willing for Fanny to read his letter, provided that she already knew something of Lincoln's own affair with a woman.

Beginning again to see Mary Todd after fifteen months of separation, Lincoln demanded of Speed in October, "Are you now in *feeling* as well as *judgement* [Lincoln's spelling], glad that you are married as you are? Please answer quickly, as I am impatient to know."

Soon after having had time to hear from Speed, Lincoln seems to have made definite moves toward making Mary Todd his wife. If they had reached a prior agreement, he did not give her an engagement ring—and there was no announcement of their intentions.

Early on the morning of November 4, 1842, Lincoln hurried to the home of James H. Matheney and arrived to find his friend still in bed. Having persuaded Matheney to be his best man, he obtained a marriage license. Mary Todd, meanwhile, called on Julia Jayne and asked her to be a bridesmaid.

Matheney later said that plans for the marriage were "quick and sudden—an affair of an hour or two." Described as "pale and trembling as if being driven to slaughter," Lincoln arrived at the Edwards home for a ceremony performed by the Reverend Charles N. Dresser. With about thirty relatives and friends watching, he presented his bride with a ring engraved "Love Is Eternal."

After the ceremony, the newlyweds drove through pelting rain to the Globe Tavern, where Lincoln had arranged for them to get a room and meals for four dollars a week. Nine months less three days after their marriage, Mary presented her husband with a son whom they named Robert Todd. Soon afterward they left the Globe for a rented three-room frame cottage. In the spring of 1844, Lincoln—now earning $1,500 to $2,000 a year from his law practice—bought a house from Dr. Dresser, who had presided over their marriage.

Herndon strongly disliked Mary Todd Lincoln; yet he considered her to have been badly neglected by her law partner. James Gourley, who lived next door to the Lincolns for nineteen years, quoted Mary as having repeatedly said that "if her husband had stayed at home as he ought to that she could love him better."

Traveling the legal circuit, most attorneys would start for home on Saturday. According to Judge David Davis, later Lincoln's campaign manager, "As a general rule, when all the lawyers of a Saturday evening would go home and see their families and friends, Lincoln would find some excuse and refuse to go." Herndon added that his partner preferred to spend his weekends with "tavern loungers"—or

Judge David Davis, who wondered why Lincoln didn't stay home with his wife, was later named to the U.S. Supreme Court by his long-time friend.
[ILLINOIS STATE HISTORICAL SOCIETY]

compatible males—rather than with his wife and children. Their observations indicate that a pattern of persistent absence from the marital bed was launched soon after Lincoln took Mary Todd as his wife.

Had Herndon kept careful records, he would have noticed a change in the rhythm of his partner's absences. Early in his marriage, Lincoln was seldom away from home more than two weeks at a time. His trips gradually increased in both number and duration. By 1854 he was so involved in his legal work that he stayed at it for more than six weeks without a single visit to his wife and children. Two years later, a twelve-month period saw him absent from home for twenty weeks.

Increasingly prosperous, in 1856 Lincoln had their Springfield home remodeled and enlarged. When the work was completed, he and Mary moved into separate bedrooms.

Spoon River Anthology author Edgar Lee Masters's least-known book deals with *Lincoln: The Man.* From an assessment of his performance as a husband—not on the basis of his prior relationship with Speed—poet-attorney Masters concluded that Lincoln was sadly deficient in his sexual drive.

According to accounts of those who knew them best, the marriage between opposites brought Lincoln and Mary little happiness as man and wife. Herndon, who never liked Mary, espoused her cause in one crucial aspect. "In her domestic troubles I have always sympathized with Mrs. Lincoln," he wrote.

*   *   *

Devoted secretaries John G. Nicolay and John Hay were in inti-mate daily contact with the Lincolns during their Washington years. Close ties with Robert Todd Lincoln gave them access to his father's papers in producing the first lengthy biography of the strange man who was the central character in the Civil War. In preparing their ten volumes, each more than 450 pages, Nicolay and Hay devoted little space to Mary Todd Lincoln, whom they privately called the Hellcat. If Lincoln frequently wrote to his wife during any of his long absences from home, most of his letters have not survived. The definitive edition of Lincoln's *Collected Works*, edited by Roy P. Basler, includes about 5,000 pages of letters, speeches, and documents. Mary Lin-coln gets brief and incidental mention on an average of once in every eighty pages.

Why did rising politician and beginning attorney Lincoln take Mary Todd as his wife?

His existing papers give few clues.

Speed never wavered in his conviction that his own successful venture into matrimony prodded his friend into following his example.

Herndon was sure he knew the unspoken motive behind the mar-riage of his partner:

> Born in the humblest circumstances, uneducated, poor, ac-quainted with flatboats and groceries, but a stranger to the drawing room, it was natural that he should seek in a matri-monial alliance those social advantages which he felt were necessary to his political advancement.

Lincoln, he stressed, was always conscious of his "humble rank in the social scale." Therefore the self-educated man and impoverished attorney married a highly educated patrician in order to foster his political fortunes!

According to the man who watched it in progress and saw its results, "On no other basis can we reconcile the strange course of his courtship."

5

*What Induced a Foe of
Slavery to Serve as*

A COUNSEL FOR
A SLAVEHOLDER?

UNDOCUMENTED TRADITION has it that at about age nineteen, Abraham Lincoln, who was living in Indiana, was shocked at seeing slaves sold at auction. According to a story told by one of his Hanks relatives, the incident, which he never forgot, took place in New Orleans.

With Allen Gentry as his only companion, the youth from near Gentryville did take a flatboat down the Mississippi River. But none of his surviving papers provide any hint that he witnessed slaves on the auction block.

His most vivid description of slavery was penned years later.

Defeated in 1832 in his first bid for a seat in the legislature, he won in 1834 and retained the seat for eight years. Probably already having his eye on Washington, he made an 1847 trip to Louisville for another visit with Joshua Speed. On the return voyage by river steamer he saw twelve slaves, shackled together six-by-six. Purchased in Kentucky, they were en route to the Cotton Belt.

Writing to Joshua's sister Mary, Lincoln gave a vivid and detailed account of his glimpse at slaves "sold down the river," yet apparently cheerful, even jolly. No doubt he saw men and women in bondage when he visited Lexington, Kentucky, with his wife; if so, he did not describe these experiences.

As a representative of Sangamon County, in 1837 he went on record as protesting resolutions passed by the legislature. Evoked by memorials from Virginia, Alabama, Mississippi, and New York, the bills to which lawmaker Lincoln objected condemned abolition societies and stressed "the right of property in slaves" as sacred.

Nearly two years after having put himself on public record concerning slavery, he again found himself in a minority in the legislature. Fellow lawmakers sided with 1839 resolutions supportive of

Tradition says that on a flatboat trip down the Mississippi River, young Lincoln gained lasting hatred of slavery from having witnessed an auction on the streets of New Orleans, similar to this auction held in Charleston, South Carolina. [ILLUSTRATED LONDON NEWS, 1856]

fugitive slave laws. Lincoln moved to postpone the matter indefinitely, but his breath was wasted.

Though slavery never prevailed in Illinois, public opinion strongly supported views commonly associated with the Deep South. Attorney John A. ("Blackjack") Logan, seventeen years Lincoln's junior and a future Union general, drafted a bill that passed by a wide majority. Under its terms, no free black was legally entitled to become a citizen of Illinois.

There is no record that Lincoln ever attempted to have the Logan measure rescinded. Yet his early opposition to slavery frequently surfaced when he took to the political platform. He publicly deplored the existence of slavery, calling it a national evil. Vehement opposition to its westward spread helped make him nationally prominent. Yet, strangely, when viewed from the modern perspective, he repeatedly stressed his conviction that abolitionists had no right to interfere with slavery where it existed. The Founding Fathers of the Republic, he noted, tolerated slavery in the South and gave it constitutional protection.

In 1847, even ardent abolitionists recognized this as reality; but Lincoln jumped to a conclusion that few Americans from the North or the South, shared. According to the man from Springfield, at least as early as 1776 framers of the Declaration of Independence and the Constitution were confident that slavery was already "in the course of extinction."

It was from this unique personal viewpoint that Springfield attorney Lincoln viewed events taking place in Coles County, where Thomas and Sarah Lincoln had settled.

Wealthy farmer Robert Matson of Kentucky purchased a tract of Coles County land in 1843. Known locally as the Black Grove, the place called for output of considerable labor. Instead of hiring local workers, Matson annually brought a group of slaves into Illinois and kept them there until harvest time. Since the seasonal work involved maintaining them at Black Grove for a few months and then taking them back to Kentucky, it was taken for granted that the slaves remained his personal property.

Four or five years after the annual pattern of migration was established, a white woman who may have been Matson's mistress became angry. She threatened to have some of the slaves sold to owners far from Kentucky. Free black Anthony Bryant, Matson's overseer for

Later a brigadier general, John A. Logan sponsored a law that barred blacks from Illinois. His friend Lincoln was largely reponsible for having a county named in his honor. [NATIONAL ARCHIVES]

work in Illinois, became alarmed and sought the aid of abolitionists in nearby Oakland.

Innkeeper Gideon Ashmore—a native of Tennessee—took the threatened slaves into his place, probably hoping soon to be able to send them along the Underground Railway to Canada. Matson tried to reclaim his slaves but failed to get them, so he decided to take the issue to court and retained the services of Usher F. Linder, who had served with Lincoln in the state legislature.

A justice of the peace held a hearing, decided he didn't have jurisdiction, and turned the contested slaves over to the sheriff. Once they were jailed, attorneys for abolitionists tried to get them released under a writ of *habeas corpus*, a move that propelled the case into the circuit court.

Great interest had been created by then. Hence, William Wilson, chief justice of the Illinois Supreme Court, decided to hear the arguments. He went to Charleston, the county seat, to share the bench with Judge Samuel H. Treat of the Eighth Circuit.

At some point in the brewing legal tempest that had already become a sideshow, Abraham Lincoln arrived at Charleston. He probably carried his personal effects in the carpetbag (actually made of carpet material) that he customarily used. Chances are also good that he brought along his faithful green umbrella with "A. Lincoln" stitched inside it in white.

Already respected throughout much of Illinois as a "lawyer's lawyer"—often called upon to assist other attorneys—Lincoln seems to have gone to Charleston upon his own volition. Once there, he soon entered into an agreement according to which he became co-counsel with Linder, who represented Matson.

With the demand for a writ of *habeas corpus* the first order of business, justices followed standard practice and heard pleas without a jury. Arguments got under way on Saturday, October 16, 1847. Spectators packed the tiny courtroom.

Orlando B. Ficklin insisted that the Illinois constitution and the Ordinance of 1787 could only be construed as requiring that Matson's slaves be set free. Abraham Lincoln countered by showing that they were seasonal workers rather than permanent settlers. Never "domiciled in the state of Illinois," they regularly returned to Kentucky. Therefore, he argued, they had been and remained slaves— lawful property of Matson and domiciled in a state where slavery was permitted.

Attorneys for both parties presented additional arguments. Then Judge Treat conferred at length with Judge Wilson before their joint finding was issued on October 17. They used formal legal language to announce that by bringing his slaves to Illinois, Matson had engaged in conduct that effectively freed them from servitude "henceforth and forever."

*   *   *

Abraham Lincoln, destined to become revered worldwide as the Great Emancipator, lost a sensational case. If he made notes concerning the case, they were destroyed. His own voluminous *Collected Works* do not include a single reference to it. Neither do pioneer biographies by men who knew him intimately—William H. Herndon, Ward Hill Lamon, John G. Nicolay, and John Hay. Whether allusions to the Matson slave case were deliberately suppressed or simply never found their way into the record, no one knows.

Perhaps attorney Abraham Lincoln felt obligated to represent anyone who requested his help, or perhaps he may have been more interested in collecting his fees than in defending his principles. Although he had spoken against slavery, it is possible that his views and actions at this time had not yet matured. It is also possible that as an attorney, he believed in finding and obeying the letter of the law, whether or not he agreed with it. Or perhaps, knowing that the case would be sensational, he couldn't refrain from getting involved for the sake of publicity.

All of these explanations—and more—have been put forward in attempting to account for actions of Congressman-elect Abraham Lincoln. Regardless, he never explained why he represented a slaveholder when he had been on record for so long as opposed to the institution of slavery.

This much is certain. In later decades, a great deal of ink has been spilled in attempting to explain why Lincoln helped to plead the case of a slaveholder.

John J. Duff, whose meticulous and detailed research for *A. Lincoln, Prairie Lawyer* yielded a step-by-step account of Lincoln's involvement in the Matson case, stressed that among chief executives Lincoln had "the most complicated personal character." Primarily interested in his legal career, Duff concluded that motives leading the future Great Emancipator to appear in court for Matson may constitute the "most profound mystery ever to confound Lincoln specialists."

6

When Did He Begin to
Dream of Becoming

THE FIRST PILOT OF THE SHIP OF STATE FROM THE WESTERN FRONTIER?

∎

"I WOULD RATHER HAVE a full term in the Senate than the presidency," Abraham Lincoln wrote on December 9, 1859.

His correspondent was Chicago attorney Norman B. Judd, long a colleague and a member of the National Republican Committee since 1856. Due to meet in only a few months, the national convention would select a nominee for the presidency. Since Lincoln never made notes about his conversations, there's no way to know what face-to-face talks prompted his formal denial of interest in winning the nomination.

During 1849 he had made a series of appearances in Kansas, Iowa, Ohio, Indiana, and Wisconsin; while his avowed goal was a seat in the Senate, voters in those states would have no impact upon the choice of an Illinois senator. His actions did not square with his words, and his terse denial to Judd simply repeated what he had said earlier.

A year earlier, fellow townsman K. N. Fell called him aside upon returning from a long trip to the East. Everywhere he went, Fell said, he heard people talking about Lincoln. That led him to wish people could know his friend's real views about slavery—highly conservative in the eyes of abolitionists. Informed that he might become a significant candidate for the presidency, Lincoln shook his head. "What's the use of talking of me," he responded, "while we have such men as [William H.] Seward and [Salmon P.] Chase."

He then added a comment that was characteristic. To modern readers it seems self-deprecating, but to intimate friends it may have been a small sample of the famous but little-understood Lincoln humor in which gross exaggeration was a key motif: "Everybody knows Seward and Chase; nobody, scarcely, out of Illinois knows me . . ."

In a July 1858 speech opposing Stephen A. Douglas, he lauded his opponent's "round, jolly, fruitful face" that seemed to promise all sorts of political offices to his followers. "Nobody has ever expected me to be president," he continued. "In my poor, lean, lank face, nobody has ever seen that any cabbages were sprouting out."

When some Illinois newspapers launched a "Lincoln for president" move in April 1859, he wrote to editor Thomas J. Pickett at Pekin, "I must, in candor, say I do not think myself fit for the presidency." Three months later, in confiding his views concerning the Ohio Republican convention, he had good words for Chase. Of himself, he repeated, "I must say I do not think myself fit for the presidency." But he felt impelled to point out that Chase, Ohio's favorite son, might not be the "most suitable candidate."

By 1859 Lincoln's protestations may have constituted a thin cover for inner yearning. If so, when did the man reared on the western frontier begin to see himself as a potential pilot for the ship of state, and how was he led to harbor aspirations that many considered to be ridiculous?

Seeking an answer to that question, William H. Herndon turned toward a woman he despised. According to him, Mary Todd "used to contend when a girl, to her friends in Kentucky, that she was destined to marry a president. I have heard her say that myself, and after mingling with society in Springfield she repeated the seeming absurd and idle boast."

Another intimate associate, Ward Hill Lamon, considered Lincoln's wife to have spurred him onward and upward. At a time when her husband really was all but unknown outside of Illinois, she told him—he insisted—that "Mr. Lincoln is to be president of the United States some day; if I had not thought so, I would not have married him."

Undocumented oral tradition, which may have taken shape years after events upon which it centers, insists that in girlhood Mary Todd often told friends she would marry a future president.

Other stories of approximately the same vintage focus not upon the woman he married, but upon the frontier youth who spent his days in manual labor. Elizabeth Crawford, a boyhood acquaintance, told Herndon, "He said he would be president of the United States, told my husband so often, said it jokingly, yet with deep earnestness. He evidently had an idea, a feeling, in 1828 that he was bound to be a great man."

If he actually had such ideas, they may have been derived from a book. In and about Gentryville, Indiana, Josiah Crawford was cele-

Mason L. Weems,
biographer of George
Washington, apparently
exerted considerable
influence upon the gifted
and imaginative young son
of Nancy Hanks.
[DICTIONARY OF AMERICAN
PORTRAITS]

brated as owner of a library, for he had an estimated twelve to fifteen books on his shelf. When Lincoln was twenty he borrowed Crawford's *The Life and Memorable Actions of George Washington*, by Mason Weems. When the prized book became soaked by rain, Crawford told him to keep it and pay for it by pulling fodder (leaves of corn, used as cattle feed).

In later life, Lincoln often referred to that biography, sometimes sounding as if he had memorized portions of it. As much as any other influence, it probably caused him to have lifelong awe for the Founding Fathers of the Republic. Since he believed himself to be descended from an unidentified Virginia aristocrat, the Weems volume may have helped him to arrive at the conclusion that he himself walked in footsteps of colonial leaders.

Regardless of where it came from, those who knew the future president well were unanimous in one verdict. Without exception, they stressed a judgment expressed by his one-time neighbor, Elizabeth Crawford: "Abe was ambitious, sought to outstrip and override others."

Herndon was not being critical, but simply analytical, when he observed that to his partner "his ambition was a little engine that knew no rest. Politics were his life and his ambition, his motive power."

Though Lamon's analysis is less familiar than that of Herndon's, it was unequivocal. "Mr. Lincoln," he wrote, "was never agitated by any passion more intense than his wonderful thirst for distinction. It governed all his conduct.

"He never rested in the race he had determined to run; he was ever ready to be honored; he struggled incessantly for place. There is no instance where an important office seemed to be within his reach, and he did not try to get it."

Whatever its source, Lincoln's ambition received a mighty boost at the first national convention of the Republican party. Seeking a vice-presidential nominee by means of an informal ballot, delegates gave William L. Dayton of New Jersey 259 votes. His runner-up, with 110 votes, was Lincoln. Though Dayton was immediately nominated by acclamation, he and other national leaders could not have failed to note that the man who described himself as unknown outside of Illinois captured delegates from Maine, New Hampshire, Massachusetts, Rhode Island, New York, Pennsylvania, Ohio, Indiana, Michigan, and California.

It was at this point that Henry C. Whitney reached a personal conclusion. Intimately acquainted with Lincoln as a result of having traveled the legal circuit with him, he decided that his friend now considered himself a serious candidate for the presidency.

Early in his political career, the future president made what appears to have been a strange choice. Continually stressing that he was poor and uneducated, he became an ardent Whig, affiliating with the party dominated by the gentry.

Illinois editors opposed to the Kansas-Nebraska Bill met at Decatur in February 1856. A single politician—Lincoln—appeared. Not knowing that the Republican party was being organized that very day, the editors suggested that Lincoln offer himself as a "fusion candidate" for governor. He showed little eagerness but responded warmly when toasted as "our next candidate for the U.S. Senate."

When a fusion convention was later held at Bloomington, delegate Lincoln realized that it "sounded the death knell of Illinois Whiggery." Not yet calling himself a Republican, he was actually state leader of the new party. During five months after the Bloomington convention—at which he was selected as a presidential elector—he made at least fifty speeches in twenty-six or twenty-eight counties. Always, he carefully avoided being labeled an abolitionist and insisted that the new Republican party would stick to constitutional measures and not challenge slavery in states where it was already in existence.

This cautious middle-of-the-road stance, many Republicans insisted, was essential for national success at the polls. Any man considered to hold extreme views would find it difficult or impossible to win the Executive Mansion in Washington.

* * *

Recollections of other persons are at sharp variance with Lincoln's insistence that he wanted a seat in the U.S. Senate, and nothing more.

Charles H. Ray of the Chicago *Press and Tribune* was with Lincoln at Freeport, Illinois, on August 27, 1858. Due to confront Douglas on the platform, Lincoln told a group of supporters that Douglas "can never be president." According to Ray, a member of the group responded: "That's not your lookout; you are after the *senatorship!*" "No, gentlemen," Lincoln reputedly responded: "*I am killing larger game* [italics added]. The battle of 1860 is worth a hundred of this!"

Another journalist, German-born Henry Villard, was with him at Petersburg sixty days later, on October 29. When a storm struck, they took refuge in a boxcar near the depot. Far more relaxed than usual, the candidate confided, "Mary insists that I'm going to be a senator and president of the United States, too." He then passed the comment off as a joke. "Just think of such a sucker as me being president!"

Lincoln's papers include at least two sets of clues that are startling by their early emergence. Speaking in the U.S. House of Representatives on July 27, 1847, he castigated Democratic presidential aspirant Lewis Cass. If he, Lincoln, were ever to take actions causing folk to make him their candidate for that office, he told lawmakers, "I protest they shall not make fun of me."

Six months later, jotting down thoughts concerning ways an influential Whig from Illinois might aid Zachary Taylor's candidacy, he prepared a brief memorandum. Talking to himself, his musings include three revealing phrases: "Were I president . . . ," "Should I come into the presidency . . . ," and "Were I President."

What may be believed? A set of protestations that run counter to patterns of action, or a group of almost-casual and seemingly incidental comments, no one of which is significant in itself?

Regardless of when Abraham Lincoln began to dream of himself as chief executive of the nation, how did so unlikely a candidate arrive at such a vision? Unqualified answers are suspect; there are too many unknowns to arrive at conclusions that cannot be challenged. He may have been influenced by daydreams concerning his lineage, by a biography of Washington, and by an aristocratic wife with high goals.

7

Why Is He Still Seen As

A HAYSEED LAWYER WHO BARELY MADE A LIVING?

■

CHARLES ALLEN, CHIEF witness for the prosecution, gave emphatic answers. Yes, he was present when James Norris and Duff Armstrong struck blows believed to have cost James Metzker his life. Correct. Norris used a weapon that looked like a neck-yoke. Certainly! He clearly saw Armstrong handling what appeared to be a slingshot.

Spectators in the Mason County circuit court shook their heads solemnly, sure that both defendants would be convicted of murder. Soon, however, defense attorney Abraham Lincoln began to question the witness: How far did Allen stand from the spot at which Metzker was attacked? Exactly—not approximately—what was the hour? Since the incident took place at night, just how much light was there at the time?

Allen answered precisely. He observed from a distance of not more than twenty yards. It was 11:00 P.M., give or take no more than five minutes. There was abundant light, for the moon shone brightly from a point close to 10:00 A.M., sun time.

Lawyer Lincoln, who entered the case after receiving an appeal from Armstrong's mother, reputedly paced back and forth as he digested Allen's data. Suddenly he wheeled, turned toward the jury, and signaled for the sheriff to hand him a pamphlet. Turning to a moon chart in an almanac he had brought from Springfield in his hat, he waved the document at jurors. At the time of the alleged murder, he told them, the moon was low in the western sky, little more than an hour from setting.

A skeptical judge demanded to see the almanac; he examined it and pronounced it genuine. In turn, it was handed to attorneys for the prosecution and to each member of the jury. Strongly influenced by it, jurors acquitted Duff Armstrong on the first ballot.

Lincoln reputedly studied law while sitting on top of a woodpile belonging to a neighbor. [EVERY-DAY LIFE OF ABRAHAM LINCOLN]

Soon the story became embellished. Shrewd Abe Lincoln, said a widely circulated tale, covered the almanac's date with his big thumb. That's why no one noticed he used an 1856 publication to discredit a witness to an 1857 brawl.

That tale, considered by his contemporaries to be complimentary, is one of many myths concerning Lincoln the lawyer. Political orators and campaign literature depicted him as a folksy, down-to-earth attorney whose practice consisted largely of participation in petty civil suits.

Actually, Lincoln was one of the most skillful and highly paid attorneys of the region. He argued criminal and civil cases; and some of his cases involved huge sums of money, and the decisions rendered set legal precedents.

He was an all-purpose attorney who was ready to support either side of any case. He argued cases dealing with disputed wills, taxation, maritime law, foreclosures, debt, slander, assault, murder, divorce, rape, horse theft, land titles, ejectment, and personal injury. During active legal practice from 1837 to 1860, he represented at least five of the most powerful corporations in Illinois—railroads.

His handling of a case for the Illinois Central Railroad has generated its own cluster of legends.

When McLean County tried to levy a tax on railroad property, all observers knew it would trigger a major legal battle. Lincoln made it clear that he wanted to participate, initially, it appears, on the side of the county. He saw the issue as the "largest law question that can now be got up in the state." As a result, he insisted that "in justice to myself, I can not afford, if I can help it, to miss a fee altogether."

Authorities of McLean County did not respond to his overture, so the man from Springfield offered his services to Mason Brayman, chief attorney for the railroad. Brayman immediately sent him his personal check for $250 as a retainer. Lincoln gave up all thought of aiding McLean County and entered the contest on the side of the biggest corporation in the state.

He and his colleagues lost in the McLean County circuit court, so the case was appealed to the Illinois Supreme Court. There two of Lincoln's former law partners, Stephen T. Logan and John T. Stuart, represented McLean County.

After three years of arguments and counterarguments, Lincoln won and immediately billed his client for $5,000. Though it was one of the largest fees ever demanded by "a Western lawyer," he pointed out that he had saved the Illinois Central at least $500,000.

Much of Lincoln's legal practice revolved around railroads— biggest land owners and wealthiest corporations of the era.
[Author's collection]

Especially during his early years as an attorney, Lincoln often
argued cases in log-cabin courthouses, such as this one in
Macon County, Illinois—still standing long after his death.
[AUTHOR'S COLLECTION]

Railroad president William H. Osborne was among those who considered the fee excessive, so he refused to pay and invited Lincoln to
sue. When he did so, the case went before Lincoln's long-time associate and friend, Judge David Davis. A citizen present at the hearing
later reported that in a matter of minutes a judgment was entered
against the railroad.

His defense of a slaveholder in a sensational case is discussed in
detail in chapter 5. That his personal sentiments were not in accord
with those of Robert Matson is shown by his having taken an op-
posite stand eight years earlier.

William Cromwell sold the papers of an allegedly indentured girl
to David Bailey. Bailey's promissory note stipulated that the seller
would produce papers showing her to be a slave. When no proof was
offered, the girl Nancy—later valued at $431.37—ran away, claiming
freedom. Bailey then refused to pay the note.

Cromwell died, and administrators of his estate brought suit in

Tazewell County. Defending Bailey, Lincoln lost the case in the circuit court, then appealed to the Illinois Supreme Court. When the high court heard the case in 1841, Lincoln argued that Nancy could not legally have been sold to Bailey because no human could be sold in a free state. Justices heard lengthy arguments, then handed down a landmark ruling: "It is a presumption of law, in the state of Illinois, that every person is free without regard to color. The sale of a free person is illegal."

Like cases involving slavery, some contests took on new meaning in the light of later events. Others are remembered chiefly for colorful incidents that illustrate Lincoln's skill in dealing with jurors.

Collapse of a Bloomington chimney in 1855 sent masonry flying so furiously that Samuel G. Fleming was crushed. Both legs were broken. A team of three physicians worked for hours to save his life, but when the accident victim began to recover, he found his right leg was crooked, and hence shorter than his left. Fleming sued his physicians for $10,000 in damages, and Lincoln gave the summation in defense of the physicians.

With jurors watching intently, he exhibited two sets of chicken bones. Then he used them to show that bones of young birds are

Attorney Lincoln appeared frequently in the courthouse of Champaign County—shown by early lithographers as flanked by the jail and the poor farm. [Author's collection]

quite pliable while those of older fowls are brittle. At his age, Fleming was fortunate that he could walk at all, Lincoln argued.

A hung jury, followed by postponement of retrial, resulted in eventual dismissal of the "chicken-bone case."

Kentucky-born John Todd Stuart, who served with Lincoln in the Black Hawk War, is credited with having encouraged his captain to seek a license as an attorney. Mustered out, the unschooled man of ambition took Stuart's advice and said he'd read law. He probably borrowed a few books from Stuart. Somehow, he got his hands upon a four-volume set of Blackstone's *Commentaries on the Laws of England.* Ninian W. Edwards, who later opposed Lincoln's marriage with Mary Todd, offered to buy a library for him and send him to a good law school. Characteristically, the man who believed no oak was too tough to split turned down aid and studied without guidance.

Soon he sought and obtained from the Sangamon County circuit court a "certificate of good character." That March 24, 1836, document was all he needed; no state bar examination was required. Licensed in September, he became a junior member of Stuart's firm early in 1837. He left after four years to work under noted Stephen T. Logan. That arrangement lasted for three years, after which he hung out his "A. Lincoln" shingle in partnership with William H. Herndon.

While he was far from being a "simple prairie lawyer," self-taught Lincoln's reputation grew steadily during his participation in several thousand cases. He appeared before the Illinois Supreme Court more than 200 times and once participated in an argument before the U.S. Supreme Court.

During the 1850s, his income reached $5,000 a year and held steady at that level—more than three times the salary of the governor of Illinois. During this time, account books of Springfield merchants showed such purchases as: pair boy's boots $1.50; pair kid gloves $1; 6 French towels $2.10; hair balsam .40; umbrella .75; pair shoes .40; 12 lbs. sugar $1; boy's hat .40; and 2 pairs boy's gloves .40. Measured in terms of purchasing power, attorney Lincoln's earnings placed him among the wealthy elite.

He went to Cincinnati in 1855 to participate in a case involving patents owned by industrialist Cyrus H. McCormick. Urbane attorneys from big cities in the East laughed when he was pointed out to them. One of them described him as "a tall, rawly boned, ungainly backwoodsman, with coarse, ill-fitting clothing, his trousers hardly reaching his ankles, holding in his hands a blue cotton umbrella with a ball on the end of the handle."

When he entered the arena of national politics, campaign workers knew that the public would be cold toward a "lawyer's lawyer" on a high income. In the heated climate of 1860, his hayseed stereotype

Lincoln traveled to Cincinnati to take part in a case that involved wealthy inventor-manufacturer Cyrus McCormick.
[DICTIONARY OF AMERICAN PORTRAITS]

was spread across the nation with such success that it has lost little of its vitality during succeeding decades.

Lincoln may have fashioned the small-time image with great care, or it could have emerged as a result of doing what came naturally. Did he deliberately dress in such fashion that he appeared to be a backwoodsman carrying hay seeds in his hair? Was his practice of stuffing letters and documents into his hat a ruse to make opponents think him inept? Were his frequent jocular references to such exploits as the "chicken-bone case" made to camouflage his courtroom skills? Only Lincoln knew the answers to such questions, and he never addressed them, even in casual conversation.

8

*Where Did He Get the Skills
That Made Him*

AN ALL-TIME
MASTER OF
PUBLIC SPEAKING?

■

"TO SAY HE is ugly is nothing," an English journalist informed his readers. "To add that his figure is grotesque is to convey no adequate impression. He has a long, scraggy neck and a chest too narrow for the great arms at his side.

"Add to this a head, coconut shaped and somewhat too small for such stature, covered with rough, uncombed hair, that stands out in every direction at once.

"Add a close-set, thin-lipped stern mouth and a nose and ears which have been taken by mistake from a head twice the size.

"Clothe this figure then in a long, tight, badly fitting suit of black that is creased, soiled, and puckered up at every salient point of the figure, then add to this a strange look of dignity coupled with all the grotesqueness, and you will have the impression left upon me by Abraham Lincoln."

Small wonder that the editor of a Democratic newspaper published in Taunton, Massachusetts, said that as a speaker, Lincoln's features "all conspire to make his hearers laugh."

German-born Carl Schurz, an ardent admirer who became a Civil War general, admitted that when Lincoln stepped before an audience, his appearance constituted two strikes against him. "His lank, ungainly body," Schurz wrote, included arms that seemed to be "so long that the sleeves of a 'store' coat could hardly be expected to cover them all the way down to the wrists.

"His black trousers, too, permitted a very full view of his large feet. On his left arm he carried a gray woolen shawl; his right hand held a cotton umbrella and a black satchel. I have seen several public men of rough appearance; but none whose looks seemed quite so un-

Edwin M. Stanton, later Lincoln's secretary of war, described Lincoln's appearance in one word— dirty. [U.S. SIGNAL CORPS]

couth, not to say grotesque, as Lincoln's."

H. C. Whitney, who rode the legal circuit with the man from Springfield, noted that his skin "was a dark, sallow color, his features were coarse, his ears were large; his hair, coarse, black and bushy, stood out all over his head, with no appearance of ever having been combed." His appearance included one set of "plus" factors, Whitney noted. He never stepped upon a speaker's platform unless he was "scrupulously clean and close shaven."

Edwin M. Stanton acknowledged the lack of facial hair, but challenged the verdict of cleanliness. After seeing Lincoln for the first time in 1858, the future secretary of war said the man destined to be the decisive figure in the Civil War was "a long, lank creature, wearing a dirty linen duster on the back of which perspiration had splotched wide stains that resembled a map of the continent."

J. H. Burnham of Bloomington concentrated upon physical features and decided that Lincoln was the "*homeliest* and the *awkwardest* man in the Sucker State."

Appearance alone should have made it impossible for Lincoln to capture listeners. But he had additional qualities that constituted a second strike against him every time he stepped before a crowd.

His speech patterns were as chaotic as his spelling. Even in the sophisticated East, he told audiences he was glad that folk who *yearned* their daily wages *keered* sufficiently for the Constitution to avoid being *hornswoggled* by Democrats. Persons not accustomed to his diction did not easily understand that he was referring to an original idea when he spoke of an "idee" that was "ra-a-ly" his.

Carl Schurz, an ardent admirer later made a general by Lincoln, penned a less-than-flattering description of the persuasive speaker. [LIBRARY OF CONGRESS]

Along with everything else he said, words labeling him "frontiers-man" were delivered with a voice heard as "high-pitched and rather strident" or "shrill and unpleasant." Newspaper reporter Horace White, who listened to a long address at Ottawa, Illinois, said his ears picked up "a thin tenor, or rather falsetto voice, almost as high pitched as a boatswain's whistle."

In spite of traits that should have defeated him as a speaker, the future president showed signs of platform greatness almost as soon as he began facing audiences. Whig attorney David Davis, later a judge, heard him in 1844 and mused that he had worked on a farm at eight dollars a month until age twenty-two. Despite the fact that he showed "the want of early education," Davis concluded that young Lincoln was "the best stump speaker in the state."

His Gettysburg Address, alone, would have been enough later to propel him into the front rank of American masters of the spoken word. Signs of literary genius emerged much earlier, however. When he addressed the Young Men's Lyceum of Springfield at age twenty-nine, Lincoln's powerful use of words promised that he would soon be recognized as both eloquent and persuasive.

Some modern analysts of his accomplishments insist that the man with access to few books nourished the "soul of a poet." He himself produced some sets of verse in his early years, but these lines are not remarkable. More than any other single source, the

Bible, as translated into English two centuries before he was born, seems to have influenced his style as a speaker and writer.

Direct quotations are rare; yet in their debates, Stephen A. Douglas more than once accused him of having a "proneness for quoting Scripture." Brief Biblical allusions such as "Mammon," "Egyptian bondage," "the blood of Abel," "hanging upon the gallows like Haman," and "numbering of the hairs of our head" appear more frequently than do entire verses or sentences.

If practice ever "makes perfect," it is small wonder that Abraham Lincoln soared when he rose to speak. During the summer and fall of 1858, he made more than one hundred addresses. In 1859, he traveled more than four thousand miles to face audiences in Ohio, Michigan, Wisconsin, and Kansas. After speaking by invitation in New York City in 1860, he toured New England in order to deliver eleven addresses in ten days.

At Hartford, New Haven, Norwich, Bridgeport, and other eastern cities he usually spoke for about two hours. Historian Albert J. Beveridge considered his address at Peoria in October 1854 to be his first great speech; it lasted fully three hours. During the debates with Douglas, he regretted that he was sometimes allocated only ninety minutes.

Much of Lincoln's power came from what he had to say.

Until "lost papers" were discovered, it was widely believed that he performed best when equipped with a complete manuscript, carefully revised several times. His partner, William H. Herndon, long ago

David Davis, a prominent Whig attorney, praised Lincoln's power as an orator. [AUTHOR'S COLLECTION]

observed that he customarily "jotted down ideas on stray pieces of paper, which found a lodgement in his hat."

Long after his death, memoranda made for speeches at Columbus, Ohio, and Hartford, Connecticut, were made public. They consist of brief phrases, punctuated with abbreviations that are all but meaningless to the modern reader. Much of the time, the man early lauded by Davis as a "stump speaker" used slips of paper rather than manuscripts—and larded his messages rather heavily with spur-of-the-moment humor.

He kept a small leather-bound notebook in which he had pasted part of the Declaration of Independence and assorted newspaper stories. A second notebook was crammed with clippings about slavery and its evils. Having scanned his notebooks, selected and perhaps memorized material he wished to use, he often strode to the speaker's platform with his huge, expressive hands empty.

Herndon attested that Lincoln "saw ludicrous elements in everything." As a result, when facing an audience he could both "narrate some story from his storehouse" and "improvise one on the spot." According to the Chicago *Journal,* a two-hour address at an 1848 Whig rally included "humorous but very appropriate illustrations." Even the Boston *Daily Advertiser* lauded his "brilliant illustrations."

Lincoln's manuscripts—if they ever existed—were rarely preserved. Reporters seldom included humorous yarns and other illustrative stories in transcripts prepared for their readers; so most used by him have been lost. Listener after listener, however, attested that part of his power as a public speaker stemmed from frequent and skillful use of humor.

Gestures played their own special role, as well. Frequently he "pointed his theories into his hearer's head with a long, bony forefinger." At what one enthralled listener called "great moments," the speaker "would fling both hands upward, to show joy—or clench his fists in silent condemnation." Often he gestured with his head instead of his hands. Sometimes when leading up to a major emphasis, he bent his knees and "then straightened them with a jerk, rising to his full height" as he made his point.

If contemporary estimates were accurate, he sometimes spoke to crowds of fifteen thousand or more. Ottawa, Illinois, was a town of about six thousand—yet an estimated ten thousand listeners crowded together in open air to listen to a three-hour debate between Douglas and Lincoln. While on his 1860 tour of the Northeast, he addressed a rally held at a railroad station. Arrival of a train full of dignitaries forced him to cut his message short—after only ninety minutes.

From Illinois to Ohio and from Wisconsin to Massachusetts, men who heard Lincoln attested that something remarkable happened to him when he was on the platform.

Attorney William H. Herndon was especially impressed by his partner's ability to use humorous stories to win audiences. [ORIGINAL IN THE HENRY E. HUNTINGTON LIBRARY]

Reporter Horace White observed that as he warmed to his subject, "The eyes began to sparkle, the mouth to smile, the whole countenance so wreathed in animation that a stranger would have said, 'Why, this man, so angular and somber a moment ago, is really handsome!'"

Herndon saw that after speaking a few minutes, Lincoln became "freer and less uneasy in his movements; to that extent, he was graceful." Donn Piatt, who labeled him "the homeliest man I ever saw," was enthralled by Lincoln the public speaker. "In action, his ugly face became animated and then brightened like a lit lantern."

When at his best on the platform, Lincoln seemed to Herndon—who never tried to conceal his partner's weaknesses—to be "inspired, fresh from the hands of his Creator." In such moments, said the man who was in intimate daily contact with him, "every organ of his body was in motion and acted with ease, elegance, and grace."

Francis Grierson, one of many who heard Lincoln at Alton, Illinois, was astonished that "the moment he began to speak, the ungainly mouth lost its heaviness and the half-listless eyes attained a wondrous power." There was something "elemental and mystical" about Lincoln the public speaker in the opinion of Grierson. As a result, "Before he had spoken twenty minutes the conviction took possession of thousands that here was the prophetic man of the present."

9

*How Did He Manage to
Occupy Center Stage in*

A SERIES OF HISTORY-MAKING DEBATES?

■

"*MY DEAR SIR:* Will it be agreeable to you to make an arrangement for you and myself to divide time, and address the same audiences the present canvass?"

Written at Chicago on July 24, 1858, Lincoln's terse note to Sen. Stephen A. Douglas was—as customary—signed simply, "A. Lincoln." It was hand-delivered to the Democrat by their mutual friend, Norman B. Judd, who at the moment called himself "an anti–Nebraska Democrat."

In his lengthy reply, penned the same day, Douglas expressed surprise that the man who proposed the arrangement had waited so long to request it. He noted that they had earlier been together in Chicago, Bloomington, Atlanta, Lincoln, and Springfield. Though he didn't say so, he knew the Republican state committee had made plans for his opponent to follow him everywhere he went. Lincoln could have challenged him to engage in public debate at any time but had failed to do so.

Nevertheless, Douglas concluded, he was willing to accommodate the man who hoped to unseat him. Since both had already spoken in quick succession in the Second and Sixth Congressional districts, he ruled out additional meetings there. But he would debate Lincoln at Freeport, Ottawa, Galesburg, Quincy, Alton, Jonesboro, and Charleston. Where the Democratic State Central Committee had already made commitments, the senator added, "I must insist upon you meeting me at the time specified."

Four days later, in a querulous mood, Lincoln agreed, "provided you name the places at once." He wanted nothing more than "perfect reciprocity," he said. Though the stipulation was not put in writing,

Stephen A. Douglas, "The Little Giant," was America's most prominent political figure when he accepted Lincoln's challenge.
[AUTHOR'S COLLECTION]

he apparently let Douglas know that he wanted them to alternate with opening and closing. Douglas assented to this arrangement, stipulating that the man speaking first should have an hour, followed by one and one-half hours by his opponent, then half an hour of closing arguments from the first speaker.

Douglas would speak first at Ottawa, he said; then Lincoln would lead off at Freeport. Such alternation would give the senator four openings and four closings to Lincoln's three.

When Lincoln agreed to these terms on July 31, the stage was set for a seven-part series of political debates unlike any that had ever taken place in the United States. Their oratorical duel would put each man on the platform—center stage—for ten and one-half hours.

Standing perhaps five feet, four inches in height and weighing only about one hundred pounds, Douglas was the nation's premier political heavyweight. Sometimes labeled "a Vermont Yankee, come to Illinois," he reached the U.S. House of Representatives at age thirty. Four years later, he moved up to the Senate to occupy a seat he would defend in debates leading up to the election of 1859. Having gained national fame through sponsorship of the Kansas-Nebraska Bill, at age thirty-nine he barely missed becoming the Democratic nominee for the presidency.

Norman B. Judd, who help to arrange the debates, later offered Lincoln's name as the Republican nominee for the presidency. [NICOLAY & HAY, ABRAHAM LINCOLN]

Deep blue eyes were set in a "shapely and well-balanced head" surmounted by a mass of curly waves. As dynamic as he was physically attractive, Douglas often used his deep bass voice to call for an "ocean-to-ocean American republic."

Even Lincoln's partner and ardent admirer, William H. Herndon, admitted that the Democrat was richly endowed with "that unique trait, magnetism." Observers of the political scene termed him "eloquent almost to the point of brilliancy," while being also "self-confident to the point of arrogance." Because of Douglas's fame, large audiences were guaranteed. As the challenger, Lincoln would share the spotlight, standing in it only because Douglas was willing to cross verbal swords with him.

Having made up his mind to campaign for the Senate seat he admitted he craved, Lincoln resigned from the Illinois legislature. In numerous counties he was endorsed as the Republican nominee. Then a precedent-making move took place. Delegates from the entire state converged upon Springfield, where the Republican convention formally endorsed his candidacy. Some analysts hold that only one other nominee for the Senate had been chosen by means of a state convention.

Everyone knew that selection of the person who would occupy the coveted seat would be made, not by the public, but by members of the legislature. This meant that despite publicity created by debates, the real electoral contest was for eighty-seven seats in the state lawmaking body. Makeup of legislative districts made it almost certain that the Democratic contender would have an easy win. Yet Lincoln set out to canvass the state as though he expected what he said to the masses might affect the outcome of the contest.

Years earlier, Douglas had moved to Chicago and allied himself with the commercial and industrial interests of the fast-growing city. Chicago's ties with New York and with Boston helped persuade such eastern Republicans as editor Horace Greeley to back the Democrat widely regarded as the "last and best hope for national unity."

On July 9, 1858, Douglas formally opened his re-election campaign in Chicago. Speaking from the balcony of the Tremont House, with Lincoln in the audience, Douglas castigated the man from Springfield for statements made earlier. Though he spoke to a different audience, Lincoln responded to Douglas within twenty-four hours. Douglas moved to Bloomington on July 16 and to Springfield the following day. On the evening of the seventeenth, Lincoln replied to both messages.

Earlier, Lincoln had delivered speech after speech in county after county. Long absences from the courtroom began to create financial problems, and so the candidate turned to friends who had provided campaign money earlier. Most appeals seem to have been made orally, person-to-person, but a June 28, 1858, letter to A. Campbell of

Because he dressed and groomed before sitting for an artist or photographer, Lincoln's everyday appearance early in his presidency remains a mystery. Here the artist shows a "pretty" person who—somehow—is without the beard he began to grow a few months earlier. [ILLUSTRATED LONDON NEWS, 1861]

LaSalle suggesting that he could use additional help has survived.

Somehow, he found the money—and the stamina—to keep going against what appeared to be insuperable obstacles. Herndon mourned that when his partner walked to the center of a platform, it was impossible to miss his "sad, pained look due to habitual melancholy." After having listened to the rich bass of Douglas for an hour, some listeners cringed at the first words delivered with Lincoln's "shrill, piping, and unpleasant voice."

Douglas was dapper; Lincoln's physical appearance had changed little, if any. Decades later, Carl Sandburg soaked up dozens of contemporary descriptions and distilled them into a single phrase. The Republican, said the poet, looked "like an original plan for an extra-long horse or a lean and tawny buffalo."

Surviving documents give no hint concerning conversations in which Lincoln must have been engaged before putting his challenge to Douglas in writing. Letters they exchanged do not indicate what motivated him to take this action, or why Douglas accepted. With the election to take place in the legislature and victory all but guaranteed, the Democrat had little or nothing to gain. Perhaps Lincoln correctly judged that many persons would consider Douglas a coward if he refused and his stance was made public, as certainly would have been the case. Again, the nation's best-known political figure may have decided that since Lincoln was dogging his heels everywhere he went, formal confrontations would be as good if not better than informal ones.

Both Lincoln and Douglas came to Illinois from other states. They first met at Vandalia when the Kentucky native was a member of the legislature and the man born in Vermont was a lobbyist. Soon, however, both occupied seats in the legislature.

In 1839 Douglas emerged as a spokesman for Democrats. Still a devout Whig, Lincoln campaigned that year for a place as a presidential elector. Both men were admitted to practice before the state supreme court on December 3, 1839. Two years later, both paid more than passing attention to Mary Todd. By 1846, both were in Washington—Lincoln for a two-year term in the House of Representatives, Douglas as a member of the Senate.

Pondering their twenty-two-year relationship in 1856, Lincoln recognized that both were highly ambitious. His own "race of ambition" he dubbed "a flat failure," but he called that of his acquaintance "one of splendid success." Viewing the Democrat's national eminence, the man from Springfield confessed that he'd rather stand where Douglas was "than wear the richest crown that ever pressed a monarch's brow."

Perhaps Abraham Lincoln correctly judged that their long-time rivalry would persuade Douglas to meet him in debate. Possibly he dogged the heels of the senator with the goal of provoking him into a

The Douglas/Lincoln debate at Galesburg on October 7, 1858.
[AUTHOR'S COLLECTION]

series of public confrontations. As early as 1854, Lincoln spoke in
Springfield for four hours on the day after Douglas appeared there.
They clashed again at Peoria less than two weeks later. As a result,
Lincoln was soon besieged by invitations to speak wherever Douglas
made an appearance. In 1858 he followed Douglas at twenty-nine
places in addition to their seven formal confrontations.

Three-hour debates that would make little or no difference in the race for the U.S. Senate attracted reporters from regional and eastern newspapers. Douglas was big news; many editors knew their readers would react strongly if his meetings with a far-behind rival were neglected.

Lincoln probably calculated in advance that he had everything to gain and nothing to lose. His exchanges with Douglas did not take him to the U.S. Senate—but propelled him into the national limelight.

Douglas was re-elected on January 5, 1859, by a vote of fifty-four legislators to forty-six. When their debates ended, Lincoln—despairing—said, "I now sink out of view, and shall be forgotten." But precisely eighteen days after Douglas won the coveted seat, his rival got busy assembling newspaper accounts of their debates.

Lincoln's speeches had been reported in great detail by the Chicago *Press and Tribune,* so he naturally used this source. For copies of speeches by Douglas, he relied upon clippings from the Chicago *Times.* Assembled without commentary, the accumulated material was offered to Springfield publishers Johnson & Bradford. On March 21, 1859, they declined to put them into print.

Through an influential friend, Lincoln then made contact with the founder of the Republican party in Ohio, Oran Follett of Sandusky, who quickly arranged for publication by Follett, Foster & Co. of Columbus. Probably because it was a Republican venture through-and-through, Abraham Lincoln's name appeared before that of Stephen A. Douglas in the title of the book. This may explain, at least in part, why the verbal encounters are today universally known as the Lincoln-Douglas debates. Had an impartial publisher issued an 1859 volume with hyphenated names, the fame of the Democrat would have dictated the usage, Douglas-Lincoln debates.

When an estimated thirty thousand copies of the debates had been circulated, Lincoln inscribed a volume "Compliments of A. Lincoln." He then had it delivered to the Springfield publishers who had rejected the project.

That characteristic bit of action came when Abraham Lincoln was politically down, but far from out. He had failed to gain the coveted seat in the U.S. Senate, but on the national scene he now towered above hosts of other Republican leaders. Defeat by Douglas made the prospect of winning the presidency loom closer than anyone would have imagined earlier. Each exchange with the Democrat had given him publicity beyond anything his most ardent backers could have expected.

10

*Who Thought of Making a
High-income Attorney*

THE RAIL-SPLITTING CANDIDATE FOR THE PRESIDENCY?

■

BENJAMIN F. BUTLER, DESTINED in the future to become a Civil War general, cast his fifty-seventh vote at the eighth Democratic National Convention. As he had done from the first ballot taken in the hall of the South Carolina Institute in Charleston, he backed Sen. Jefferson Davis of Mississippi.

Butler wasted his time, his effort, and his paper ballots. Hopelessly divided over interpretation of Stephen A. Douglas's "popular sovereignty" slogan, the convention adjourned on May 3, 1860, without selecting a nominee. Delegates already had decided to make a fresh start in Baltimore on June 18. There anti–Douglas Democrats boycotted the session. Hence, the Little Giant was nominated for the presidency on the second ballot.

Five days later, Democrats calling themselves "independent" but actually advocating extension of slavery into territories also met in Baltimore. They took just one ballot to put John C. Breckinridge of Kentucky into the presidential race. Within the week, dissidents making up the Southern Democratic party added their support to Breckenridge.

On May 9 a third national political convention convened in Baltimore. Members of the Constitutional Union party professed to ignore the slavery question, while stressing the Constitution and law enforcement. On the second ballot they chose John Bell of Tennessee as their candidate for the Executive Mansion.

Republicans everywhere whooped with delight when they learned that their man would not face Douglas alone. Instead, a trio of strong candidates, each with a distinct following, would draw votes from him. With at least 800,000 voters committed to Breckenridge

Benjamin F. Butler, first Democrat to be made a brigadier general by Lincoln, was an ardent backer of Jefferson Davis for the presidency. [BRADY STUDIO, LIBRARY OF CONGRESS]

and perhaps 500,000 to Bell, Douglas was described as having "about the same chance as a snowball in Hell."

Civil service not yet having been established, entrenched Democrats had for decades controlled and dispensed patronage. Their party split meant that their candidates were all but certain to lose. Such a prospect promised that the November election would put thousands of jobs into the hands of Republicans, whose party was barely six years old.

Already flexing mighty industrial and financial muscles, Chicago badly wanted the second Republican National Convention. In a fervent bid to get it, civil leaders made an extravagant promise; they would erect a special building to house the convention—something never before done.

That inducement was almost enough to sway the national committee. When Norman B. Judd of Chicago confided that the Illinois delegation would not enter a candidate for the presidency, the issue was decided. Chicago it would be, on May 16. Delegates would convene in a new structure already named the Wigwam, not simply to agree upon a candidate, but to choose the man all but certain to be the next president of the United States.

Eight days prior to the Chicago convention, Illinois Republicans gathered in Decatur, a town into which young Lincoln had come years earlier in an ox-wagon. Early on the second day of the conclave, Richard J. Oglesby gained the floor. Widely known as an ardent admirer of the Sangamon County attorney who was often called Mr. Illinois Republican, Oglesby announced that a long-time Democrat had expressed a desire to come forward to make a contribution.

When assent was given, fifty-eight-year-old John Hanks started down the aisle. Heavily bearded and wearing the clothing of a "dirt farmer," he carried in his arms two old fence rails. A sign attached to the rails proclaimed:

ABRAHAM LINCOLN
The Rail Candidate
FOR PRESIDENT IN 1860
Two rails from a lot of 3,000
made in 1830 by Hanks and Abe Lincoln
whose father was the first pioneer
of Macon County

Pandemonium broke out as Hanks walked slowly toward the platform. Before he reached it, shouts of "Lincoln! Lincoln" prompted a self-appointed committee to escort the man from Springfield to the podium.

Reaching the platform, Lincoln's second cousin turned solemnly to him and demanded, "Identify your work!"

"I cannot say that I split these rails," the aspirant for office responded. "Where did you get them?"

"At the farm you improved down on the Sangamon River."

"That was a long time ago," Lincoln mused. "It is possible that I

John C. Breckinridge as he appeared during his tenure as Buchanan's vice president. [LIBRARY OF CONGRESS]

split these rails, but I cannot identify them. What kind of timber are they?"

"Honey locust and black walnut."

Turning from his rail-bearing relative to the ecstatic audience, Abraham Lincoln ended the dialogue, "Well, boys," he commented, "I can only say that I have split a great many better-looking ones!"

In the aftermath of that hour, it was inevitable that delegates should instruct those bound for Chicago to enter the name of Abraham Lincoln for the presidential nomination.

Once the Illinois convention made its choice, for campaign purposes Lincoln ceased to be a high-income attorney. At rallies throughout the nation, he was hailed as the Rail-Splitter. Campaign buttons and tobacco pipes were inscribed with symbols that depicted rails. At party headquarters in New York, two weathered rails were put on display.

Noted cartoonist Frank Bellew produced a sketch he called "A 'Rail' Old Western Gentleman"—a "stick body" of rails surmounted by Lincoln's head. In Chicago a campaign newspaper appeared from June through October under the masthead *THE RAIL SPLITTER*. Cincinnati Republicans who saw it were so impressed that they launched their own paper of the same name in August.

A political club in New England gleefully announced that it held the ax used by Lincoln to split rails. Currier and Ives issued a Louis Maurer lithograph that depicted Lincoln riding a rail labeled "Republican platform."

Some Democrats tried to turn the slogan to their advantage, mocking the Republican candidate as the Prince of Rails. Readers of the Chicago *Herald* were informed that at age eighteen, Lincoln regularly split 76,000 rails each working day. In New Albany, Indiana, the editor of the local newspaper hoped that all the rails ever split by Lincoln might be brought into one pile. If so, he calculated, there would be enough of them to build a ten-foot rail fence all the way from the North Pole to the South Pole.

Republicans responded to taunts by enlarging upon imagery of the Rail-Splitter. That was Lincoln's title, they gloated, but Douglas was the Party-Splitter! Lines of doggerel derided Douglas as being the greater of the two because he managed to split a party while Lincoln only split rails.

At least as early as 1847, a few Illinois Republicans were calling their favorite political candidate Honest Abe. Elihu B. Washburne credited orator Lisle Smith with having coined the nickname in 1847. When first used, said Washburne, it identified a "tall, angular, and awkward" man who strolled about while wearing "a short-waisted swallowtail coat, thin pantaloons scarcely coming to his ankles, a straw hat, and a pair of brogans with woolen socks."

"Honest Abe" was a natural, almost an inevitable, accompaniment

*Uncle John Hanks made
the Rail-Splitter image
public but almost certainly
did not conceive of it.*
[NICOLAY & HAY, *ABRAHAM
LINCOLN*]

of the Rail-Splitter. Though in almost universal use by persons who
supported him for the presidency, intimates of Lincoln were unanimous in saying that in his adult life, no one ever dared to call him
Abe in face-to-face conversation.

His earliest political nickname, Long Shanks, was well adapted to
his stance, which today would be called populist. Lincoln dressed to
appear to be the laborer he often described himself as having been—
"hired on a flatboat at eight dollars a month, with only one pair of
breeches to my back." When possible, he liked to make speeches
while standing in a wagon. In Springfield he once used such a platform to address an estimated fifteen thousand persons.

Traveling to Washington as president-elect, he denounced the national crisis as the work of "politicians"—skillfully using the term in
such fashion that he indicated he did not belong to that tribe. Earlier, he denounced all holders of the nation's chief office. "An honest
laborer digs coal at about seventy cents a day," he observed, "while
the president digs abstractions at about seventy dollars a day."

Throughout the North, ardent young party workers organized
torchlight parades, demonstrations that were quickly dubbed the
"work of wide-awake Republicans." In many localities, bands of Wide
Awakes walked through streets carrying rails—authentic or simu-
lated. Citizens of some urban centers were treated to strings of
horse-drawn wagons on which Rail-Splitter floats had been created.

Colorful though they were, these demonstrations were not seen by
experts as necessary. Once nominated, Lincoln's election was an all
but foregone conclusion, though no one dared to predict by what
majority. An outright split in the Democratic party meant that the

Republican didn't need the image of the Rail-Splitter to win. Once fashioned, however, it stuck to him for the remainder of his life and has continued long after his death.

It was Hanks who burst into the Bloomington convention with two rails and a placard. Few who knew him credited the illiterate long-time Democrat with having devised the ruse. His most notable achievement in the aftermath of the convention was to go around the region peddling old rails for one dollar each.

Undocumented Republican tradition credits Richard J. Oglesby of Decatur with having concocted the drama in which weather-beaten rails were central. Later a governor of Illinois, he is said to have gone to Hanks with his idea. According to this story, Oglesby and Hanks found old rails ten miles from Decatur at or near the site of a one-time Lincoln cabin. They fastened their trophies to the axles of their buggy, then hid them in Oglesby's barn until they were ready to use them.

That account may be authentic and accurate. If so, it is incomplete.

Regardless of the pledge made to the national committee by Judd, Abraham Lincoln didn't want to be ignored in Chicago. Writing to Judd one month before the Illinois state convention, he suggested that it wouldn't do his career great damage if he failed to win nomination "on the national ticket." But he stressed that it really would hurt if he didn't get the support of the Illinois delegation. "I mean this to be private," he concluded.

Admittedly eager to be his adopted state's favorite son in Chicago, he needed something special—something extra—to be sure of gaining that spot. Cousin John Hanks and his rails proved to be that "something extra."

Speaking in New Haven, Connecticut, just ninety days before the Republican convention in Decatur, Lincoln told his sophisticated eastern audience that he wasn't ashamed to confess that twenty-five years earlier, he was "a hired laborer, mauling rails." That theme surfaced frequently during earlier speeches. He especially liked to tell of having earned the material with which to make a pair of brown jeans trousers by splitting four hundred rails for each yard of cloth.

Regardless of who conceived it, the Rail-Splitter image bore all the earmarks of having come from a master of ideas and audiences. Those who knew Abraham Lincoln well remembered him as having been a top-rank political genius almost from the time he first won a seat in the Illinois legislature in August 1834—about four years after he split his last batch of rails. That he may have been the inspiration for the idea of presenting himself as the Rail-Splitter candidate should come as no surprise.

11

*At the Wigwam, How Did a
Minor Contender Achieve*

A SWEEPING VICTORY ON THE THIRD BALLOT?

■

GALVANIZED BY SYMBOLISM of the rail-splitter, Abraham Lincoln's supporters rejoiced that the 1860 Republican National Convention would be held in Chicago. Editorial endorsement had been given to him there as early as February.

A campaign team was hurriedly but carefully assembled. Led by Lincoln's long-time associate David Davis, it included William H. Herndon and Ward Hill Lamon, plus Lincoln's second law partner, Stephen T. Logan. Norman B. Judd, chairman of the Illinois state committee and a member of the national committee, cooperated closely but often made decisions without consultation. Joseph Medill and Charles H. Ray of the Chicago *Press and Tribune,* invaluable because of their many press contacts, were supplemented by Leonard Swett, who only a few months earlier had tried to become governor of Illinois.

Numerous persons headed toward the fast-growing city of 110,000 expected the Chicago conclave to be perfunctory. So many of the 466 delegates expected William H. Seward of New York to become the nominee that their attention focused upon the choice of his running mate.

Conductors of several trains converging upon the convention site took informal polls among their passengers. One found 127 Seward supporters, with just 44 persons backing all other candidates combined. On another train, 240 passengers indicated a seven-to-one preference for the New Yorker. Still another train, coming from Milwaukee, carried 368 supporters of Seward and 93 for Lincoln, plus 46 for all others combined.

Chicago's Wigwam building was erected especially for the purpose of selecting a Republican nominee for the presidency.
[NICOLAY & HAY, ABRAHAM LINCOLN]

Seward's ardent supporters considered it "singularly appropriate" that the convention would be called to order on his fifty-ninth birthday. In its issue of May 15, the New York *Tribune* advised readers that the New Yorker would have little opposition. Editor Horace Greeley, who backed Edward Bates of Missouri, discussed the backgrounds of candidates in some depth. Of the suddenly introduced man from Springfield he only said, "Mr. Lincoln of Illinois, however, is rising in prominence."

When the convention opened on Wednesday morning, May 16, ten thousand people packed the Wigwam, while an additional twenty thousand stood outside. Four years earlier in Philadelphia, Republicans drew no more than two thousand to their national convention.

Governor Edwin D. Morgan of New York called the body to order; then David Wilmot of Pennsylvania delivered a stirring address. At 5:00 P.M. George Ashmun of Massachusetts was elected permanent chairman. A committee on resolutions was instructed to draft a platform, and the convention adjourned for the evening.

Most of Thursday was devoted to adoption of the platform, to which Greeley contributed freely. As modified after presentation, it approved the right of each state to "order and control its own domes-

In Chicago's cavernous Wigwam, Lincoln, who was in Springfield, was nominated on the third ballot. [LIBRARY OF CONGRESS]

tic institutions according to its own judgment exclusively." It backed protective tariffs, a transcontinental railroad, and a program aimed at providing free land to settlers in the West. Delegates from slaveholding states such as Virginia, Maryland, Kentucky, and Texas were heartened that the document included a solemn warning: "We denounce the lawless invasion by armed force of the soil of any State or Territory, no matter under what pretext."

With the first ballot scheduled for Thursday evening, many expected Seward to be chosen by a landslide. A chorus of groans ensued when chairman Ashmun announced that printers had failed to deliver tally sheets, so no vote could be taken. Once the turmoil subsided, a motion was adopted to adjourn until Friday morning.

Rejoicing, Lincoln's manager hailed the delay as an act of God. Led by Lamon, John H. Marshall and a group of his youthful friends scrawled names of convention officers on admission tickets. Simultaneously, Judd—a railroad attorney—arranged for special trains to haul Lincoln supporters into the city.

Boisterously confident, Seward's followers put a brass band into the streets on Friday morning. Then they marched from their hotel to the tune of "Oh, Isn't He a Darling!"—only to find the Wigwam so crowded that few people other than delegates were able to find seats.

Edward Bates of Missouri, who helped swing the West to Lincoln, soon became a member of the new president's cabinet. [NICOLAY & HAY, ABRAHAM LINCOLN]

Bogus tickets passed out by Davis, Swett, and their lieutenants had been used so well that the convention hall was packed with supporters of Lincoln.

Nominations were limited to single sentences. Presentation of Seward's name by William M. Evarts was followed by thunderous applause. When Judd reached the podium, he shouted, "I desire, on behalf of the delegation from Illinois, to put in nomination, as a candidate for president of the United States, Abraham Lincoln of Illinois!" Before he finished speaking, hundreds of small hand-colored wood engravings showing Lincoln's face as depicted by E. H. Brown showered down like confetti.

The roll call of states, later alphabetical, was then geographical, with New England at the head of the list. On the first ballot, Seward received 173.5 votes; 236 were needed to win. Lincoln followed with 102 votes, while Simon Cameron of Pennsylvania, Salmon P. Chase of Ohio, and Bates of Missouri each received about 50 votes.

Recognizing that Pennsylvania was crucial, David Davis had arranged for delegates from the state to be seated between Illinois and Indiana, both strongly backing Lincoln. Since many Hoosiers felt that Republicans would be defeated at the state level if Seward should be the presidential nominee, Indiana went for Lincoln on the first ballot. Davis, Judd, and other members of Lincoln's team then persuaded the Pennsylvania delegation that Seward's name on the ballot would cost Republicans the Pennsylvania state house. As a result, Cameron withdrew.

When the second ballot was tallied, it offered a stunning surprise.

Seward gained only 11 votes, while Lincoln's total jumped by 79. That left Chase of Ohio in third place, with 42.5 votes.

Other key workers in the Lincoln campaign had been busy contacting delegates from every state. Their strategy was deceptively simple. Instead of asking for votes on the first ballot, they had persuaded as many men as possible to take Lincoln as their second choice.

With Seward's lead slipping, Lincoln's followers stressed the contrast between the two men. Seward had made his positions clear on most or all major national issues; Lincoln had been guarded in his speech and had followed a deliberate policy of trying to offend no one.

Seward was the only nationally known Republican alleged to have lauded John Brown after the raid upon Harpers Ferry; in addition, he had hinted at civil war by warning that an "irrepressible conflict" seemed to be looming because of the slavery issue. While Lincoln was on record as opposing extension of slavery into territories, the Illinois candidate had also underscored his conviction that where slavery existed it was lawful and could not be challenged. In addition, he supported enforcement of laws concerning fugitive slaves.

Sharp contrast between a candidate with universally familiar and often controversial views and a rival not nearly so well known or so

William H. Seward of New York, "Mr. Republican," was expected to win the nomination without a fight. [LESLIE'S ILLUSTRATED WEEKLY]

Stephen T. Logan, an early law partner of Lincoln, joined the team working for nomination of the Rail Splitter. [Nicolay & Hay, *Abraham Lincoln*]

clearly a foe of the South was significant, but not enough. Lincoln's managers seem to have been willing to promise almost anything to anyone who would back him. Oral tradition says that from Springfield the candidate sent a telegram to Davis that instructed him to make no bargains. If so, that telegram has vanished. Lincoln used the margin of a newspaper said to have been carried by his friend Edward D. Baker to order, "*Make no contracts that will bind me.*"

Such a notation was precisely what Davis needed to show to persons who hesitated about backing Lincoln for fear he was offering positions with a free hand. What arrangement, if any, prevailed when Lincoln and Davis talked preconvention strategy is unknown. In Chicago, rumor said Davis persuaded delegations to abandon their favorite sons in return for promises that these men would be chosen as members of Lincoln's cabinet.

Whatever took place in smoke-filled rooms of Chicago's forty-two hotels where delegates paid $1.50 to $2.50 per day for room and meals, the third ballot proved decisive. When the tally was completed, Seward had lost 4.5 votes and now needed 56 to win. Lincoln, on the other hand, had gained 53.5 votes and was within 1.5 votes of the nomination.

As soon as he could be heard above the commotion, ex-minister to Bolivia David K. Cartter of Ohio jumped up and shouted that five members of the Buckeye delegation had switched their votes to Lincoln! Reporter Murat Halstead wrote, "Imagine all the hogs ever slaughtered in Cincinnati giving their death squeals together, and a score of big steam whistles going together! Lincoln boys gave a concentrated shriek and stamping that made every plank and pillar in the building quiver."

When the tumult subsided sufficiently for speakers to be heard, other states jumped on the Lincoln bandwagon as rapidly as possible. After all 466 votes had been cast, the man from Springfield had 364 of them—128 above the number needed to win.

Abraham Lincoln chafed at remaining in Springfield but took the advice of his lieutenants and did so. When a telegram arrived with announcement of victory, he was sitting in a hickory chair in the office of the *Sangamon Journal.* An admirer who was present recalled that he scanned the telegram, then smiled, stood up, and remarked, "Well, there's a little lady down on Eighth Street who'll want to hear the news."

What, if anything, was said about trading positions for votes in conversations between Lincoln and his campaign staff?

No one knows. Neither is it possible to document promises made—or hints offered—by Davis and his aides at Chicago.

Journalist Charles H. Ray, a member of Lincoln's inner circle, later said his managers promised Indiana and Pennsylvania anything and everything they wanted. Cartter of Ohio, who started the dramatic third-ballot turn around, is alleged to have been guaranteed a high post in the administration. Other rumors abound; none can positively be proved or disproved.

One thing is clear from the record, however. Many who gave way to

Simon Cameron of Pennsylvania lost the nomination for the presidency but was named U.S. secretary of war.
[NICOLAY & HAY, *ABRAHAM LINCOLN*]

the Lincoln momentum or who worked for him behind the scenes were chosen by him for important posts. Seward was made secretary of state; Chase received the Treasury Department portfolio; Cameron became secretary of war; and a fourth contender for the nomination—Edward Bates—became Lincoln's attorney general.

Campaign manager Davis had hoped to become a federal judge; in 1862 he was appointed to the U.S. Supreme Court. Judd, who presided over the convention with a heavy hand, was named as U.S. minister to Prussia four days after Lincoln's inauguration.

Ward Hill Lamon, of bogus admission ticket fame, became marshal of the District of Columbia in April 1861. Jesse W. Fell of Bloomington, who secured and circulated a brief Lincoln autobiography, won appointment as a U.S. Army paymaster. William P. Dole, credited with having gained the support of both Indiana and Pennsylvania, was named commissioner of Indian Affairs. Editor Thomas J. Pickett of Rock Island, Illinois, who put all the resources of his *Weekly Register* behind candidate Lincoln, became custodian of the local army quartermasters' depot. Another pro–Lincoln editor, William O. Stoddard of Champaign, went with the president-elect to Washington as one of his secretaries and later was appointed U.S. marshal for Arkansas.

Cartter of Ohio was famous only briefly for having delivered the votes that took the Lincoln nomination over the top. Many who knew him as U.S. minister to Bolivia or as chief justice of the District of Columbia Supreme Court, didn't even remember that he had been in Chicago a few days during May 1860.

Thus did one-term Congressman Abraham Lincoln—out of elected office for a dozen years—snatch the nomination from William H. ("Mr. Republican") Seward.

Nathaniel Hawthorne, who didn't claim to be an experienced politician, pondered the outcome at Chicago and wrote:

> It is the strangest and yet the fittest thing in the jumble of human vicissitudes, that he, out of so many millions, unlooked for, unselected by any intelligible process that could be based upon his genuine qualities, unknown to those who chose him, and unsuspected of what endowments may adapt him for his tremendous responsibility, should have found the way open for him to fling his lank personality into the chair of state—where, I presume, it was his first impulse to throw his legs on the council-table and tell the cabinet ministers a story.

PART TWO

Six Fateful Months

U.S. secretary of the navy Gideon Welles was positive that the ships and men needed to take Fort Sumter by force were not available. [NICOLAY & HAY, ABRAHAM LINCOLN]

12

Why Did He Ask His Advisers,

"IS IT WISE TO ATTEMPT TO RELIEVE FORT SUMTER"?

■

STANDING CLOSE TO a horsehair bench just inside Willard's Hotel, John G. Nicolay signaled to a porter. "Be sure there are plenty of spittoons," he instructed.

Consulting his watch, the private secretary of the president-elect mused, "Twenty minutes to go. Wonder who will be first? Seward, for sure. He'll be here within ten minutes!" Pacing back and forth, Nicolay went over his list: "Seward, Chase, Welles, Blair, Cameron, Smith, and Bates."

Suddenly he stopped, realizing his list showed complete disregard for protocol. Until Lincoln, cabinet members were listed in the order of their importance: state, treasury, war, attorney general, postmaster general, navy, and interior.

"The new sequence hasn't been changed since the Tycoon put it together," he reflected. "Must be a reason for it. He said he wanted diversity, and he has it. Seven men, seven states. He owes most of these men, and tonight is their first payment."

William H. Seward of New York was, indeed, first to arrive for the March 3, 1861, cabinet dinner. Others were close behind. Soon the mahogany walls echoed to laughter and small talk, while blue cigar smoke swirled about as waiters came and went.

Eight years older than Lincoln, Seward had long been known as Mr. Republican. Now he had a new nickname: Prime Minister. He went to Chicago with nearly enough votes to win the nomination on the first ballot, and it was demeaning to serve in the cabinet of the Westerner who had beaten him. But as senior statesman, he expected to make the crucial decisions.

Tall and portly Salmon P. Chase hadn't wanted to give up his Senate seat in exchange for treasury. His forty-nine ballots for the

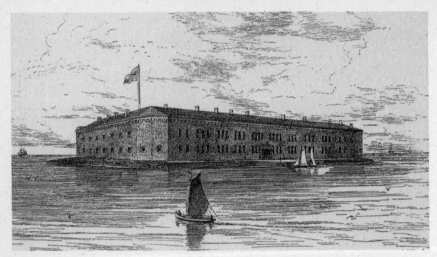

Fort Sumter at the time Major Anderson moved his men there. On an artificial island of granite "leavings," the installation had never before been occupied. [THE GENESIS OF THE CIVIL WAR]

presidential nomination had led him to expect to become secretary of state. Passed over for that post, at the last minute he learned that the "Illinois baboon" had drafted him for treasury.

Simon Cameron of Pennsylvania had launched the stampede for Lincoln by releasing fifty delegates after the first ballot. Boss of his state for twenty years, he had no military background or experience, but his influence put him in the cabinet as secretary of war.

Montgomery Blair, slated to become postmaster general, was the only man at the dinner under fifty years of age. Everyone knew he was there because his wealthy and powerful father had thrown his support to Lincoln when members of the Republican convention wavered.

Edward Bates was told by the Republican nominee that he could choose any cabinet post he wanted. Because of his legal experience, he seemed right for attorney general.

Gideon Welles of Connecticut seemed out of place at the dinner. His long, white beard was surmounted by a smooth-shaven upper lip. His clumsy old wig required frequent straightening, but New England was owed a cabinet post, and he would run the U.S. Navy.

Caleb B. Smith, due soon to become secretary of the interior, was there because Indiana had called in her markers soon after the state's delegation went for Lincoln in Chicago.

Nicolay, who was in and out of the room several times, noticed that conversation was dominated by Seward. Small wonder that Seward stood out above the rest. He had spent more time with Lincoln—one-on-one—than all of his colleagues combined. He was jovial, knowing that everyone knew he would be the power behind the throne. But he didn't conceal his anxiety over the plight of the Federal garrison at Fort Sumter in Charleston Harbor; these men were becoming desperate.

Reluctantly, it seemed to Seward, the president read to the cabinet on March 11 a report from Gen. Winfield Scott. According to the army's head, Maj. Robert Anderson and his men could hold out only a short time. But a relief expedition headed to Charleston would have to include 25,000 men and a fleet of warships.

Blair was less pessimistic. His brother-in-law, Gustavus V. Fox, had eighteen years of naval experience and was working on a plan to rescue the Federals and save face for the Union.

Lincoln met with Fox on March 14, heard his plan, and on the following day summarized it for his cabinet. After his advisers went their separate ways, the president drafted a memorandum asking each of them for a written opinion on the wisdom of attempting to resupply Fort Sumter.

Replies came in during the next twenty-four-plus hours.

Seward noted that use of military forces could trigger civil war, so he voted a resounding No. Welles pondered political and military aspects of the question before concluding, "I do not think it wise."

Blair's yes was as firm as Seward's no. What's more, he noted, he had a brother-in-law ready and willing to head a relief expedition. Cameron had conferred with army officers and had found them supporting the judgment of Scott, so he registered his opinion as no. Smith, who used guarded language, didn't think the proposal wise. Bates went directly to the heart of the matter by saying he favored evacuation of the fort as preferable to launching civil war.

Only Chase gave a qualified verdict. He opposed any move that might require enlarging military forces . . . but did not believe that a mere resupply effort would have that effect.

The total was five negative votes against one positive vote from the postmaster general, plus a no/yes from Chase. Pressed for their opinions, members of the cabinet had spoken clearly and distinctly on the most pressing issue of the day.

Having read all seven replies to his question by March 16, the president found time to attend to other matters. To Welles he penned a respectful note asking him to find a job for William Johnson, a servant who had been with him for some time.

Two days later, Lincoln committed to writing his own thoughts concerning the remote installation he consistently called Fort "Sumpter." There were eight separate "considerations in favor of withdrawing the troops," he concluded. Against these were two powerful objections: withdrawal might demoralize the Republican party, and it would be considered a victory by secessionists.

*   *   *

Since sons Willie and Tad were suffering from the measles, official business in the Executive Mansion was restricted to a minimum for several days.

On March 29 the president interviewed army engineer Montgomery Meigs concerning the re-enforcement of Fort Sumter and Fort Pickens in Florida. By then he had requested and received a second set of opinions from cabinet members. With Bates taking no clear stand and Cameron's views not recorded, the cabinet had made an about-face and now favored doing everything possible to hold Fort Sumter.

When the earlier tally of five and one-half negative votes versus one and one-half positive votes became known, Lincoln's displeasure was vividly evident. He said nothing for the record and wrote no letters asking for a reversal of judgment. But he must have hinted that his own position was outlined in his inaugural address. Some who switched positions may have gone back to that message to read it more carefully.

Now having a majority of advisers behind him, Lincoln reported to the cabinet about plans already formulated. Contested forts in South Carolina and Florida would be held, regardless of the consequences. Late on March 29, a terse memorandum went to Secretaries Welles and Cameron: "I desire that an expedition, to move by sea, be got ready to sail as early as the 6th of April next."

No one who learned of that order was under any delusions. Armed conflict was practically certain; the probability that secessionists would suddenly reverse their stance was all but nil. There was no longer a question of whether war would erupt in Charleston Harbor, but only a matter of when the first shots would be fired and who would be blamed for igniting the tinderbox.

In his Inaugural Address, Lincoln labeled himself president of all thirty-three states. No secession had occurred, he said. Hence, "The power confided to me, will be used to hold, occupy, and possess the property and places belonging to the government.

This was not a new position. By late December 1860, he had told intimates that he would "maintain the Union at all hazards." Scott and the U.S. Army should be prepared "to either hold, or retake the forts, as the case may require, at, and after the inauguration."

In light of his announced views and intentions, one cannot help but wonder why Abraham Lincoln consulted cabinet members concerning Fort Sumter. Various motives have been attributed to his actions—from exposing Seward as favoring peace at any price to provoking the South to fire the first shots to believing that the mere show of force would bring the secessionists to their senses. In reality, since he never publicly wrote or commented about the incident, his reasoning is unknown.

13

What Led Him to Call for

75,000 MEN FOR NINETY DAYS?

■

"MR. ASHMUN INSISTED I come."

"Splendid! He knows I value your advice, Mr. Douglas. Please help me look over the situation," Abraham Lincoln responded.

For two hours, the men whose rivalry had grown more keen as the years went by remembered the past and contemplated the future. Often bent over documents and maps, they paid little attention to Republican national chairman George Ashmun, who noticed that Stephen A. Douglas did most of the talking.

Scanning a presidential proclamation scheduled to go out on Monday morning, April 15, Douglas repeatedly expressed doubts, which Lincoln brushed aside. So the Democrat eventually agreed to prepare for the Associated Press a statement of support. In it he said he remained strongly opposed to Abraham Lincoln's political views. But, recognizing that the division of the nation now threatened to become permanent, he gave his personal support to the president's decision to call for troops.

Cabinet members converged on the Executive Mansion early Monday morning and remained there most of the day. They heard Gen. Winfield Scott's report that Washington City was vulnerable to attack and were troubled by news that secessionists seemed to be planning to take over the Gosport naval base near Norfolk.

William H. Seward affixed his signature to Lincoln's document, which included a paragraph calling for Congress to convene on July 4. Secretary of War Simon Cameron arranged for his list of quotas to be transmitted to governors in conjunction with the presidential proclamation.

In it Lincoln pointed out that execution of laws had for some time been opposed and obstructed in seven states: South Carolina, Georgia, Alabama, Florida, Mississippi, Louisiana, and Texas. Their actions created a combination "too powerful to be suppressed by the

Congress, shown here as the body appeared in 1858, had just adjourned. Instead of calling lawmakers back immediately, the president chose July 4 as the date on which they would reconvene. [LIBRARY OF CONGRESS]

ordinary course of judicial proceedings." Hence he demanded from the several states of the Union 75,000 militia "in order to suppress said combinations, and to cause the laws to be duly executed."

Having resorted to an obscure 1795 statute for his authority and having summoned Congress to meet in ninety days, the president dated his order "in the eighty-fifth year" of United States independence.

Almost everyone, Douglas included, was surprised at the action taken by the president. Persons who learned of the proclamation firsthand or from newspaper accounts shook their heads in bewilderment.

Earlier, Gen. Winfield Scott had estimated that resupply of Fort Sumter would require five thousand regulars, one-third of the entire U.S. Army. These professionals would need the support of twenty thousand volunteers, for whose transportation a fleet would be required. In Scott's opinion, such an undertaking could not be launched without an act of Congress. Facing the impossible, the army's head drafted an order requiring Maj. Robert Anderson and his men to evacuate the disputed fortification. When he learned the president's strong views, Scott did not dispatch his message.

Now that secessionists had seized Fort Sumter, Scott agreed that action was necessary. But he considered the call for 75,000 men to be "only a drop in the bucket." To make matters worse, raw members of the militia would be out of uniform before they learned how to use

Virginia's governor John Letcher indignantly refused to supply troops. Strong Unionist sentiment in the state gave way to anger over the call for militia, and Virginia seceded from the Union. [AUTHOR'S COLLECTION]

muskets and respond to commands. Under the act to which the president resorted, militia could be employed no more than thirty days after the next session of Congress.

Keenly aware of Scott's doubts and knowing that Douglas had argued for calling up at least 200,000 men, the secretary of war followed the president's instructions and asked for 75,000—no less, and no more. Governors were given their quotas and asked to deliver infantrymen or riflemen "for three months' service, unless sooner discharged."

Because Michigan's treasury was empty, the governor reported that he was unable to act. In Pennsylvania the small quota was accepted with eagerness and the legislature enacted a bill designed to punish secessionists. Hastily dispatched, a Pennsylvania unit of 460 men was first to reach the threatened capital, but volunteers failed to bring along weapons. Largely through the influence of powerful Democratic leader Benjamin F. Butler, Massachusetts managed to get its quota doubled. Under the enlarged assignment the state began taking steps to provide a four-thousand-man brigade—commanded by Butler.

Cameron obediently refused numerous companies that would have caused their states to exceed their quotas. In spite of his vigilance, about eighty thousand ninety-day men were assembled by July 1.

Leaders in the South and the four border states were even more taken aback by Lincoln's call than were their counterparts in the North. But their reactions were quite different.

Gov. Isham G. Harris of Tennessee reported that the state "will not furnish a single man for coercion, but fifty thousand if necessary for the defence of our rights." "Kentucky will furnish no troops for the wicked purpose of subduing her sister Southern States" was the word from Frankfort. Gov. John W. Ellis of North Carolina called the proclamation a violation of the U.S. Constitution "and a great usurpation of power."

Gov. Clairborn F. Jackson of Missouri denounced the president's call as "illegal, unconstitutional, revolutionary, inhuman, and diabolical." From all-important Richmond came the calmly worded response of Gov. John Lechtner: "The militia of Virginia will not be furnished to the power at Washington for any such use or purpose as they have in view."

Far more significant than the refusal of militia, Virginia's previously wavering leaders reacted by clamoring for secession. Earlier, Lincoln reputedly offered to give up Fort Sumter in return for a pledge that the Old Dominion would remain in the Union, a strong possibility until April 15. Two days after the call for militia, members of the Virginia State Convention voted eighty-eight to fifty-five for secession. Plans were laid for Virginia troops to march upon the Federal arsenal at Harpers Ferry, and Col. Robert E. Lee of the U.S. Army was invited to head the state's forces.

Word of Virginia's actions had a domino effect. One after another, states known to have strong Unionist sentiment followed her into the Confederate alliance: Arkansas, May 6; Tennessee, May 7; North Carolina, May 20.

Congress having just adjourned for the spring recess, many lawmakers were on the way home. Those who were approached by reporters were reluctant to talk, but in their journals and memoirs many expressed consternation that Congress had not been consulted. Power to make war was specifically assigned to that body, but the president was taking care to talk only of dealing with an insurrection.

July 4 was many weeks away, but in a national emergency even the president's vocal foes were reluctant to criticize him. To many lawmakers, it seemed just as well that the chief executive had acted summarily. By doing so he had relieved representatives of the people from the necessity of registering their views.

In the opinion of Horace Greeley, editor of the New York *Tribune*, the real surprise in the proclamation rested in its numbers. Lincoln, said he, should have called for 500,000 men. Simultaneously, he should have secured a loan of $100 million with which to purchase in Europe 100,000 firearms and 1,000 choice pieces of artillery.

While editors throughout the North echoed Greeley's sentiments, Ohio leaders approached William T. Sherman about raising and

Washington was so unprepared for a flood of volunteers that men of the Eighth Massachusetts regiment bivouacked in the Rotunda of the Capitol. [HARPER'S WEEKLY]

leading a regiment. He refused immediately. In his opinion, there was no hope of subduing secessionists by using 75,000 poorly trained men for three months. "You might as well attempt to put out the flames of a burning house with a squirt gun," he said.

Most who didn't question the president's judgment did not expect his new troops to be used. According to the New York *Times*, the "local commotion" far to the South would be put to rest "effectually in thirty days"—a view echoed by the Philadelphia *Press*. In Chicago, the influential *Tribune* scoffed at the national call for men and boasted that in sixty or ninety days the West alone could put an end to the disturbance.

A tiny minority, South and North, held views expressed by Nathaniel Hawthorne: "I don't quite understand what we are fighting for or what definite results can be expected."

Nine days prior to Lincoln's call, Jefferson Davis requested 100,000 volunteers to serve for twelve months. He did not, however, announce state quotas or establish a mechanism for recruitment. Pierre Gustave Toutant Beauregard, having resigned after five days as superintendent of the U.S. Military Academy, was made head

In Ohio, William T. Sherman indignantly refused to raise a regiment, comparing Lincoln's plan with an attempt to put out a fire with a squirt gun.
[LIBRARY OF CONGRESS]

of the Provisional Army of the Confederate States of America—organized, Davis repeatedly said, for defensive purposes only.

Davis called the Lincoln proclamation "a presidential declaration of war." C.S.A. Vice President Alexander H. Stephens said it "showed the party in power intended nothing short of complete centralization . . . and the erection of a centralized empire."

Virginia state troops moved into Harpers Ferry two days after Lincoln's proclamation. On Saturday secessionists burned railroad bridges to prevent troops from reaching the capital. While bridges were in flames, commandant Charles S. McCauley of the Gosport Navy Yard torched the facility and ships lying at dock to prevent Confederate seizure.

Alarmed government officials suddenly inquired about the condition of the U.S. Army. They found it included just 16,364 men, a majority of whom were foreign born. With 197 companies listed on the rolls, 179 were on duty at isolated western posts and 18 constituted garrisons along the Canadian border and the Atlantic coast.

On Friday, April 19, a letter from Mayor George W. Brown of Baltimore was hand-delivered to the president. According to it, any additional troops designed for the capital would have to "fight their way at every step." Probably at Brown's orders, telegraph wires were cut and bridges were burned—effectively isolating Washington.

If Abraham Lincoln had misgivings about the wisdom of his decision, he concealed them. A memo to customs collector Henry W. Hoffman asked that any secessionist be removed and the place given to S. C. Atkinson. Concurrently he wrote his intimate young friend and protégé Elmer Ellsworth that he was asking senior military officials to place him in some satisfactory position. He endorsed George Ashmun's request that Newell A. Thompson be made agent of the U.S. Navy at Boston. Gideon Welles was requested to give a commission to Eugene L. Sullivan, who had been a delegate to the convention at which Lincoln was nominated.

Before the day of the proclamation ended, the president had made ten New York appointments, ranging from revenue collector to postmaster. Early the next day, he reminded the secretary of war that he wanted Mrs. Lincoln's brother-in-law, Benjamin H. Helm, to be made an army paymaster. So far as the flood of patronage appointments was concerned, the Executive Mansion seemed to be occupied with business as usual.

Confederate leaders were clearly ready to fight, if necessary, and Lincoln's warmest supporters considered his measures inadequate. That being the case, it seems strange that he asked for so small a body of volunteers for so short a term of service. While it is possible that he pared his request to the bone, realizing that he was on questionable legal ground, it is also possible that he still was confident that a show of strength would end the rebellion and did not expect to use the men he requested. Once again we are left to conjecture since he never explained the basis for his decision.

14

*Why Was John Brown's Captor
Picked to Become*

FIELD COMMANDER
OF THE U.S. ARMY?

■

"YOU WILL TOMORROW TAKE COMMAND of a contingent of U.S. Marines," Robert E. Lee was informed by Secretary of War John D. Floyd in 1859. "Proceed at once to Harpers Ferry, where an insurrection is reported to be in progress. You are to quell the disturbance promptly and deliver any persons captured to stand trial under the statutes of the state of Virginia."

On October 16 fervent abolitionist John Brown had led his tiny army of twenty-one against the federal arsenal at the railroad and river junction. He seized weapons, hoping to provide them to the thousands of slaves whom he expected to flock to him. Barricaded inside a sturdy building, he disregarded Lee's October 18 order to give himself up.

At the head of his marines, the cavalry officer, whose leave had been interrupted, stormed Brown's sanctuary. Ten members of the insurgent band, including two of Brown's sons, died. Among the captives was Brown himself, notorious in Kansas for having led raids in which persons believed to have proslavery sentiments were hacked to death with swords.

Brown's trial was the legal sensation of the day. Found guilty of treason against the Commonwealth of Virginia, he was sentenced to die. Much of the northern press gave repeated page-one space to the trial; at his execution on December 2, 1859, he became an instant martyr in the eyes of abolitionists everywhere.

It was quite possible, Lee realized, that he had been denied a long-deserved promotion because he was seen by many as a key figure in the martyrdom of Brown. But because he was an officer from the sole of his foot to the crown of his head, he would never, never complain—or even ask questions.

*   *   *

Harpers Ferry, where Robert E. Lee captured abolitionist John Brown, was the site on a major Federal arsenal. [AUTHOR'S COLLECTION]

"Gen. Winfield Scott instructed me to report to him no later than April 1, 1861," Lee told relatives and friends. "I left Fort Mason, Texas, on February 13—using an ambulance as a vehicle.

"By the time I reached San Antonio on the sixteenth, the place was in turmoil. Gen. David Twiggs had surrendered his entire command to secessionists. That made my uniform conspicuous, and I was uncertain as to whether or not I might be arrested.

"Leaving San Antonio without incident, I reached the coast on Washington's birthday, where I took passage on the steamer *Indianoloa*. We reached New Orleans on February 25, and on the first day of March I arrived at Arlington.

"Since General Scott was then in New York, I reported to the War Department on March 5 and was listed as 'awaiting orders.' Clearly, something involving me was in process—but I had no idea what it might be."

Lee had been a professional soldier for thirty-two years. Deep-chested and long-waisted, he looked almost like a professional athlete of later times. Only his iron-gray beard gave a terse hint that he might be a year or two older than the new president of the United States.

During four years at the U.S. Military Academy, he did not receive a single demerit. Graduating second in the class of 1829, the new second lieutenant was assigned to the elite Corps of Engineers.

Waiting to see Scott as soon as the aging brevet lieutenant general came to the nation's capital, Lee wondered if the course of his career would be altered. Promotions had come slowly: first lieutenant after seven years in uniform, then a jump to captain in just two years. But it took seventeen years to make the leap from captain to lieutenant colonel.

His Mexican War record included one wound and three brevets for gallantry. Yet he was practically unknown except among his relatives and comrades until propelled into the spotlight by events over which he had no control.

Uncertainty concerning his call from the Texas frontier vanished during the second week of March. Reporting to Scott's Washington office, Lee was met by his friend Erasmus D. Keyes, military secretary of the commanding general. After pleasantries had been exchanged and Lee had received news of comrades in arms, Scott rose to his full six feet, four and one-half inches, leaned toward Lee, and confided that there was serious talk of a promotion that was calculated to provide "an opportunity for some real action."

On March 16 President Abraham Lincoln signed the parchment by which Lee became a full colonel. He was immediately assigned to the command of the First Cavalry, but it was twelve days before he received and accepted his new commission. Scott had told him nothing specific, but Lee reasoned that talk of "real action" plus his sudden promotion could mean only one thing. He was likely to be deeply involved should there be a military clash between federal forces and those of the just-formed Provisional Army of the Confederate States of America.

Leaders of his beloved Virginia took a test vote on April 4. Much to the astonishment of many in the nation's capital, delegates to a special convention voted two to one against secession.

Then came Lincoln's surprise call for 75,000 militia. One day later, the Virginia convention—meeting in secret session—switched from opposition to support of secession. Simultaneously, state militia began to move against Harpers Ferry—so deeply etched into the memory of Lee.

On Thursday, seventy-two hours after the president's call for militia with which to subdue elements too powerful for ordinary processes of law, Washington resident John Lee transmitted to his cousin Robert a request that he call upon Francis P. Blair, Sr., at his earliest convenience.

Like everyone else close to the nation's hub, both Lees knew that Blair was the former editor of *The Congressional Globe.* He had played a significant—perhaps a key—role in the nomination of Abraham Lincoln by the Republican National Convention. From his base in Missouri, he had established a network of relationships that made him among the most powerful political leaders in the nation.

Robert E. Lee, only recently made a colonel, considered his first duty to be loyalty to the state of Virginia.
[NATIONAL ARCHIVES]

When he agreed to go to the Pennsylvania Avenue home of Blair's son Montgomery, his long-time friend, Lee was positive that he would be hearing from Lincoln—through Blair. His intuition proved correct, he later wrote. Their conversation was "at the instance of President Lincoln."

Blair informed his guest that he had been authorized to offer field command of the U.S. Army to the man who had held the rank of colonel for only one month. Lee was surprised but was not caught off guard; he knew that Scott would like to have him as his chief subordinate. Under other circumstances, nothing would have given him equal delight. But it took Robert E. Lee only an instant to reject the offer. "If the Union is dissolved," he said, "and the government is disrupted, I shall return to my native state and share the miseries of my people and save in defence will draw my sword no more."

Leaving the Blair mansion, Lee went immediately to the office of General Scott to tell him what had taken place. Scott was blunt. "There are times when every officer should fully determine what course he will pursue and frankly declare it," he said. Then he suggested that if Lee contemplated resignation, he should act promptly. "Your present attitude is equivocal," said the aging warrior who was second only to George Washington in rank and prestige. Lee thanked Scott for his words of wisdom and promised to act soon.

Well after midnight on the following day, he penned a single sentence to Secretary of War Simon Cameron: "I have the honour to tender the resignation of my commission as Colonel of the 1st Regt of Cavalry."

To General Scott he sent a much longer message: "Since my interview with you on the 18th instant, I have felt that I ought not longer to retain my commission in the army. I therefore tender my resignation, which I request you will recommend for acceptance. It would have been presented at once, but for the struggle it has cost me to separate myself from a service to which I have devoted all the best years of my life and all the ability I possessed. Save in defense of my native state, I never desire again to draw my sword."

Concurrently, he wrote much the same thing to his sister and to his brother, Smith. On the following day—wearing civilian clothes—he attended worship services in company with his daughter. Late that evening he received an urgent summons to go to Richmond to confer with the governor.

On April 23 he received and accepted an offer to command Virginia's military forces. Two days later, officials of the U.S. War Department formally accepted his resignation.

Retaliation was swift in coming.

When the president's frequently repeated pledge that Federal forces would not invade territories in rebellion was pushed aside, the Arlington mansion inherited by Mrs. Robert E. Lee was seized on the day following Virginia's formal secession. John G. Nicolay—Abraham Lincoln's intimate, confidential secretary, and biographer—wrote that Lee was full of "weakness and defects" and should have been treated as a deserter.

Only Abraham Lincoln knew precisely why a colonel with thirty days' seniority who was anathema to abolitionists was offered field command . . . and he never committed his thoughts to writing. Dozens of veteran officers had greater seniority; Lee's old commander, Albert S. Johnston of 2nd Cavalry fame was a Kentucky native who was conspicuously capable of top leadership. But the offer transmitted through Blair went to Lee.

15

*What Induced a Landlubber
to Announce That*

The entire coastline of the seven states be under blockade?

■

NEWS FROM MONTGOMERY, Alabama, reached Washington very late on Wednesday, April 17, or early on Thursday, April 18, 1861. According to it, Jefferson Davis had issued an open invitation.

Realizing that the Confederate navy consisted of one barely usable side-wheel steamer and a few revenue cutters and coast-survey vessels seized from Federal hands, Davis took dramatic action. Any owner or master of a ship, said the head of state, could apply for "letters of marque and reprisal." With such a document in hand, the recipient would—by Confederate standards—be legally authorized to become a privateer on the high seas.

Neither Abraham Lincoln nor his closest advisers preserved for posterity the slightest hint of his immediate reaction to the Davis announcement. But on Friday the president touched the match to a verbal bombshell at least as powerful as his stunning call for 75,000 men to take up arms against insurgents.

Lincoln enumerated the seven states in which federal revenue could not be effectively collected. He cited the granting of "pretended letters of marque" as a new and serious offense. Then he said he had "deemed it advisable to set on foot a blockade of the ports" in offending states. This was done "in pursuance of . . . the law of nations." Any person molesting a vessel of the United States, he warned, "will be held amenable to the laws of the United States for the prevention and punishment of piracy."

Maritime experience of the president was limited to two river trips

In a futile bid to prevent rebels from seizing ships and guns,
Federal forces tried to destroy Gosport Navy Yard. [VICTOR'S
HISTORY OF THE REBELLION]

by raft and boat—as a young civilian. His secretary of the navy had
experience as a journalist, Connecticut officeholder, postmaster, and
head of the Naval Bureau of Provisions and Clothing. But Gideon
Welles hardly knew the bow of a warship from its stern.

If Abraham Lincoln consulted Welles or anyone else, there is no
record of their conversations. His April 19 proclamation appears to
have been a personal reaction to the threat that Confederate pri-
vateers might operate on the high seas.

William H. Anderson, later an officer on a vessel of the Federal
blockade, recalled reaction of comrades to the news. "We threw our
glove to the world on the strength of a few decrepit and superannu-
ated hulks," he said.

Editors A. H. Guernsey and Henry M. Alden of influential *Harper's
Weekly* warned readers not to expect too much from the "paper
blockade." Little or no preparation had been made in the North, they
said, and the South could be expected to take strong counter-
measures.

Since Welles was a man of scrupulous exactness, he probably
knew the approximate strength of the U.S. Navy. With ninety wooden
vessels listed, twenty-eight were dismantled for repairs. Four of the
twelve ships comprising the Home Squadron were in northern

Savannah was guarded by Fort Pulaski, upon whose plans engineer Robert E. Lee had worked. Rebels seized the pentagonal fortress soon after Georgia seceded. [HARPER'S WEEKLY]

ports, while one was on the Great Lakes and another was at Pensacola. Experienced leaders were in even shorter supply than were vessels. Resignations began in March; within four months, 259 officers resigned or were dismissed for having shown sympathy for secessionists.

It would take weeks or months to send orders to frigates of the East Indian, Mediterranean, Brazilian, and African squadrons. Even when these vessels again sighted home shores, most of them would prove too big for use in coastal waters. No one had any idea how long it would take to rebuild the leadership structure.

It was not surprising that T. C. DeLeon of Richmond spoke for secessionists everywhere when he reported that the presidential proclamation "was laughed to scorn." According to him, the tiny Federal navy was impotent to do more than "keep loose watch over the ports of a few cities."

By far the longest blockade in the history of warfare, Lincoln's announcement involved 3,549 miles of coastline. Veterans of southern waters estimated that bays, rivers, lagoons, and channels provided just under 200 "openings for commerce." So when news of the plan to close all of them with a handful of ships reached England, naval experts labeled it "a salt water joke."

Gustavus V. Fox, a former lieutenant in the U.S. Navy for whom a new position was soon created, was an enthusiastic backer of the announced blockade. [NICOLAY & HAY, ABRAHAM LINCOLN]

Gustavus V. Fox didn't laugh.

Despite the fiasco of his attempt to resupply Fort Sumter, the man who entered the U.S. Navy in 1838 as a midshipman remained in the president's highest esteem. With a dozen years of experience on the sea behind him before resigning to become agent for Bay State Mills of his native Massachusetts, he had a unique asset. Montgomery Blair, U.S. postmaster general and son of the man by whom Lincoln's offer to Robert E. Lee was transmitted, was his articulate and persuasive brother-in-law. In only a few months the president would create for Fox a new position—assistant secretary of the U.S. Navy.

Records are distressingly silent. Logic suggests that Lincoln, who had consulted Fox frequently in the immediate past, again relied on the judgment of a man who hadn't been aboard a warship in five years. If Fox made unrecorded visits to the Executive Mansion, he probably stressed rapid growth and improvement of the U.S. Navy during recent years.

Work was started on the heavy side-wheel steamers *Mississippi* and *Missouri* in 1847. By the time the most powerful vessels then in the federal fleet were launched in 1850, two sister ships—the *Powhatan* and the *Susquehanna*—were nearing completion.

Fox knew that six screw frigates, equipped with the very latest of propulsion systems, were authorized in 1855. All were above 3,000 tons and all heavily armed; the 4,500-ton *Niagara* was the biggest of the lot. Though vessels such as these could not enter shallow water, they were capable of standing beyond range of shore batteries to prevent ships from leaving or entering Confederate ports.

Perhaps Lincoln learned from Fox or an unknown adviser that the immense Confederate coastline was not as formidable as it appeared on paper. To bar overseas commerce to insurgents effectively, it would be necessary to close only those ports that had rail or water links with the interior. On April 19 there were just ten major ports of such description: Charleston, Savannah, Mobile, New Orleans, and Norfolk; Jacksonville, Fernandina, and Pensacola in Florida; Wilmington and New Bern in North Carolina.

Neither Lincoln nor Fox nor Welles nor anyone else who may have had inside knowledge of the blockade before it was announced anticipated Virginia's response. On April 20 militia units so threatened the immense Federal navy yard near Norfolk that its commandant gave up hope of saving it. Eager to prevent it from becoming an asset to secessionists, Charles S. McCauley decided that destruction was the best alternative.

During the afternoon and early evening, ten vessels of the U.S. Navy were set afire, then scuttled. Officers and men of the undamaged *Pawnee* and *Cumberland* came ashore at 9:00 P.M. Saturday and spiked as many guns as possible. At 10:00, marines set fire to their barracks and went aboard the *Pawnee.* Officers raced from building to building and from ship to ship, spreading turpentine-soaked waste. They laid a trail of powder to the dry dock and at 2:00 A.M. on Sunday put a match to it.

According to the New York *Times* of April 24, "At this time the scene was indescribably magnificent, all the buildings being in a blaze, and explosions here and there scattering the cinders."

Despite destruction estimated by newspaper editors at the then-astronomical figure of $50 million, Gosport Navy Yard was far from totally demolished. Virginians who had left the Union in response to Lincoln's call for troops recovered nearly one thousand heavy guns that later played key roles in major battles.

More important for the moment, leaders of the vessel-scarce Confederacy decided to raise, repair, and refit the forty-four-gun USS *Merrimac.* Renamed the CSS *Virginia,* within months it was destined to become an ironclad. In conjunction with its Federal counterpart, the *Monitor,* it made wooden ships instantly obsolete.

On the day after the blockade was proclaimed, officers at Annapolis decided that a famous Revolutionary warship might be endangered. So they had the USS *Constitution* towed out of Chesapeake Bay to prevent its seizure.

If Attorney General Edward Bates or future Secretary of War and former Attorney General Edwin M. Stanton saw the April 19 document before it was made public, no records of talks with the president have survived. Both veteran attorneys had at least a bit of knowledge about international law, an area with which Abraham Lincoln had never been concerned.

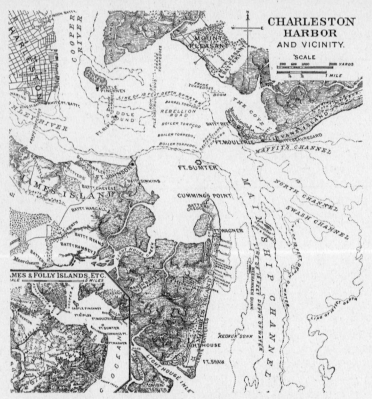

*Charleston had so intricate a system of waterways
that Gideon Welles knew it would take many
warships to effect its blockade.* [BATTLES AND LEADERS]

Bates or Stanton, or both, could have told him at a glance that "the
law of nations" limited a blockade to a belligerent nation. Since no
war had been declared and because the Confederate States of America were officially branded as insurgents, an international high
court would have pronounced Lincoln's actions illegal.

The blockade was not subjected to a legal test in 1861. But piracy,
stipulated as the crime committed by any Confederate who served
aboard a privateer, was another matter. Soon it would rise to haunt
and to humiliate the administration headed by the attorney from
Illinois.

Destined months later to become perhaps the most effective of all
measures designed to subdue states claiming to have seceded, the
blockade was for the moment impotent as well as illegal. His official
papers and letters give no hint as to why he decided to announce a
blockade just four days after having startled the world with his call
for militia.

16

*What Persuaded a Veteran
Attorney to Order*

SUSPENSION OF THE WRIT OF *HABEAS CORPUS?*

■

BALTIMORE ERUPTED A FEW hours before Abraham Lincoln announced his blockade of the southern coastline. On Friday evening, April 19, 1861, members of the Sixth Massachusetts piled off the train at a depot of the city. Marching toward a second depot at which they expected to assemble on another train for the last leg of their journey to Washington, they were attacked by pro-secessionist civilians. In the ensuing melee, at least thirteen persons died and an unknown number were injured. As the Washington-bound train pulled out of Balitmore, bands of secessionists prepared torches and gathered inflammables. By morning, every railroad bridge of the city was in ruins.

Twenty-four hours after the blockade was announced, the cabinet held a long emergency session—not in the Executive Mansion, as usual, but at the Navy Department. While there, they learned that the insurrectionists seized the Baltimore telegraph office after burning the bridges.

Consternation reigned.

Washington seemed to be in a vise—isolated from the North by both wire and rail so that even mail could not get through. Gov. Thomas H. Hicks called a special session of the Maryland legislature for April 26; Lincoln and his advisers feared that lawmakers would adopt an ordinance of secession.

Meanwhile, railroad executives worked out a plan by which troop trains could bypass Baltimore, taking the route Philadelphia-Perryville-Annapolis-Washington. That meant armed defenders could reach Washington, but it in no way reduced the tension in all-important Maryland.

Right to the writ of habeas corpus, *by which a prisoner could win a discharge from prison, was rooted in the time-honored Magna Carta, signed centuries earlier by England's King John.*
[AUTHOR'S COLLECTION]

So on Thursday, April 25, the president drafted in his own hand an urgent memorandum to Gen. Winfield Scott. In it, he intimated that the meeting of the Maryland legislature on the following day might involve "in the extremest necessity, the suspension of the writ of *habeas corpus.*"

Embodied in England's Magna Carta and subject to suspension only by Parliament, *habeas corpus* was debated by the Founding Fathers of the United States. Members of the Constitutional Convention initially voted unanimously that the privilege "shall not be suspended." At the insistence of Gouverneur Morris, a qualifying clause was added: ". . . unless when in cases of rebellion or invasion the public safety may require [suspension]." By a vote of seven states to three, the amended provision became a part of Article I, Section 9.

Until Abraham Lincoln reached a different conclusion, constitutional experts and national leaders had taken it for granted that only Congress could temporarily suspend the writ. Even with what the president insisted upon calling "an insurrection—not a war" in progress, many legal scholars held to the accepted view. So did Secretary of the Navy Gideon Welles and Secretary of the Treasury Salmon P. Chase. In Philadelphia Gov. Andrew Curtin tried to calm fears by assuring the legislature that only Congress could suspend *habeas corpus.*

On April 27 Scott was formally authorized to suspend the writ at any point along the improvised rail route at which resistance occurred. Soon Baltimore police marshal George P. Kane and Mayor George W. Brown of Baltimore were under arrest. Later, nine members of the Maryland legislature and the chief clerk of the Maryland senate were put behind bars.

*   *   *

Suspension of *habeas corpus* in Baltimore and other trouble spots established a precedent. For the remainder of the conflict, the president and his secretary of state apparently acted to void the civil right with little or no hesitation. Nearly a dozen additional executive authorizations are on record.

Suspension by presidential proclamation—not afforded the secrecy of a military order—came on May 10. That day, civil rights were curtailed throughout Florida. In addition, commanders were authorized to remove all suspected persons from the vicinity of the state's fortifications.

June 20 brought a puzzling and unduplicated suspension that applied only to a Major Chase. Formerly in the Engineering Corps, U.S. Army, he was believed to be guilty of treason—hence he was denied *habeas corpus* by order of the nation's chief executive. Twelve days later, a sweeping edict extended suspension of the writ to New York.

There was no additional action for three months, at which time a document prepared by William H. Seward but issued in the name of Lincoln made suspension possible as far north as Bangor, Maine. With Washington still considered to be in great danger, on October 23 the personal liberty provision for all military-related cases in the District of Columbia was suspended.

In Baltimore men of the Sixth Massachusetts took careful aim upon civilians, then fired. This riot led to Lincoln's first suspension of the writ of habeas corpus. [HARPER'S WEEKLY]

August 8, 1862, brought the greatest expansion of the suspension yet. For the first time, the entire United States was cited: "The writ of *habeas corpus* is hereby suspended in respect to all persons arrested and detained [as evaders of the compulsory conscription act] and in respect to all persons arrested for disloyal practices."

Six weeks later, mere suspension of *habeas corpus,* though reiterated, was not enough. This time, a September 24 proclamation stipulated that "during the existing insurrection . . . all rebels and insurgents, their aiders and abettors, within the United States" were also subject to martial law. So were "all persons discouraging volunteer enlistments, resisting militia drafts, or guilty of any disloyal practice."

Martial law meant that offenders—who could not gain freedom by means of a writ of *habeas corpus*—"shall be imprisoned in any fort, camp, arsenal, military prison, or other place of confinement by any military authority." Though not specified in the proclamation, this meant that persons suspected of guilt were subject to imprisonment without trial for the duration of "the rebellion."

Approximately one year later, national suspension of *habeas corpus* was repeated in yet another presidential proclamation. Strangely, since Kentucky was never numbered among seceded states, the region of Lincoln's birth was specified in a proclamation of July 5, 1864. According to it, the president had concluded that "the public safety especially requires the suspension of the privilege of the writ of *habeas corpus* [plus establishment of martial law] in and throughout Kentucky."

Nothing remotely comparable to this succession of proclamations had been experienced in the United States.

Fourteen months after Lincoln's first order, the Thirty-seventh Congress took belated action. On July 3, 1862, lawmakers empowered the president to suspend the writ when the public safety was imperiled by rebellion or invasion. A second congressional step was taken on March 3, 1863. After an all-night session, passage of the Trumbull Bill authorized the chief executive to suspend *habeas corpus* "in any case throughout the United States or any part thereof."

Repeal of these congressional acts, approving what the president had already done, did not come until all the guns fell silent.

No one knows precisely how many citizens were arrested and imprisoned without a judicial hearing during the war. A few who had influential friends and relatives gained quick release; some were held for four years.

Throughout the North, the majority of Democrats denounced "presidential usurpation of power." Printing presses turned out tract after tract. Some writers endorsed the curtailment of personal liberty in a time of national peril; others agreed with the author of *The*

Abraham Lincoln was steadfast in his insistence that a "state of rebellion" justified measures that ran contrary to the letter and spirit of the U.S. Constitution. [NATIONAL ARCHIVES]

American Bastille that the price of stifling opposition was far too high.

In 1991 noted Lincoln scholar Mark E. Neely, Jr., published the results of a painstaking study of *The Fate of Liberty*. In it, he listed names of approximately 150 "prisoners of state" who represent less than 2 percent of the cases he examined. In an apology for wartime encroachment upon freedom, he suggested that the vast majority of persons who were imprisoned without trial were avowed secessionists or were outspoken sympathizers of the southern cause.

At some periods in his life, Abraham Lincoln would have challenged Neely's defense of his actions. Speaking to representatives of Massachusetts, he promised, "As president, in the administration of the government, I hope to be man enough not to know one citizen of the United States from another, nor one section from another." Had that promise been kept, a citizen who shouted "Hurrah for Jeff Davis!" would have been in no greater danger of arrest than a fellow townsman who eagerly responded to a call for volunteer soldiers to "put down the insurrection."

*   *   *

During the war years, courts seldom dealt with the constitutionality of the suspension or with the legality of arrests made under declarations of martial law. Had they done so regularly, and had rulings adverse to the president's position been rendered, all the evidence indicates that he would have ignored them.

Requested to give an opinion on bypassing the Fifth Amendment in order to declare martial law in Maryland, Attorney General Bates delegated the task to Titian J. Coffee. Lincoln glanced through the brief on the morning of April 20—the day after having proclaimed the blockade and the day the Gosport Navy Yard went up in smoke. There is no record that his judgment was influenced by the arguments cited. In July Bates himself completed a twenty-six-page opinion. In it he held that each of the three branches of the federal government is empowered to interpret the Constitution independently.

The veteran attorney who occupied the Pennsylvania Avenue mansion had not waited upon such support to act. Circulation of the Bates opinion meant, however, that legal authorities could be cited to buttress the argument that neither Congress nor the courts could challenge the executive department.

Though he never claimed to be a constitutional scholar, attorney Lincoln many times went on record as desiring to uphold all the laws. He knew that *habeas corpus* is the only personal liberty law mentioned in the body of the U.S. Constitution. But he never explained why he suppressed this crucial law from the start of hostilities until his death.

17

How Did a Novice Get

THE UPPER HAND OVER CONGRESS?

■

IF ABRAHAM LINCOLN checked his calendar after having suspended *habeas corpus* by proclamation, he found that it was sixty-eight days before Congress would assemble in special session.

Detailed records list only one consultation with a lawmaker that focused upon the special session. That was on the evening of July 3 when Kentucky-born Sen. Orville Browning of Illinois went over the message his friend had prepared for Congress.

Lincoln's experience at the national level consisted of a single term in Congress, after which he held no elected office for a dozen years. Now he would be forced to deal with powerful political veterans, many of whom were opposed to some of his views. His preparation for potential confrontation consisted of carefully preparing a special message for Congress.

During more than two months after his final executive action of the period, the president devoted most of his time and energy to a few central matters. He held numerous talks concerning military matters and paid a surprising number of visits to newly arrived units of fighting men. He reviewed troops on an average of once every three days, and he pored over lists of regiments before repeatedly authorizing states to exceed their quotas. He talked patronage—civilian and military—until sometimes he confessed weariness. And somehow he found time to be involved frequently in a new and absorbing interest—specifications and performances of weapons.

It was almost as though the nation's lawmaking body didn't exist —or was of such little importance and power that strategy sessions with leaders were not needed.

Members of the Frontier Guard, temporarily quartered in the Executive Mansion, vacated it on April 26. After having formally suspended *habeas corpus* the following day, Lincoln talked military matters over with Carl Schurz, the German-American leader who had helped to elect the first Republican president and who was being

Orville H. Browning seems to have been the only member of Congress who actually heard Lincoln's message of July 1861 from the lips of the president. [NICOLAY & HAY, *ABRAHAM LINCOLN*]

rewarded with appointment as minister to Spain.

He found time to see New York Congressman Charles H. Van Wyck, who wanted temporary active duty while waiting for his regiment. He issued instructions that a "war steamer" should be placed on Potomac duty, to check the situation daily in the vicinity of the Executive Mansion. He listened to Sen. Henry Wilson of Massachusetts, who came to urge more aggressive war measures.

May 3 brought the North another surprise. That day, the president announced an increase in the size of the regular U.S. Army by ten regiments, or 22,714 men. At the same time he called for 42,034 volunteers for land fighting, plus 18,000 seamen. Most officials and editors who doubted that the executive department was empowered to take these actions kept very quiet.

One day later, he met with Gen. Benjamin F. Butler to discuss the military situation in Baltimore and at the Gosport Navy Yard. He sent Vice President Hannibal Hamlin a personal report of troop movements in New York. On May 7 he authorized Maj. Robert Anderson of Fort Sumter fame to recruit three-year volunteers in Kentucky and western Virginia.

While waiting for Congress to answer his call, he received daily military reports from Gen. Winfield Scott and sometimes met with him to discuss them. He interviewed Judge William F. Arny of Kansas who came to offer three regiments for the protection of northwestern Missouri. He discussed with F. B. Cutting the possible use of the Rothschild organization in a bid to gain popular support in

Europe; he gave command of Chicago's Sturgis Rifles to George B. McClellan. He interviewed Emerson Etheridge concerning distribution of arms being sent to Cairo, Illinois, and discussed formation of a regiment of sharpshooters with Hiram Berdan.

Still not having conducted a single recorded political conference, on June 24 he interviewed Commodore Silas H. Stringham who was preparing to lead an expedition to the North Carolina coast. Three days later, he was quoted as having expressed a strong desire "to bag Thomas J. Jackson"—destined soon to become known as Stonewall Jackson.

During this period, the president paid personal visits to quarters of the Seventh New York Regiment, volunteers from the District of Columbia, the Sixty-ninth New York, the Thirty-seventh New York, and the Eleventh Massachusetts regiments plus the First Brigade of New Jersey volunteers. He was at the navy yard repeatedly, sometimes for more than two hours. He visited encampments in City Hall Park, on the Virginia side of the Potomac, and near the chain bridge over the river.

So many troops were reviewed—often two or three times—that it was difficult or impossible for anyone to remember all of them: the Rhode Island Marine Artillery, Ellsworth's New York Fire Brigade, New Jersey volunteers, the Seventy-first New York Regiment, the Seventh New York Regiment, the Garibaldi Guards, and a dozen other units.

Between military conferences, visits to encampments, and reviews of troops, the president took time personally to approve acceptance

Owen Lovejoy of Illinois urged a war against slavery, despite Lincoln repeatedly going on record as upholding it where it existed. [NICOLAY & HAY, *ABRAHAM LINCOLN*]

Thaddeus Stevens of Vermont, a leader of radicals called Black Republicans, did not want the Constitution to stand in the way of getting rid of slavery. [NATIONAL ARCHIVES]

of regiments from states already having met their quotas: fourteen from New York, six from Indiana, two from Illinois, one from Michigan, ten from Massachusetts, three more from both Indiana and Ohio. By presidential directive, a cavalry unit was accepted as one of Indiana's regiments.

In at least a dozen instances, he devoted time and energy to the making of appointments: the New York custom house, quartermaster general of the army, promotion and field command for Erasmus D. Keyes, and selection of brigadier generals. He even managed to endorse Horatio N. Taft, Jr., to be a page boy "as he is a playmate of my little boys."

Sandwiched between activities that directly involved troops, he gave personal attention to weapons. Aboard the USS *Pensacola,* he watched target practice with the eleven-inch Dahlgren gun. He boarded the steamer *Monticello* to see for himself the effect of shots from Sewall's Point. At least twice he watched experiments with rifled cannon, and he was intrigued by a demonstration of the "coffee-mill gun" that was a predecessor of modern machine guns. He watched a demonstration by inventor Orison Blunt, then wrote that "I think it worthy the attention of the government." He found time to listen to Thaddeus S. C. Lowe, who came forward with a proposal that—for the first time, ever—observation balloons should be used to gather battle information for use by Federal commanders.

Although men who would sit in the special session of Congress were conspicuously absent from activities, Abraham Lincoln had their upcoming conclave on his mind at least as early as May 7. On June 19 he made an official announcement that he would see no more visitors until Congress convened. By July 3, his carefully crafted special message for lawmakers—written without assistance— was shared with members of the cabinet. That evening he personally read it to Orville Browning.

Only his old associate from Illinois heard the message from the lips of its author. Congress convened July 4, and the following day announced to the president that lawmakers were "ready to receive communications." Shortly afterward, Lincoln's explanation of what he had done and why he had done it was read to a joint session of Congress in what one listener described as "a droning monotone."

Convening on the eighty-fourth anniversary of the Declaration of Independence, the Thirty-seventh Congress was heavily Republican. In the Senate, the party held thirty-two of forty-eight seats and in the House had a comparable majority. House chaplain T. H. Stockton offered a prayer that "if there must be war . . . may it not be bloody and ruinous." Galusha Grow of Pennsylvania defeated Frank Blair and won the speakership. Eventually the purity of the Congress was established by purging ten senators and one representative, all Southerners except for Jesse Bright of Indiana.

Abraham Lincoln's message was long and detailed; in many printed editions, it runs to twenty-eight or more pages. A single issue was at stake, the president declared. That issue was prevention of disunion. Democracy itself—not simply the American form of it—was on trial; failure would have worldwide consequences.

During the eighty days since the special session of Congress was announced, said the chief executive, he had been forced to take a number of executive acts; now he wanted them approved. To guarantee a swift conclusion to the matter, he requested at least 400,000 more men in uniform and $400 million.

He branded so-called secession as illegal and added that border states could not claim "armed neutrality."

He made no allusion to the slavery issue, stressing that suppression of the insurrection was necessary for preservation of the Union. Since he proposed to deal with rebellious citizens only, he had concluded that it was not necessary to ask for a declaration of war, which required armed opposition to an enemy nation.

On the third day of the session, Sen. Henry Wilson of Massachusetts introduced a resolution approving of everything the president had done. Opposition was so strong that the measure lay in "unfinished business" until within hours of adjournment.

Provision of men and dollars was a different matter. Lincoln's request was overwhelmingly and enthusiastically approved despite the

Although Congress had not authorized enlargement of the U.S. Army, Robert Anderson of Fort Sumter fame was authorized by the president to recruit three-year volunteers. [NICOLAY & HAY, *ABRAHAM LINCOLN*]

fact that a few members feared it threatened subjugation of the South. Andrew Johnson of Tennessee framed a resolution blaming the war upon secessionists. Clement L. Vallandigham said he was not concerned with placing blame; he wanted mobilization to end. Hence he requested that a peace commission be named, with hostilities suspended until it could meet and act. Only twenty colleagues joined him in voting for the measure.

Many fiery abolitionists, widely known as Black Republicans, largely held their peace for the moment; they would make great trouble for the president later. Owen Lovejoy of Illinois went on record as being ready and willing to destroy the South for the sake of abolition. James Dixon of Connecticut was sure that people of the North were ready to do away with slavery. After lengthy debate, a statute was enacted under whose terms the owner of a slave employed in military work would lose possession. No slaves in Northern or border states were set free.

When Vallandigham tried to censure Lincoln for executive actions taken without congressional approval, his motion was tabled. Thaddeus Stevens went on record as believing that the Constitution should never stand in the way of dealing with an enemy.

To many lawmakers, suspension of *habeas corpus* was the president's most troubling action. It was debated at length, but Congress neither approved the actions of the president nor rebuked him for what he had done.

Vice President Hannibal Hamlin, who seldom saw the president, received a detailed report of early troop movements. [NICOLAY & HAY, ABRAHAM LINCOLN]

On July 27 Abraham Lincoln refused a request for papers showing the grounds, reason, and evidence upon which Baltimore's police commissioners were arrested. Earlier, he had told the Thirty-sixth Congress that he would not provide letters and papers relating to Major Anderson's actions at Fort Sumter. Having established a precedent in the Anderson matter, he followed it in the case of Baltimore, then refused to provide an explanation of the establishment of martial law in Kentucky.

With Congress due to adjourn on August 7, an act came to the floor on August 6 "to increase the pay of the privates and volunteers in the service of the U.S." A rider attached to that bill stipulated that all actions of the president after March 4 concerning the armed forces, militia, and volunteers "are hereby approved and in all respects legalized and made valid . . . as if they had been issued and done under the previous express authority and direction of the Congress." Only the bravest could object to a boost in military pay. With no mention of *habeas corpus* in the rider, the bill to which it was appended passed the Senate by a vote of thirty-seven to five and the House by seventy-four to nineteen.

Abraham Lincoln had twenty-four outspoken opponents in Congress. But close to the zero hour, he won after-the-fact approval of questionable, extralegal, and illegal actions! That placed him in the driver's seat permanently; for the duration, he would conduct the executive department of the government as though it were all but independent of other branches.

18

Why Was Bull Run Made

THE POINT OF NO RETURN?

■

WITH THE SPECIAL session of Congress more than two months away, on May 3, 1861, the president signed the most revealing document yet. In his earlier call for 75,000 militia, he gave "insurrectionary combinations" twenty days to disperse. With most of that time having elapsed and the rebellion growing, he pored over the latest intelligence.

According to Lincoln's reports, states claiming to have seceded planned to expand their military strength. If reports were accurate, the "so-called Confederacy" had ambitious aims:

Confederate troops in South Carolina when Fort Sumter was attacked—5,000; March 9 requisition for volunteers—8,000; April 8 requisition—20,000; April 16 requisition—34,000; new requisitions, April 16 to 29—15,000; Jefferson Davis's request to C.S.A. Congress April 29—100,000; *Total manpower wanted by insurgents:* 182,000.

Lincoln's private secretaries summarized the U.S. manpower position after the May 3 call as: April 4 report of navy—7,600; April 5 report of regular army—17,113; April 15 request for three-month volunteers—75,000; May 3 call for three-year volunteers—64,748; May 3 enlargement of regular army—18,000; *Total manpower needed by the United States:* 182,461.

Aside from the indisputable recognition that the president was carefully responding to perceived Confederate actions, his new proclamation was remarkable. It was intended only for governors and not released to the public, with fresh language of tremendous import used in the call:

"Now, therefore, I Abraham Lincoln, president of the United States, and commander in chief of the army and navy therefore, and of the militia of the several states, when called into actual service, do hereby call into service of the United States . . ."

Probably because all knew that George Washington would be the

A seasoned and proven leader, it was natural that George Washington was made commander in chief as well as president. [AUTHOR'S COLLECTION]

first chief executive, framers of the Constitution stipulated that the president should also be commander in chief. Abraham Lincoln took the clause literally. Although his military experience was limited to fifty-one days during the Black Hawk War, without combat, he very early made it clear that he and he alone would make the crucial decisions concerning conflict with the insurgents.

In a preliminary draft of his upcoming congressional message, he initially planned to ask for 300,000 more men. Raising that request to 400,000 meant that by July 4 he envisioned a 2,300 percent increase in U.S. military strength over its April 21 base. Calls for more and more men for longer periods of service were clear indications of the commander in chief's intentions.

In addition to establishing ever-higher goals, he dealt with matters that many would have relegated to subordinates. Less than pleased with a list suggesting officers to be added to the regular army, the commander in chief penned eight paragraphs as a response. Changes he requested ranged from making Col. Robert Anderson a brigadier general to asking that Francis E. Brownell be promoted to second lieutenant. A few days later, he wanted three men made lieutenants, one made captain.

Already he was receiving and considering daily reports made by Gen. Winfield Scott. Soon he asked for precise accounting: exact number of men enlisted in the army and navy, or entering Federal

Against advice of Gen. Winfield Scott, ninety-day volunteers under the leadership of Brig. Gen. Irvin McDowell moved against Confederates. [LIBRARY OF CONGRESS]

service as volunteers or members of state militia units. He wanted to know about the equipment and drill of all these men and the time of their probable readiness for active service.

In an undated memo, apparently a "reminder note" to himself, he listed officers to remember: Major Anderson, Captain Doubleday, Captain Foster, Major Hunter, and Lieutenant Slemmer—whose "pretty wife says major or first captain." Slemmer got his promotion, along with all the others listed, except Foster.

Keenly aware that Southerners held "long-cherished dreams of peaceable secession," the president's secretaries took care to note that not all secessionists were beating war drums. After Fort Sumter Howell Cobb of Georgia, they recorded, assured folk of the Deep South that there would be no war. Hence he urged them to go home and cultivate their crops. In a proclamation of April 24, Gov. John Letcher of Virginia counseled citizens not in military service to resume their normal ways.

Cobb and Letcher could cherish pipe dreams of peace if they wished. One man—Lincoln—knew that a decisive conflict would be fought.

General Scott's daily report No. 22, dated April 27, briefly outlined a plan drafted by George B. McClellan. If adopted, Scott warned, it would involve trying to "subdue the seceded states, by piecemeal." He had already recommended securing the Mississippi River from

Cairo, Illinois, to New Orleans while blockading more and more southern ports. By fall, reasoned the head of the U.S. Army, strangled seceded states would be ready to talk terms.

Knowing that plans had been drafted to move in force soon against insurgents at the Virginia railroad junction of Manassas, about twenty-four miles southwest of Washington, Scott voiced objections when a council was held at the Executive Mansion on June 29. He wasted his hard-to-get breath. Supported by members of the cabinet, the president pressed for immediate action.

Brig. Gen. Irvin McDowell, age forty-two, had been lauded for his leadership of the first invasion into Virginia. Tendered a major generalship in reward, he turned it down "because fellow officers might become jealous." Now he had in hand a scheme for effecting the speedy end to hostilities that the president had promised.

Federal forces, said McDowell, should move against Manassas in three columns of ten thousand men each. Another ten thousand men should be held in reserve. Meanwhile, sixty-nine-year-old Maj. Gen. Robert Patterson should use his Pennsylvania troops to prevent units under Joseph E. Johnston from joining the main Confederate army commanded by P. G. T. Beauregard.

Records leave no doubt concerning the dominant voice in the council of war. Expecting simultaneously to crush opposition and encourage Unionists in the South, "the administration [that is, the president] was responsible for the forward movement," his secretaries noted. The campaign was formally approved, to begin five days after the opening of Congress.

By the time troops began moving, days behind schedule, lawmakers were debating a resolution by Sen. John J. Crittenden of Kentucky. Early in the year, a compromise measure that he had framed had been considered but never adopted. Now he won thirty to five approval of a measure. It stipulated that the war for which 400,000 more men had been voted would be fought to preserve the Union and to uphold the Constitution—not to alter slavery where established.

If abolitionists learned of the measure adopted by the U.S. Senate, they ignored it. Editor Horace Greeley of the New York *Tribune* spoke for multitudes whose first priority was destruction of "a slave-based society" when on June 26 he thundered:

"Forward to Richmond! Forward to Richmond! The rebel congress must not be allowed to meet there on the 20th of July. By that date the place must be held by the national army!"

Weeks earlier, pressure for "active aggressive measures" had grown strong. In June a cabinet member confided to an intimate that "we will very probably soon have a fight." Repeatedly, the president stressed that the speedy victory he promised would be effected to save the Union—a goal quite different from that for which many who

Because he had the strong support of the president, Senator John J. Crittenden won easy Senate approval for a bill that insisted the war would be fought for the preservation of the Union, slavery to remain undisturbed where it already existed. [NATIONAL ARCHIVES]

had helped to elect him now clamored loudly.

Even in the increasingly heated climate of confrontation and challenge, fatalities were few. Soldiers clashed with civilians in Alexandria, Baltimore, and St. Louis; five soldiers and at least forty-six civilians died. In nearly a dozen small military encounters, neither Federals nor Virginians accumulated a total of one hundred fatalities. All clashes combined caused only about one-tenth as many deaths as an 1865 accident to a steamboat.

Lincoln had been firm in declaring there would be no invasion of the South. Southerners had responded by abstaining from killing as they continued to seize installations within seceded states. Suddenly the situation changed—after 2:00 A.M. on May 24, when Federal columns crossed two Potomac River bridges and filed into Arlington Heights and Alexandria. Though viewed from windows of the Executive Mansion as purely defensive, to Virginians in particular and to Southerners in general, the troop movement was an invasion, pure and simple. There still might have been time for a national peace conference such as envisioned by Clement Vallandigham—if only the key policy maker would agree to seek mutual concessions and accommodations.

Since Abraham Lincoln was in no mood for compromise of any

sort, men he had called into uniform would soon be veterans of the battlefield. Many of McDowell's recruits, just learning to march, found it hard to keep up with their units as they moved toward Manassas Junction. Scouts found that Confederate forces were massed behind a small waterway, Bull Run. When Federal forces launched an all-out attack on Sunday, July 21, it was estimated that the enemy line stretched for eight miles.

Though Patterson failed to block the movements of Johnston as planned, after several hours it appeared that Federals had won. Richmond was reputedly "in a state of terror" at tales of defeat. In Washington the chief executive rejoiced over a steady stream of optimistic reports. After supper, victory seemed so sure that he went for his customary evening drive. But on returning from it, he learned that McDowell was in chaotic retreat, with only his broken army protecting the capital itself.

Learning of the debacle, Horace Greeley admitted himself to be "hopelessly broken." Not so the chief executive. On the night after Bull Run, he stretched out on a sofa in the Executive Office and napped at intervals. During periods of wakefulness, he may have

Horace Greeley, editor of the New York Tribune, *strongly urged implementation of plans to capture Richmond and end the rebellion immediately.* [NEW YORK PUBLIC LIBRARY]

studied census reports to rediscover that the free states held 3,778,000 white males age eighteen to forty-five—against only 531,000 in states that seceded prior to Fort Sumter. Before morning, he completed a set of notes that were expanded into formal memoranda. In them the commander in chief outlined his basic military strategy and gave detailed plans calling for a joint movement upon Memphis and Cincinnati—while recapturing and permanently holding Manassas for the sake of its railroads.

Conflicting reports make it impossible to know the extent of the human toll at Bull Run. There may have been as few as 3,900 casualties or as many as 5,300. Whatever the number, both sides left the battlefield with heightened determination to fight.

Keenly aware that the point of no return had been reached, with talk of peace ceasing for now, Lincoln decided that the next phase of the war required a new field commander. Since George B. McClellan had won a string of small victories in western Virginia, a message dispatched the day after the battle called him to Washington. After conferring with him and cabinet members—Lieutenant General Scott not having been invited to be present—the chief executive ousted McDowell and began to call McClellan "general in chief." Theoretically subordinate to Scott, in practice he took his orders from the president.

Instead of being interpreted as an imperative demand for new and productive peace talks, Bull Run was taken to mean that the war might last as long as a year. Whatever its duration, it would be pursued with even greater determination than in the weeks leading up to the disastrous first large-scale conflict.

PART THREE

■

Questions the
Commander in Chief
Did Not Address

Abraham Lincoln's military experience consisted of seven weeks in the field against warriors led by Chief Black Hawk. [NICOLAY & HAY, *ABRAHAM LINCOLN*]

19

*Why Was an Overworked
Commander in Chief Also*

GENERAL IN CHIEF AND CHIEF OF STAFF?

■

SECTION 2 OF ARTICLE II, the Constitution of the United States, requires the president "to take care that the laws be faithfully executed." Becoming commander in chief of U.S. armed forces at the instant he assumed the presidency, Abraham Lincoln considered his oath of office as overwhelmingly important—"registered in heaven."

During his tenure, he devoted substantially more than half of his time to the war effort. Often working sixteen to eighteen hours a day for weeks on end, from start to finish he did not limit his participation to shaping of long-range military goals. Instead, he devoted enormous time and energy to roles then associated with that of the commanding general and now linked with the chief of staff.

Just across the lawn from the Executive Mansion, the telegraph office of the War Department was his command post. From it he often directed the movements of several armies. Very early, he made it clear that he, and he alone, would make final decisions. Having dispatched elsewhere troops that Gen. George B. McClellan wanted at hand, Lincoln noted the pressure upon him and suggested that if his general knew all the facts he would approve "even beyond a mere acknowledgement that the commander in chief may order what he pleases." Soon it became customary for him to speak of Confederates simply as "the enemy." In July 1862 a frequently repeated motif was underscored: "As commander in chief of the army and navy in time of war, I suppose I have a right to take any measure which may best subdue the enemy."

Emphasizing his decisive role, he concluded, "If I had fifty thousand additional troopers here now, I believe I could substantially close the war in two weeks." It was in this mood that he confided to his assistant private secretary John Hay, "I who am not a specially brave man have had to sustain the sinking courage of professional fighters in critical times." Contemplating the actions of the military leader whom he first knew as a Springfield attorney, Hay mused, "The Tycoon is in fine whack; he is managing this war. The most important things he decides and there is no cavil."

Decisive action started very early. General in Chief Winfield Scott balked at attempting to resolve the Fort Sumter dilemma by military action. His commander in chief then turned to civilian Gustavus V. Fox and authorized him to lead—not an army but a naval expedition. He did so knowing that Confederates had earlier turned back by gunfire the supply ship *Star of the West* and were showing no signs of taking a more moderate course. Dispatch of a relief force meant that rebels were likely to be provoked into firing the first shots of "a small and short war."

When Scott hesitated to send raw troops against Confederates at Bull Run, Lincoln pondered a plan offered by Brig. Gen. Irvin McDowell, then ordered McDowell to proceed. In the aftermath of defeat, Scott castigated himself: "I deserve removal, because I did not stand up, when my army was not in condition for fighting, and resist it to the last." Resenting the implication that he had forced the battle, the commander in chief protested. Too polite to demur, Scott said no more. But members of Congress engaged in empty debate about whether or not Lincoln should have overruled his general in chief.

Accepting defeat with the stoicism for which he became famous, Abraham Lincoln did not go to bed the night after First Bull Run. He busied himself with pencil jottings that a few days later became detailed memoranda of military policy. He stressed the blockade and training of volunteers, then enumerated plans for use of troops in Baltimore, western Virginia, Missouri, and Arlington. He wanted Manassas Junction seized immediately while simultaneously striking toward Memphis and East Tennessee.

Almost without exception, analysts have insisted that he engaged in self-study of military leadership much as he had earlier done with law. His "borrowing of military treatises from the Library of Congress" and "study of strategical works" has been emphasized by observers ranging from his own secretaries to present-day commentators upon the Civil War.

A Library of Congress list of "Borrowed Books in the White House" tells a different story. According to it, from April 19, 1861, through June 6, 1865, only four military works were sent to the Executive Mansion. These were: Henry W. Halleck, *Science of War* (January 8, 1862, to March 24, 1864); *Book on the Rifle* and Stonehenge, *On the Rifle* (March 20, 1863 to May 31, 1864); and Domini, *Operations Militaire*. The French-language treatise was returned on March 18, 1865, after having been sent on March 1.

Initially an ardent admirer of George B. McClellan, Lincoln castigated him for action he called "having the slows" and removed him after four months as commander of Federal forces. [LIBRARY OF CONGRESS]

If Lincoln actually studied strategy and command, he used sources of which there is no record. His personal military experience was limited to fifty-one days as a member of the Illinois militia during the Black Hawk War. Reputedly sworn into service by Robert Anderson, later to become the hero of Fort Sumter, Lincoln was proud that his sixty-man unit elected him as captain. He confessed, however, that he was never engaged in combat.

It is no wonder that his orders were sometimes confusing. Because of a mixup in his own directives, in April 1861 the warship *Powhatan* went to Fort Pickens rather than to Fort Sumter, as expected. When Lincoln gave McClellan a plan for simultaneous frontal and flank movements against the railroad at Manassas, his general held it for ten days then tactfully suggested, "They could meet us in front with equal forces, nearly."

Commanders found it impossible to obey his General War Order No. 1 of January 1862. It directed "a general movement of the land and naval forces" against insurgents on February 22. When it was seen that this could not be done, a supplemental order directed the Army of the Potomac to move against the railroad south of Manassas Junction on highly symbolic Washington's birthday.

Specific directives were typically sent as "suggestions" or as "recommendations" rather than as orders, but recipients knew that seemingly soft language was deceptive. Gen. David Hunter was too high in rank to be ordered to Missouri to aid John Charles Frémont. So Lincoln wrote, "Will you not serve the country and oblige me by taking it voluntarily?"

War literature includes wide criticism of the Union army for lack of

Maj. Gen. John Pope's tenure as titular head of the Army of Virginia lasted from June to September 1862. [AUTHOR'S COLLECTION]

centralized command. Actually, for most of its duration it had a highly centralized command—a lonely amateur alternating between the Executive Mansion and the telegraph office and trying to run the entire operation.

Interference with the command structure was commonplace. War Department orders required governors to control men from their states, but the commander in chief bypassed Gov. John A. Andrew of Massachusetts and gave Benjamin Butler permission to raise an army. While Scott was still general in chief, Lincoln brought McClellan to the Executive Mansion and conferred with him without inviting Scott to participate. Later he didn't ask McClellan's approval when he detached a large body of troops for the protection of the capital and another contingent to help subdue rebels in Tennessee. With Gen. Ambrose Burnside heading the same army, he had a subordinate general—Joseph Hooker—report directly to him.

Though seldom mentioned, the "Harney affair" may have included the most un-military exploit by the commander in chief. From Washington it appeared that Gen. William S. Harney was not performing satisfactorily in Missouri. Col. Francis P. Blair was given discretion whether or not to deliver to him an order relieving him of command. No ordinary colonel, Blair was the son of a powerful editor who helped to win the nomination of Lincoln.

Few details were too small for Lincoln's attention. He requested that a first cousin of his dead friend Elmer Ellsworth be made a second lieutenant. On the recommendation of a Father O'Hara, he requested that a brother of the priest be made quartermaster of a brigade. During a single week, he sent fifty telegrams to half a dozen

generals, instructing them concerning movements against Stonewall Jackson in the Shenandoah Valley.

Not surprisingly, Union military leaders rotated in and out of office
at short intervals. When Scott was eased out in favor of McClellan in
November 1861, his successor as general in chief lasted only four
months. From March 1862 until July, there was no general in chief
to take instructions from Lincoln; he issued them above his own
signature. Gen. Henry W. Halleck survived as titular head of armed
forces for eighteen months, but he seldom argued with his commander in chief. As head of the Army of Virginia, Gen. John Pope
lasted just over two months. Burnside's tenure as commanding general of the Army of the Potomac was only a few days longer. Hooker
held the same post for about half a year, and Gen. George G. Meade
was in full command for nine months, until Grant was elevated.

Matters changed, most commentators agree, when Ulysses S.
Grant was made lieutenant general and placed in command. According to this view, Lincoln saw Grant as a man of decisive action and
hence gave him a free hand.

Almost, perhaps, but not quite. "Your three dispatches received,"
he wired his general in March 1865. "From what direction did the
enemy come that attacked Gen. Charles Griffin?" With the Army of

*Henry W. Halleck, author of
one of a handful of military
texts Lincoln may have
read, typically did as he
was told and thus held the
title of general in chief for a
relatively long time.* [U.S.
MILITARY INSTITUTE]

Lt. Gen. Ulysses S. Grant received relatively few directives from the president—possibly because Lincoln was busy preparing for the election of 1864. [LIBRARY OF CONGRESS]

Northern Virginia about to collapse, Lincoln directed Grant not to confer with Gen. Robert E. Lee "unless it be for capitulation." In addition, he ordered him not to "decide, discuss, or confer upon any political questions" since he held these matters in his own hands and would "submit them to no military conferences or conventions."

Grant's elevation and his relatively free hand may have stemmed from political rather than military considerations. With the administration in deep trouble, Lincoln's re-election became doubtful before the end of 1863. Forced to give increasing attention to political matters, the new hands-off attitude of the commander in chief who often functioned as general in chief and as chief of staff may have come about by default. He simply no longer had time to direct what had become the largest-ever body of troops under one command.

T. Harry Williams spent years studying Lincoln as a military leader and concluded that he was "a great natural strategist, a better one than any of his generals." He simply echoed the verdict of England's Gen. R. Colin Ballard, who said, "Lincoln was solely responsible for the strategy of the North and proved himself very capable."

More recently, others have seen things differently. Lincoln seems often to have made matters difficult for his own troops as a result of bypassing commanders to deal with subordinates and frequently countermanding orders.

The overwhelming superiority of the Union in terms of manpower, money, and industrial resources has never been disputed. Had Lincoln established a chain of command and contented himself with outlining major goals, would the conflict have cost an average of 3,000 lives each week for 208 weeks?

It was Lincoln who launched and pursued what was—in its broadest outline, rather than its minute details—an offensive war. Initially judged sure to be small and short, it became immense and lengthy. But from start to finish, he never wavered from insisting upon unconditional surrender by insurgent forces. Perhaps this consuming goal rather than his "suggestions," directives, and specific demands constitutes his outstanding and enduring contribution to the Union war effort.

20

*How Did He Develop Enthusiasm
for Testing*

WEAPONS OF EVERY KIND AND SIZE?

■

AFTER ABRAHAM LINCOLN's death, dozens of persons told what they remembered of him during his prepresidential years. No one described him as having been even a casual hunter. If he was ever seen taking a musket into woods or fields, the incident was not recorded. His constant stream of quips and witticisms seldom included a reference to firearms.

His life was abruptly transformed by the third ballot at the Wigwam. Within months, at age fifty-two, he developed a keen and lasting interest in weapons of every kind, shape, and size. Any person who perfected a gun called new and revolutionary could gain a hearing at the Executive Mansion simply by appearing at the door.

This abrupt change in interests and habits took place some time between the unsuccessful attempt to relieve Fort Sumter and the Union debacle at First Bull Run. So powerful was his absorption with offensive weapons and defensive equipment that during the remainder of 1861 it often seemed almost dominant. Although this interest gradually dwindled, it was still vital at war's end.

New Hampshire native Thaddeus Sobieski Coulincourt Lowe may have been the first entrepreneur of his kind to gain Lincoln's interested attention. On the day a blockade of Confederate ports was proclaimed, Lowe landed in Charleston from a balloon—ecstatic at having made a successful test flight of nine hundred miles. Accused of being a Yankee spy, he headed for Washington as soon as he managed to talk his way out of the dilemma.

Joseph Henry of the Smithsonian Institution introduced him to the president on June 11. Before they parted company, Lincoln agreed to let Lowe make a test flight aimed at showing the military capability of the inflated bag.

130

One of Thaddeus Lowe's balloons being filled with hydrogen from portable generators. [U.S. MILITARY HISTORY INSTITUTE]

June 18 brought a telegram from the pioneer who was in the balloon *Enterprise* over grounds of the Columbia Armory: "This point of observation commands an area nearly 50 miles in diameter. I have the pleasure of sending you this first dispatch ever telegraphed from an aerial station."

Lincoln assigned the civilian aeronaut to the Army of the Potomac where his "aerial corps" eventually grew to seven balloons. Lowe once gave directions to an artillery battery and several times provided early information regarding movements of enemy troops. Total impact of the balloonist sponsored by the president was insignificant, however.

That was not the case with Orison Blunt of New York. A prominent Republican who had launched a gun manufacturing plant, Blunt showed the president a prototype rifle on June 10. Probably a modified Enfield, it seems to have awakened in Lincoln an absorbing interest in rifles of every description. Just ten days later, the door of the Executive Mansion opened to admit Robert McCarty. His multiple-shot weapon, clumsily cranked by hand, promised to mow rebels down like ripe wheat. Though McCarty's invention never performed well, the rifle zealot who occupied the mansion remained mentally poised to look for a good "repeating rifle."

He believed he had found it when he accompanied J. D. Mills to a loft near Willard's Hotel late in June. Invited to turn the crank of the queer contraption, the president saw cartridge cases drop into a revolving cylinder at regular intervals. When struck by a firing pin, each empty cartridge was ejected. Delighted with what he dubbed "a coffee-mill gun," the president arranged for it to be fired before a group of cabinet members and army officers. They were impressed but said a possible purchase would have to proceed through regular channels.

No order had been processed when Mills returned to the capital four months later. This time he brought along ten finished weapons. The president bought them on the spot at $1,300 each—consummating the first recorded purchase of what later came to be called machine guns. In mid-December, Gen. George B. McClellan ordered fifty "coffee-mills." Under battle conditions, they proved to be dangerous and inefficient, so they went into Union warehouses for the duration.

Not all weapons that won early presidential recommendations proved useless, however. A Springfield rifle that had been converted into a breechloader seemed to Lincolon to represent an important innovation; in combat, it could be fired much more rapidly than any muzzleloader. He personally tested it in the Treasury Park, allegedly using a small portrait of Jefferson Davis as his target. Though the weapon he used that afternoon was never mass produced, its principle was basic to the Spencer carbine, which he approved later in the year.

Work on his post–Bull Run memoranda concerning tactics was briefly interrupted on July 24. "A fellow at the door, named Sherwin, wants you to see his rifled cannon," the president was told. He inspected the weapon, agreed with the inventor that addition of rifle grooves to the barrel would boost accuracy of fire, and ordered the construction of a six-pounder. His decision to try the invention was based partly on earlier experience. Having seen the James rifled cannon on July 6, Lincoln considered [first name unknown] Sherwin's model to be superior.

Early in August he persuaded Postmaster General Montgomery Blair to go with him to see tests of a Maynard rifle and Alexander's cartridge. The following month brought Eli Thayer to his interested attention. His four-foot cannon with a bore of just 1.5 inches, the entrepreneur urged, could be pulled into place by men rather than by horses. His demonstration was so persuasive that on September 24 Lincoln ordered twenty of the guns at $350 each. Simultaneously, he personally investigated a steam cannon captured near Baltimore. Produced by wealthy pro-Confederate Ross Winans, it needed no gunpowder.

Before the war's end, Robert Parrott's banded gun was hurling missiles that weighed three hundred pounds. [U.S. MILITARY HISTORY INSTITUTE]

Not even Lincoln's secretaries noted how many hours the president spent examining claims made for the Perkins steam gun. A twelve-pounder, it could get off ten balls per minute and required only 1,500 pounds per square inch of steam. Reluctantly, this brilliant innovation was not pursued because it would require the service of a steam boiler in every battery that included it.

October 14 saw decisive action. Convinced that the muzzleloading rifle would soon be obsolete, the president directed his chief of ordnance to order 25,000 Marsh breechloaders. Three days later, he participated in a demonstration of W. B. Chace's special projectile for muskets. He found it to carry "a full third, or more" beyond an ordinary round ball cartridge fired from the same smooth-bore weapon. Hence he wrote Secretary of War Simon Cameron that he believed it to be "worthy of a regular test."

Before October ended, he also examined a chaplain's plan for a worm-gear elevating mechanism designed for use with coastal cannon. Enthusiastic about what he now called "repeating guns," he arranged for a battery to be displayed at the arsenal and urged McClellan to take a look. It was also in October that he pored over plans for iron warships, examining and approving a model described as "resembling a cheese-box on a raft."

In November he personally authorized purchase of thirty pieces of experimental light artillery, known as Woodruff guns. He then devoted much of a day to a breechloading cannon developed by George A. Rollins of Nashua, New Hampshire.

Old-time ordnance experts were dubious, but Abraham Lincoln had spent so many hours with inventors that he believed the era of the single-shot muzzleloading weapon to be over. Eager to get the Spencer into action, on December 26 he directed his chief of ordnance to purchase ten thousand. A cartridge box holding ten to thirteen bullet tubes was to accompany each weapon. Popularly known as a carbine, it was the Spencer that gave Union cavalry units a significant advantage over mounted Confederates. By war's end, an estimated 200,000 Spencer carbines and rifles were in the hands of fighting men in blue.

During 1862 the president tested the chemical called Greek Fire, hoping that it could be used to manufacture incendiary shells. He offered to provide "fire shells" to McClellan and purchased a thousand after his ordnance chief balked. He investigated the use of chlorine as well as a breechloading cannon invented by George Ferris of Utica, New York. Judged to be inferior to competing models, no Ferris guns were ordered. But Horatio Ames so impressed the president with his wrought-iron cannon that he gave instructions to buy ten of them at one dollar per pound.

He tested Samuel Strong's breechloading carbine and paid a visit to Robert P. Parrot's foundry near West Point, New York, to examine the inventor's rifled cannon. Most of an afternoon was spent at the navy yard testing the Rafael repeater cannon. Peter Peckham's rifles and special cartridges were also given careful attention. In his only international arms purchase, the president accepted Solomon Dingee's offer of 50,000 Austrian rifles at nineteen dollars each.

Accompanied by two members of his cabinet, late in the year the chief executive presided over a test of Joshua Hyde's rocket, whose warhead with adjustable time fuse was designed to make it detonate at a predetermined point. When the rocket exploded in its stand, an observer wryly noted, "The war very nearly ended on November 25, 1862; along with Secretaries Seward and Chase, Lincoln probably would have been killed, had he been a few feet closer to the demonstration."

Months before the election of 1864, retention of the Executive Mansion became Lincoln's top priority. As a result, his personal inspection of weapons and his hours spent with inventors diminished—but did not cease. He examined George W. Beardslee's electric detonating system for cannon, saw that the Amsterdam projectile was tested, and ordered a thousand pounds of experimental gunpowder from Capt. Isaac Diller. He instructed a board of officers to inspect and to test the Ames wrought-iron cannon of seven-inch calibre and pored over a diagram of an "improved shell" perfected by Quaker Samuel Gardiner. An explosive bullet attracted

The USS Monitor, *for a time the most deadly warship afloat,
was built against the advice of many veteran naval officers but
with the hearty approval of Abraham Lincoln.* [LESLIE'S
ILLUSTRATED NEWSPAPER]

Lincoln's interested attention, whose personal test of the Marsh
breechloading rifle led to purchase of 25,000.

Sometimes termed "a one-man Office of Research and Development," the president considered the use of iron body armor and may
have tried it on himself. He pondered field tests of more than one
kind of portable breastworks and gave early sanction to experiments
that led to development of submarines. No flame thrower, land mine,
or rocket was too bizarre to warrant his attention.

Perhaps his most significant contribution was encouragement.
He backed those who envisioned the USS *Monitor*, was an early en-
thusiast for machine guns, and played a significant role in supplant-
ing muskets with rifles.

Sudden but lasting interest in new weapons on the part of the
president may have been an outgrowth of his long-established
fondness for inventions.

Again, it could have stemmed from his realization very early in the
war that the military bureaucracy was inordinately reluctant to try
anything new. He listened to radical ideas because no one else
would.

Or his focus upon weapons could have been a fruit of his passionate and never-modified insistence that he would halt the war only
after enemy troops laid down their arms without condition.

If anyone ever knew precisely why a busy and burdened chief executive devoted so much time and energy to instruments of death,
that person was Abraham Lincoln. He never explained his actions.

21

What Led Him to Countermand

EARLY EFFORTS TO FREE SOME SLAVES?

■

BEFORE HE LEFT Springfield for Washington, Abraham Lincoln realized that something must be done for John Charles Frémont. Famous as the Pathfinder who had explored the West, Frémont had been the 1856 Republican nominee for the presidency. Numerous party members wanted Lincoln as his running mate; though not chosen for that role, he delivered an estimated fifty campaign speeches for Frémont. Now the Pathfinder must have an appointment of significance, but precisely what should that be?

Some leading Republicans wanted Frémont in the cabinet; Lincoln did not. Perhaps he was influenced by the pressure of promises made by managers in Chicago. A self-made man who grew up in poverty may have winced at working closely with a millionaire who had been nationally famous for years. Whatever the case, the new president leaned toward naming his fellow Republican as U.S. minister to France. William H. Seward objected, so that idea was dropped.

Outbreak of the Civil War provided an opportunity to placate Frémont and his followers, without putting him in a post that would involve frequent contact with the president. One month after Fort Sumter, Lincoln made the Pathfinder a major general. On July 3 he sent him to take command in St. Louis.

A border state with many slaveholders, Missouri was a focal point of strife. Guerrilla activity was so threatening that on August 30 Frémont declared martial law. Expecting to break the back of resistance, he announced that property of all who had taken up arms against the government would be confiscated. Since slaves were property, he said slaves of rebels "are hereby declared free men."

Almost a week passed before news of his actions reached the Executive Mansion. Abraham Lincoln reacted with uncharacteristic speed. "In a spirit of caution and not of censure," he dispatched a

John Charles Frémont, the first to proclaim that some slaves were free, saw his military career suffer badly as a result. [LESLIE'S ILLUSTRATED NEWSPAPER]

September 2 letter that urged Frémont to reconsider. Slaves belonging to non-Unionists were not affected, but Lincoln warned that the action with regard to dissident slave owners "will alarm our Southern Union friends and turn them against us; perhaps ruin our rather fair prospect for Kentucky." Then the commander in chief requested Frémont, of his own volition, to modify his proclamation to conform with an August 6, 1861, act of Congress.

On May 21, 1861, the Confederate Congress had taken action by which all debts due to Northerners were "confiscated," or made null and void. Possibly in retaliation for this step, the U.S. Congress had passed the Confiscation Act of 1861, under whose terms owners of property devoted to "hostile use" forfeited their titles.

Perhaps Frémont considered his edict to be legal. Or he may have decided to stand his ground because he felt his decision was right and proper. In any case, he refused to act upon Lincoln's "suggestions" and prepared a response. Instead of entrusting it to the mails, he persuaded his wife—daughter of the famous senator Thomas Hart Benton—to act as courier.

She reached the capital late on September 10 and sent a note to the Executive Mansion, asking when she could see Lincoln. When he responded, "Now, at once," she was led into his office about midnight to deliver her husband's message. In it, General Frémont said he considered his proclamation to be "as much a movement in the war as a battle." Should his commander in chief decide, after reflection, that the step toward liberation of slaves was wrong, wrote Frémont, "I have to ask that you openly direct me to make the correction."

When Frémont refused to
rescind his proclamation of
emancipation, he was
succeeded by David Hunter.
Hunter later issued a
proclamation of his own
and was forced to withdraw
it. [HARPER'S WEEKLY]

September 11 saw Lincoln prepare and dispatch another letter.
This time the commander in chief transmitted an order rather than
a request. Frémont was told to modify his proclamation and to pub-
lish it along with the text of the congressional act of August 6. One
day after this order went out, Lincoln sent Judge Advocate General
Joseph Holt to St. Louis as his personal representative. Having already gone on record as denouncing Frémont's position, Holt was
instructed to urge him to adopt a course of "moderation and modification."

Frémont ignored both Holt's urging and Lincoln's order.

It took an agonized commander in chief six weeks to arrive at a
course of action. After consultation with members of his cabinet, he
selected his long-time friend Leonard Swett to serve as a messenger.
To Swett he entrusted a parcel addressed to Samuel R. Curtis, a
brigadier general of U.S. Volunteers. Curtis was informed that one
enclosed letter meant for Frémont would relieve him of command. A
second enclosure, for Gen. David Hunter, made him Frémont's successor. Curtis was told to take "safe, certain, and suitable measures"
to see that Frémont received his dismissal, provided that he had not
in the meantime fought and won a battle or was about to engage the
enemy.

Fearing that he could not gain admission to Frémont's camp, Swett

persuaded Curtis to consign Lincoln's letter to Capt. Thomas J. Mc-
Kenney. Disguised as a farmer, he succeeded in delivering it to Frémont
on October 24, after which the document making Gen. David Hunter
his replacement was also delivered.

Revocation of the emancipation clause of Frémont's proclamation
led to a storm of indignant protest. Senator Charles Sumner said
that actions of the commander in chief showed how vain it was "to
have the power of a god and not use it godlike." Senator Benjamin F.
Wade declared that the revocation could only have come from a person "born of 'poor white trash' and educated in a slave state." William P. Fessenden, chairman of the Senate Finance Committee,
called Lincoln's actions "a weak and unjustifiable concession to
Union men of the border states."

Despite the barrage of criticism, Lincoln briefly assigned the Department of the West to Hunter. Five months later, would-be emancipator
Frémont was given a new command—the Mountain Department—
which meant he was now expected to defeat Stonewall Jackson.
After three months, he transferred to the First Corps, Army of Virginia. When his personal enemy, Gen. John Pope, was elevated to
command of the army, Frémont resigned.

Eighteen months later, Isaac N. Arnold suggested that Gen. Henry W.
Halleck should be dismissed. Responding on May 26, 1863, the commander in chief demurred. Defending his course of action in dealing
with top military leaders, he wrote that "Frémont was relieved at his
own request."

Secretary of War Simon Cameron probably saw the Frémont-
Lincoln clash as an opportunity for personal political gain. Hence
his annual report to Congress included arguments for immediate
emancipation of slaves. Newly free males "capable of bearing arms"
should be inducted into the military, he urged.

A few newspaper reporters learned of the impending verbal bombshell as early as November 25, 1861. Edwin M. Stanton, special
counsel for the War Department, was identified as the legal expert
who had read and approved the final draft.

Cameron took his entire report to the Executive Mansion on Saturday, November 30. Occupied with his own message to Congress,
difficulties with Mexico, and the *Trent* affair, Lincoln was too busy to
read it immediately. On Sunday morning the Cameron report was
mailed to postmasters of major cities, who were instructed to deliver
it to newspapers as soon as Lincoln sent his annual message to
Congress. That meant numerous copies were en route and a few had
been delivered by the time Lincoln realized what Cameron had done.

Furious, he forced his secretary of war to accept substitute language for the offending paragraphs. On Monday, acting as president
of the United States, he had Postmaster General Montgomery Blair

telegraph postmasters to return packages containing the Cameron report.

Some postmasters claimed never to have received Blair's instructions, and others ignored them. As a result the Cameron proposal for emancipation and for use of black soldiers appeared in the Cincinnati *Gazette*, the New York *Herald*, and other media. A few days later, Cameron's report, as revised by Lincoln, was widely published.

In Chicago, Charles H. Ray of the *Tribune* recalled how hard he and colleagues had worked for the nomination of Lincoln. Astonished at learning about the revocation of Cameron's proposals, Ray wrote to a friend, "Old Abe is now unmasked, and we are sold out."

Lincoln had not wanted Cameron in his cabinet but put him there to keep promises made in Chicago. Embroiled in controversy, Cameron was already slated for dismissal at the first opportunity. His emancipation proposal provided the opportunity; so he was named U.S. minister to Russia. Stanton, who helped to phrase Cameron's controversial proposals, succeeded him in the War Department.

Hunter, who assumed command of the Western Department when Frémont was demoted, was sent from Missouri to Kansas and then to the South. There he took charge of coastal areas of South Carolina, Georgia, and Florida on March 31, 1862.

Ten days after he assumed command, his troops captured Fort Pulaski near Savannah. Twenty-four hours later, Hunter issued an order that conferred freedom on slaves then held by units under his control. Union victory in the Port Royal campaign had swelled the number of fugitive slaves immensely; so Hunter authorized their enlistment in the army and formed the First South Carolina regiment. As though he knew nothing of what had happened to Frémont in Missouri, on May 9 Hunter issued his General Order No. 11— more sweeping than that of Frémont. Under its terms, all slaves in Union-held regions of three states were "declared forever free."

Abraham Lincoln took the Hunter proclamation to his cabinet on May 17 and seems to have met no outspoken opposition to his insistence that it could not be allowed to stand. Three days later, again acting as commander in chief, he revoked the emancipation order of Hunter.

During a ten-month period, repeated efforts at emancipation were thwarted by Abraham Lincoln. Why such actions on the part of the man destined to become the Great Emancipator barely four months after having overruled Hunter?

Speculation has abounded for 130 years; firm answers are not readily found. Here is an area of mystery about which so much is known that questions are as numerous now as they were in 1861–62.

Powerful Senator Charles Sumner raged that Abraham Lincoln had godlike power to abolish slavery but refused to use it. [NICOLAY & HAY, *ABRAHAM LINCOLN*]

On the day that the Cameron proposal went into the mail, Abraham Lincoln was working very hard on a document aimed at persuading the divided nation that gradual emancipation—with compensation— would solve the slavery problem. Was he so convinced of the correctness of this course that he refused even to consider any other? Perhaps.

Or was he—as he repeatedly insisted—so concerned about keeping the border states in general and Kentucky in particular in the Union that he felt this matter to be more important than emancipation? Maybe.

Again, in his dual roles as military and political head of the Union, he may have been angered at the insubordination of Frémont, Cameron, and Hunter—sufficiently angered to force each of them to retract and retrench.

Finally, astute politician Lincoln was keenly aware that the North he guided was far from unified concerning emancipation. Many members of both major political parties despised abolitionists fully as much as—perhaps more than—they despised the rebels. Hasty action could have strengthened his political opposition, so the Rail-Splitter may have postponed emancipation of relatively few slaves in order to retain the support of a great many Northern voters.

22

*Why Was Preservation
of the Union*

THE DOMINANT
GOAL OF THE
COMMANDER IN
CHIEF?

■

DURING THE TURBULENT 1850s, with sectional tensions rising, many Americans hoped to preserve the Union. Many were unwilling to go to war to do so. Among those ready to use military force was Abraham Lincoln. His near obsession was clearly expressed in 1854 when he proposed to repurify the robe of state and make it white "in the spirit, if not the blood, of the Revolution."

Adamantly opposed to the extension of slavery, he saw it as the "only thing that ever endangers the Union." Evil as slavery was, in the scale of values it loomed far below dissolution of the Union. Much as he hated slavery, said the man from Springfield, "I would consent to the extension of it rather than see the Union dissolved."

Though he heard much talk of separation, he regarded this as "humbug, nothing but folly." A vast majority of Americans, he told Galena, Illinois, listeners in 1856, didn't want dissolution. Should a minority attempt it, "We won't let you. With the purse and sword, the army and navy and treasury in our hands, you could not do it."

Breakup of the Union was the talk of the nation during the journey of the president-elect from Springfield to Washington early in 1861. On the first day he told Indiana lawmakers that to secessionists, "the Union, as a family relation, would seem to be no regular marriage, but rather a sort of 'free-love arrangement.'"

This analogy emerged in his carefully prepared and edited inaugural address. "A husband and wife may be divorced, and go out of the presence and beyond the reach of each other," he pointed out. "But the different parts of our country cannot do this. They cannot but

Preparing to take the oath of office, the rough-looking Westerner carried in his pocket a manuscript with no mention of the nation and twenty-three references to the Union. [LESLIE'S ILLUSTRATED NEWSPAPER]

remain face to face, and intercourse, either amicable or hostile, must continue between them."

That is, according to the man who within minutes would take the oath of office, the marriage Union of the states could not be dissolved. Divorce in the form of fracturing the Union was not an alternative.

En route to the capital, his language had been less explicit, but his consuming goal was not. At Indianapolis he challenged listeners to rally to the protection of the Union—a theme repeated in Cleveland, Buffalo, and Albany. In New York City he cried, "There is nothing that could ever bring me to consent—willingly to consent—to the destruction of this Union." Then he stressed the same concept at Trenton and Philadelphia.

In his inaugural address, the president-elect did not refer to "our nation" even once but spoke of the Union almost two dozen times. By July 4, 1861, when for the first time he prepared a message for Congress, Lincoln made articulate the conviction that had guided him for years. No portion of the Union could be separated from it without destroying the whole, he declared. His expedition sent to Fort Sumter was, therefore, not aggressive in nature. Rather, it went

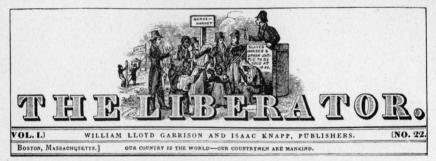

Masthead of William Lloyd Garrison's newspaper in which he advocated the abolition of slavery but suggested that peaceful separation of regions was preferable to civil war. [New York Public Library]

forward "to maintain visible possession, and thus to preserve the Union from actual and immediate dissolution."

Probably no man in America knew better than Lincoln that he was a political knight errant fighting for a minority view.

Sentiment supporting the course that editor Horace Greeley called "a peaceable separation," strong everywhere, was overwhelming in the thought of many leaders. Writing to William H. Seward on the eve of Lincoln's inauguration, General in Chief Winfield Scott urged, "Say to the seceded states—wayward sisters—depart in peace."

U.S. Supreme Court Chief Justice Roger B. Taney regarded peaceful separation preferable to "union under a military government and a reign of terror—preceded by a civil war with all its horrors." Ardent abolitionists William Lloyd Garrison and Wendell Phillips welcomed secession because it would sever the regions that differed so greatly in social structure. Garrison considered it "self-evident" that the free North and the slaveholding South constituted two nations.

Seward, who failed by a hair's breadth to win the Republican nomination and the presidency, advocated compromise and conciliation that included peaceful secession. Salmon P. Chase was regarded as Seward's rival when delegates converged upon the Wigwam with seven states already having seceded. Chase thought it better to let them "try the experiment of a separate existence, rather than incur the evils of a bloody war." Seceded states, Chase insisted, "would soon come back, chastened, and the cause of liberty would be all the stronger for it."

In Chicago industrialist Cyrus H. McCormick led a mass meeting at which voters registered their support for "peaceful separation of the states." In New York City editor James Gordon Bennett consistently advocated secession of the North from the South. His mayor, Fernando Wood, went a step further and proposed that the city secede from the state to gain independence. Bizarre as Wood's view seemed at the time to many, his principle later prevailed when western Virginia withdrew from the Old Dominion and became a separate state.

Public sentiment in the North and in the South notwithstanding, the president-elect made it clear that he expected to preserve the Union intact. No state had seceded, he insisted; those claiming to have done so had not actually withdrawn because such a course of action was impossible.

Many in the North did not accept this line of reasoning. On the contrary, said editors of Washington's *States and Union* newspaper:

> The Constitution is a rope of sand, the government a system of courtesy. Vermont, New York, and Virginia, upon entering the Union, were wise enough to distinctly enunciate this principle in setting forth the independent sovereignty of a state, when they reserved the right to "resume the power delegated to the federal government" whenever they were found to be used in an oppressive manner.

Having taken his oath of office and having become commander in chief of the U.S. Army and Navy, Abraham Lincoln did not think military force would be necessary but was prepared to use it if other options failed. He did not suggest a U.S. Supreme Court test of the legality of secession; he felt that such was not needed despite James Madison's strong statements concerning states' rights. In his heart, Lincoln knew beyond a shadow of a doubt that the Union was indissoluble. His call for 75,000 militia to serve under him was not an acknowledgement that secession had taken place. Rather, he saw it as a prelude to chastening of insurgents and quick restoration of normal conditions.

Viewed from the perspective of many decades, some of Abraham Lincoln's views concerning the Union were highly unusual.

Repeatedly, he insisted that the Union existed before the Constitution was framed and adopted. "The Union is much older than the Constitution," he held. "It was formed, in fact, by the Articles of Association in 1774." Two years later, he said, the Declaration of Independence matured and continued the Union. This mystical bond "was further matured by the Articles of Confederation in 1778."

According to Lincoln's line of thought, the Constitution was secondary to the Union because it succeeded it in time. Though the Constitution should be respected and followed, "a little bending of it" was justified if that was needed to preserve the Union.

Seeing the pre-constitutional Union as eternal, the commander in chief repeatedly stressed that states in rebellion had not seceded; they only sought to do so. Seldom using the word *war* or an exact

Abolitionist editor William Lloyd Garrison welcomed secession because he felt that would enable North and South to go their separate ways in peace.
[LIBRARY OF CONGRESS]

synonym, he declared that men called upon to fight would do much more than keep intact a nation made up of thirty-four states and located in North America. If the Union should be broken, Lincoln solemnly warned, the entire world would be the worse for it.

Some persons argued that states came together in order to form a Union. Not so, declared Lincoln; the preexistent globally significant Union served to bring the states into being. No voluntary association or partnership that could be terminated, he considered the Union to be perpetual. Therefore it could not be divided. Even if he, Lincoln, were willing to consent to such division, it would be impossible. Hence it was the sworn duty of the commander in chief to preserve the Union unimpaired.

Secession he labeled a "farcical pretense." Consequently, the "combined government" of states claiming to have seceded was neither more nor less than an illegal organization. "So-called seceding states" that made up "the so-called Confederate States of America" were "out of their proper practical relation with the Union." Still, they remained part of "our one common country."

According to Lincoln, after hostilities began, masses of citizens erred by speaking of civil war. No civil war, fighting between Federal forces and those of the South was the result of seeking to quell an insurrection. Success in this enterprise would force insurgents to confess that they belonged to the Union as fully as did fighting men clad in blue.

Citizens of states claiming to have seceded were to Lincoln "erring brethren" and "dissatisfied fellow countrymen" whom he invited to join with him in a national day of thanksgiving in November 1863. This day, said the commander in chief and the president, was a time for God's mercy to be "reverently, and gratefully acknowledged by the whole American people"—not simply those who made their homes in states listed as loyal to the Union.

It was this set of unalterable convictions that caused Lincoln to refuse in 1864 to sign a congressional bill whose preamble asserted that seceded states were not in the Union.

Lincoln's last public address was delivered on April 11, 1865. Speaking from an upstairs window of the Executive Mansion, he did not swerve from earlier views and labeled the question of secession as "a merely pernicious abstraction." So-called seceded states, he said, were "out of their proper practical relation with the Union." In regard to these states, his sole personal object, and the sole object of the government he headed, "is to again get them into that proper practical relation."

From Fort Sumter to Appomattox, the Federal commander in chief refused to acknowledge that a brutal civil war was being fought. His paramount task was to preserve the mystical Union—challenged, perhaps, but not broken by "so-called secession."

In light of his passionate stance, it is not strange that some contemporaries voiced their belief that Lincoln's views were unique. "The Union, with him," wrote Alexander H. Stephens, "in sentiment rose to the sublimity of a religious mysticism."

In 1876 Frederick Douglass was given the honor of unveiling a Lincoln statue. Using nearly forgotten language, Douglass called black Americans "Lincoln's step-children" as a prelude to emphasizing that to the Civil War president "the union was more to him than our freedom or our future." Ardent admirer Walt Whitman observed Lincoln closely for months before concluding, "The only thing like passion or infatuation in the man was the passion for the Union of these States."

Modern psycho-biographer Dwight G. Anderson has gone beyond the verdicts of those who actually saw the dominant figure of the Civil War in action. "By the end of 1864," he concludes, "the identification between himself and the Union had become so complete that he *was* the Union."

Even if the Anderson verdict is rejected as extreme, it is impossible to fathom the mystery of how Abraham Lincoln arrived at his views concerning the Union and became absolutely devoted to it. At most, a few tentative conjectures can be made, without expecting any or all of them to yield firm answers.

His treasured biography of Washington by Mason Weems described disunion followed by civil war as the greatest dread of the first president. Did Lincoln's conviction that he was a biological, as

U.S. Supreme Court Chief Justice Roger B. Taney preferred "peaceful separation" to military conquest of states claiming to have seceded. [LIBRARY OF CONGRESS]

well as political, successor to the nation's Founding Fathers lead him to his views of Union?

If not, could he have been influenced by ambition? Always hungry for office, perhaps he saw preservation of the Union as a political slogan that would help to win elections. Could it be that a concept he set out to use eventually became his master—using him rather than being used?

Or is it remotely possible that he was more deeply influenced by family scars than is generally recognized? He knew that his grandmother never entered into a marriage union and he was unable to find proof that his parents had done so. Overwhelmed by the solemnity of this sacred bond, did he equate it with Union of the states, to make preservation of the political Union his all-consuming goal?

23

*What Accounts for His
Dealings with*

THE FIRST
NATIONAL DRAFT FOR
MILITARY SERVICE?

■

LESS THAN THREE months after assuming leadership
of the U.S. Army, Commander in Chief Lincoln had only about
15,000 men in its ranks. On April 15, 1861, he called for 75,000
additional soldiers who would serve for three months. Though enlisted in state militia systems, these volunteers would be under his
command. Despite the fact that many offers of units were rejected,
about 80,000 men were eventually accepted with the hope that their
presence in uniform might lead so-called secessionists to reverse
their stance. Otherwise, volunteers would have to use force to effect
a speedy resolution of difficulties.

Two weeks after his dramatic first call to arms—without prior
congressional approval—the commander in chief enlarged the U.S.
Army by 40 percent and the U.S. Navy by 250 percent. At the same
time, he requested more volunteers for the militia; this time men
were asked to serve three years "unless sooner discharged."

By the time he sent his July 4 message to Congress, it was apparent that the end of the struggle might be more distant than it had
seemed on the day after the fall of Fort Sumter. Hence he informed
lawmakers that he now needed an additional 400,000 men who
would be willing to wear uniforms for an unspecified period. Enthu-
siasts responded by promising "Father Abraham" [Lincoln] that
"600,000 more" would hasten to enroll at his beckoning.

According to the provost marshal general, 637,126 men were in
uniform by spring 1862. So many had volunteered that on April 3,
Secretary of War Edwin M. Stanton called a halt to recruitment.
Soon the entire system designed to produce soldiers was scrapped;
just three months later, Federal generals found themselves facing a

FOURTH REGIMENT
NEW HAMPSHIRE

DOWN WITH THE REBELLION.

VOLUNTEERS.

ABLE BODIED MEN WANTED
FOR THE FOURTH REGIMENT.

The subscribers having been appointed Recruiting
Officers, will open a Recruiting Office at

Where they will enlist all who would like to rally around the OLD STARS
AND STRIPES, the emblem of America's Freedom.

$10 BOUNTY WILL BE ALLOWED!
Regular Army pay and Rations to commence on taking the oath.

Lieut. J. M. CLOUGH,
Sergt. W. B. ROWE.

Sept. 1861.

Even Halley & Co., Printers, Concord.

*Recruitment posters such as this one failed to attract
sufficient men to meet increasingly heavy Federal
demands.* [AUTHOR'S COLLECTION]

severe shortage of manpower. Recruitment efforts had been abandoned at the beginning of a period not foreseen; military defeats, delays, and desertions caused enthusiasm to wane. Recruitment was therefore resumed on June 6.

Under the prevailing system of placing state militia in Federal service, governors organized new units and issued commissions for their officers. On July 1, 1862, eighteen heads of Northern states joined in urging Lincoln to make a new call for men whose officers they would choose. He responded by asking for 300,000 three-year volunteers "so as to bring this unnecessary and injurious civil war to a speedy and satisfactory conclusion."

Congress moved quickly to support the commander in chief; on July 17 a Militia Act was passed. Yet only about 87,000 fighting men were gained as a result. Lincoln reacted by ordering a draft—conducted by state authorities—of 300,000 men for nine months of service.

So far, it appeared that men were voluntarily flocking to Federal colors in vast numbers. Actually, the new statute was a thinly disguised move toward conscription. Six weeks before Congress acted, through the War Department a sweeping set of orders was prepared. "By direction of the president of the United States" all citizens subject to draft into the militia were forbidden to go to a foreign country or to leave their states before the draft was made. Disobedience carried a penalty of an automatic arrest and fine. To make certain that the presidential edict was not circumvented, orders stipulated that "The writ of *habeas corpus* is hereby suspended in respect to all persons so arrested and detained and in respect to all persons arrested for disloyal practices." Made public on August 8, the stern edict was supplemented by an order giving military commissions authority to try civilian offenders.

For practical purposes, a national draft was under way, with a goal of 300,000 "to meet deficiencies in quotas under the call for volunteers."

Indiana, Wisconsin, and other states formulated and implemented systems of conscription. In Wisconsin, noncitizens posed a special problem. Responding to it, the U.S. secretary of state ruled that regardless of citizenship, all who had voted were subject to the draft. *Habeas corpus* was suspended nationally, rather than along limited lines as in the past. A draft dodger or a person accused of being less than loyal would now be tried before a military tribunal.

Following a longstanding practice used in recruiting militia, volunteers were offered bounties. Trying to avoid making drafted men go to war, many states and localities boosted the Federal inducement. Some three-year enlistments brought total bounties of $1,500 or more in 1863–64.

Seven months after the Militia Act proved ineffective, Congress

Among those who escaped military service by hiring substitutes was Grover Cleveland of Buffalo, New York, destined to become the twenty-fourth president. [NATIONAL ARCHIVES]

passed new legislation over strenuous objections from Sen. William A. Richardson of Illinois and others. This time, the statute was labeled as what it was—a national conscription act. There was no mention of the militia; all males of age twenty through forty-five became subject to service in the national army.

Under terms adopted on March 3, 1863, a major hole in the existing system was plugged; most residents who were citizens of other countries were made subject to the draft. In a bid to soften the blow, draftees were offered the alternative of hiring substitutes or paying $300 commutation fees.

Prominent spokesmen throughout the North labeled the edict a "giant step toward despotism." Horace Greeley called the draft "an anomaly in a free state; it oppresses the masses." Editor Joseph M. Medill of the Chicago *Tribune*—influential in securing Lincoln's nomination—especially objected to the commutation provision. It made things easy for the rich, he argued, while a laboring man earning one dollar a day would find it impossible to buy his way out of service. He went to the capital to protest and four times was not allowed to see the man he had helped to put in office.

In New York the *Evening Express* called conscription "slavery, accursed slavery, in its most frightful form." Voters of the state had recently defeated pro–Lincoln candidate James S. Wadsworth for governor in favor of Democrat Horatio Seymour. In his inaugural the new chief executive of the most populous state noted, "The conscription act was believed by one-half the people of the loyal States a violation of the supreme constitutional law."

In spite of the hue and cry, the Conscription Act of 1863 was never subjected to test by the U.S. Supreme Court. In his First Inaugural Address the president who was determined to preserve the Union regardless of every other consideration made his personal views clear:

> If the policy of the government, upon vital questions, affecting the whole people, is to be irrevocably fixed by decisions of the Supreme Court, the instant they are made . . . the people will have ceased to be their own rulers, having, to that extent, practically resigned their government into the hands of that eminent tribunal.

A Pennsylvania court ruled that the conscription act went beyond the Constitution, and an unpublished decision by Chief Justice Roger B. Taney labeled it "unconstitutional and void." Abraham Lincoln said he would welcome a court test—but coupled that assurance with insistence that he could not afford "to lose the time while it is being obtained."

Under the commutation provision, about 86,000 men paid $300 each to avoid the draft—boosting Federal revenue by $26,000,000. Among men who paid to dodge the draft were J. Pierpont Morgan,

Having escaped battle-line military service, Robert Todd Lincoln later became the president of the Pullman Company.
[DICTIONARY OF AMERICAN PORTRAITS]

Protesters against the draft even made the office of the New York Tribune a target—perhaps because editor Horace Greeley had urged that war be fought to bring an end to slavery. [NEW YORK PUBLIC LIBRARY]

John D. Rockefeller, and Grover Cleveland. Though this feature of the act aroused more anger than any other provision, Lincoln strongly defended it. As though to prove that he meant what he said, he paid for a substitute although he was personally exempt from the draft. Pennsylvania native John S. Staples received at least $500 and perhaps as much as $750 to fight in Lincoln's stead. Along with 117,985 others, the substitute for the commander in chief was duly inducted into the armed forces.

Resistance to the draft was as widespread as it was deep. There was violence in Ohio and Illinois, coupled with "disturbances" in parts of Kentucky, Indiana, Pennsylvania, and Wisconsin. Riots were reported from Troy and Albany in New York and from Newark, New Jersey. Far the most serious riot broke out in New York City when names of a few draftees were drawn on July 11, 1863. Three days of burning and looting, largely directed toward black residents, left more than one hundred persons dead before order was restored by four thousand Federal troops.

So many judges defied previous orders by issuing writs of *habeas corpus* that they seemed to the commander in chief to be "defeating the draft." Attorney General Edward Bates noted that on September 14, Lincoln was "more angry than I ever saw him." Blaming Copperhead Democrats with having "formed a plot," the president called a cabinet meeting on the following day. Over strong objections from Salmon P. Chase, he decided to deal with *habeas corpus* by authorizing military officers to resist civil officials who were carrying out judicial orders.

Draft resistance was so pervasive and commutation so frequent that of at least 250,000 men whose names were pulled from revolving drums by blindfolded officials, only about 6 percent were inducted.

Presidential secretaries John G. Nicolay and John Hay compiled figures for the entire conflict. Less than 15,000 draftees went into combat. This meant that the chief effect of conscription was a surge in volunteers, whose number included substitutes. Recognizing that "bounty jumpers" and many other men enlisted two, three, or more times, Executive Mansion insiders reported that 2,975,000 men were called and 2,653,000 enlisted.

Robert Todd Lincoln personally approved the voluminous record compiled by Nicolay and Hay. Hence it is not strange that they made no mention of the fact that the oldest son of the commander in chief

One victim of mob anger in the New York draft riot was an aged resident who was attacked for no reason except the color of his skin. [HARPER'S WEEKLY]

was carefully shielded from the draft. Illinois was among the states most desperate for men, yet young Lincoln remained at Harvard until his graduation in 1864. He then prepared to enter the school of law.

Having learned of the high-placed evader of the draft, editors of the Philadelphia *Argus* published a stinging rebuke that was widely reprinted. Even the proadministration Indianapolis *Sentinel* called attention of readers to the fact that "Robert Lincoln is still not in uniform."

His father then wrote to Ulysses S. Grant, not as commander in chief, but "only as a friend." He didn't want his twenty-two-year-old son put in the ranks, he said. Neither did he wish him to receive a commission that should go to better qualified men. Could Grant "without embarrassment to you or detriment to the service," let Robert "go into your military family with some nominal rank?"

On January 21, 1865, with all signs pointing to an imminent Confederate collapse, Grant responded that he'd be happy to have Robert in his "military family." It would be appropriate, said the general, to give the untrained and inexperienced son of the commander in chief the rank of captain.

Captain Robert Todd Lincoln became an assistant adjutant general on Grant's headquarters staff. His duties consisted largely of serving as an official escort to notables—his father included—and ended when he resigned his commission in April.

After having lost two boys as a result of illness, it is not surprising that—prodded by his wife—Abraham Lincoln was reluctant to send his oldest son to face Confederate bullets. His action with regard to nineteen-year-old Staples is not so readily understood. Since he never explained why he chose to pay twice the standard rate for a substitute he didn't need, this aspect of his dealings with conscription remains a total enigma.

Was he encouraged to launch the draft because Confederates had already done so on April 16, 1862? If so, he left no record of this influence. Perhaps his consuming motive in resorting to the constitutionally questionable draft—indeed, his only motive—may have been his burning desire to defeat forces of "so-called seceded states."

Whatever the reasons for the course he took, once Abraham Lincoln introduced conscription into the United States it was here to stay. He made it a permanent aspect of American life many decades before it was endorsed by a Supreme Court ruling.

24

How Did a Tenderhearted
Man Direct

WHOLESALE SLAUGHTER FOR MONTH AFTER MONTH?

■

A few days before the completion of his eighth year, in the absence of his father, a flock of wild turkeys approached the new log cabin, and Abraham with a rifle-gun, shot through a crack and killed one of them. He has never since pulled a trigger on any larger game.

At the request of Jesse Fell, Lincoln prepared a campaign autobiography in December 1860. Written in the third person, it is one of the most valuable sources about his early life. Brief as it is, the aspiring politician included in it his account of once having shot a big bird.

Years earlier, as a one-term Congressman, he wrote to William H. Herndon about a moving speech delivered by Alexander H. Stephens of Georgia. He was so affected by Stephens that he confessed that "my eyes are full of tears yet."

With the Civil War barely under way, New York native Elmer Ellsworth led his Fire Zouaves to Alexandria, Virginia. Finding a rebel flag in front of a hotel, Ellsworth ripped it from its pole on May 24, 1861. Before the flag hit the ground, hotel owner James W. Jackson shot and killed the Union soldier.

Only a few months earlier, twenty-four-year-old Ellsworth had begun reading law in Lincoln's office. Soon the man a trifle more than twice his age developed great fondness for him. So the news of Ellsworth's early death brought a vivid public display of grief by the commander in chief.

*Youthful Col. Elmer Ellsworth was killed by the owner of an
Arlington, Virginia, hotel.* [LESLIE'S ILLUSTRATED WEEKLY]

Again he wept openly when the telegraph brought news that
his long-time friend Edward Baker had been killed at Ball's Bluff
in October of the same year. An observer reported that Lincoln
"stumbled as he left the telegraph room," having mumbled that the
news "hit him like a whirlwind from the desert."

Four months later, Lincoln's fourth son contracted "bilious fever."
Earlier, he had lost Eddie—named for Baker—from undiagnosed
causes. When the commander in chief learned that Willie had joined
Eddie in death, he was inconsolable for days.

After the first battle of consequence, Bull Run, commanders reported 2,896 Union and 1,982 rebel casualties—nearly one-third of
the total for the entire U.S. Revolution and two-thirds as many casualties as were inflicted in the War of 1812. Yet no one who spent July
21–23, 1860, with Lincoln reported anything approaching a public
display of emotion. He was agitated, but remained sufficiently calm
to spend many hours drafting plans for new movements against the
enemy.

As weeks passed, the casualty list grew with astonishing rapidity.
Long before the end of 1861, it exceeded the 17,435 total of those
killed and wounded in the Mexican War. Before the carnage was over,
combined deaths among Union and Confederate forces reached at

least 623,000. Another 471,000 or more were wounded in action, for a conservative total of 1,094,000 casualties.

Only once did the commander in chief briefly consider the possibility of an armistice leading to a negotiated peace. Very late in the conflict, he pondered this option briefly. Then he resolutely put it aside and resumed his announced course: a war to the finish with weapons to be laid aside only after unconditional surrender "by forces of seceded states, so-called."

Famous humorist Petroleum V. Nasby went on record as being positive that "No man on earth hated blood as Lincoln did. He was as tenderhearted as a girl."

That verdict is clearly in accord with his guilt-ridden recollection of once having shot a turkey and with his occasional public demonstrations of great sorrow. Yet except for his law partner who remained in Springfield, no one close to Lincoln seems ever to have tried to reconcile his tenderheartedness with his role as commander in chief.

Col. Edward Baker died at Ball's Bluff when making an unauthorized foray into Confederate-held terrain. [LESLIE'S ILLUSTRATED WEEKLY]

His compassion for persons facing execution or imprisonment became legendary long before the conflict was over. He often pored over summaries of court-martial sentences for hours at a time in order to deal with thirty-five or forty in a day. In all, he processed thousands of them—no one knows precisely how many.

He suspended or commuted death sentences for Union soldiers convicted of offenses that ranged from sleeping on duty to desertion to murder. Many of his verdicts were written in the margins of judicial summaries; some were penned on scraps of paper. One, still preserved, pardoned an unnamed wounded man lying in a City Point, Virginia, hospital. Some of Lincoln's memos were lost; many deal with persons whose names appear nowhere else except in company or regimental rolls:

Daniel Sullivan, Samuel Wellers, Thomas Sands, James Haley, H. H. Williams, Mathias Brown, H. C. Beardsley, George F. Perkins, William Griffin, Thomas Lowery, Lorenzo Stewart, Rhett Bannister, James R. Mallory, August Bittersdorf . . .

Over and over, he considered appeals from Confederate prisoners and repeatedly showed leniency for otherwise forgotten men: George S. Herron, Corporal Hardy, Louis A. Welton, Theophilus Brown, Jesse A. Broadway, Horace H. Lurton, J. Hirman Hubbard, Job Smith, Thomas Bennington, John Russell . . .

Other special requests reached him from civilians. Most Confederates who managed to make contact with the commander in chief had already been convicted or faced trial. A majority of Union civilians who appealed to him had been sentenced by courts-martial. These folk constituted a cross section of the nation, South and North alike: two ladies from Tennessee whose husbands were imprisoned; a District of Columbia resident convicted of having delivered ammunition and quinine to the enemy; Sioux Indians charged with having gone on a rampage of murder when Federal troops were withdrawn from the West; T. W. Johnson and R. M. Sutton, who had been found guilty of selling goods to a blockade runner; twenty-year-old Alfred Rubery—convicted on a charge of giving comfort to the rebellion . . .

Many cases involved multiple defendants. The fate of multitudes of men and women was in the hands of Abraham Lincoln when documents reached him. Many friends and relatives managed to get his ear for a personal appeal. If all names he processed were inscribed in stone, the resulting wall would be like the Vietnam Memorial.

Reactions to clemency on the part of the commander in chief were vivid and highly critical. Schuyler Colfax, who was numbered among the Radical Republicans, concluded that "No man holding in his hands the key of life and death ever pardoned so many offenders, and so easily." Edward Bates, who didn't permit close friendship to interfere with his dutes as attorney general, called his chief "pigeon-hearted." He went on record as having "sometimes told him that he was unfit to be trusted with the pardoning power." What's more, Bates pointed out, "If a wife, mother, or sister gains access to him, in nine cases out of ten, her tears, if nothing else, are sure to prevail." Gen. Daniel Tyler was outright disgusted. "If we attempt to shoot a deserter," he protested to Lincoln, "you pardon him, and our army is without discipline."

Some Washington insiders thought it laughable that Abraham Lincoln refused to order the execution of any man under age twenty-one; a few military leaders cursed instead of smiling at the eccentricities of the commander in chief.

Although easily swayed by a woman's grief, and troubled at permitting capital punishment for an offender who had not attained his majority, Abraham Lincoln did not swerve from his goal of military victory, so he almost daily issued orders that he knew might result in sending thousands to death on the battlefield.

To Gov. Horatio Seymor of New York, he justified conscription on the grounds that "We are contending with an enemy, who, as I understand, drives every able-bodied man he can reach into his ranks, very much as a butcher drives bullocks into a slaughter pen."

One of his personal secretaries, William O. Stoddard, was so awed by the reasoning of the commander in chief that he penned a precise summary of one period of meditation:

> We lost 50 percent more men than did the enemy, and yet there is sense in the awful arithmetic propounded by Mr. Lincoln. He says that if the same battle were to be fought over again, every day, through a week of days, with the same relative results, the army under Lee would be wiped out to the last man, the Army of the Potomac would still be a mighty host, the war would be over, the Confederacy gone, and peace would be won. No general yet found can face the arithmetic.

Informed of utter devastation in the Shenandoah Valley brought about by marauding Federal troops whose leader had vowed not to leave enough food for a bird, the commander in chief formally conveyed the thanks of the nation to Gen. Philip Sheridan, then added his personal gratitude. Knowing that a vast portion of Georgia had been laid waste, he sent Gen. William T. Sherman and his men "grateful acknowledgement" for the march to the sea.

When sacrifices of Union soldiers came up in conversation, Lincoln customarily pointed out that they were "endeavoring to purchase with their blood and their lives the future happiness and prosperity of this country." This despite the fact that tens of thousands favored a peaceful solution to the sectional conflict and donned uniforms only under compulsion.

Were his views strangely inconsistent? Of course!

That he himself recognized inconsistences and paradoxes in his views about suffering and his conduct of the war is shown by a terse comment to Congressman Daniel W. Voorhees of Indiana: "Doesn't it seem strange that I should be here—I, a man who couldn't cut a chicken's head off—with blood running all around me?"

Despite his recognition that he held a strangely mixed set of emotions and goals, Abraham Lincoln never tried to explain how a man of tender heart persisted for month after month in sending men to their deaths.

Had he, as Herndon repeatedly insisted, arrived at a point of view according to which "Men were but simple tools of fate, shaped and moved by forces set in motion millions of years ago and causing an individual to be a mere cog in one wheel"?

In all likelihood, yes.

If this supposition is valid, it explains in part his apparent indifference to battlefield carnage. For from certainty that events were irresistible and inevitable, it followed that actions of the commander in chief were all but incidental. If Hiram Q. Bosomworth was destined to be felled by a minié ball, nothing that Abraham Lincoln did or did not do would significantly affect the message written long ago by the finger of fate.

Was his conduct also affected by a pattern of dealing in one fashion with individuals and in quite another fashion with masses of men whom he never saw and who were therefore merely statistics?

Probably so.

Was he so totally convinced that "insurrection" must be crushed as a prelude to restoration of the Union that other considerations were secondary?

Almost certainly so. Though additional aspects of his emotional and intellectual life probably affected his willingness and capacity to direct the course of the Civil War, this may have overshadowed all other factors, combined.

25

*What Led the Tycoon to Risk
a New Response to*

EMANCIPATION— THE BURNING ISSUE OF THE DAY?

■

"LIBERATION OF SLAVES is purely political and not within the range of *military* law or necessity," Abraham Lincoln wrote on September 22, 1861. His letter to his long-time friend Orville H. Browning was penned in response to Browning's reaction to revocation of John C. Frémont's order concerning slavery in Missouri. No thought had yet been given to the possibility of relieving Frémont from command.

"Can there be a pretense that the Constitution and laws govern," the man whom his secretaries called the Tycoon mused, "when a general, or a president, may make permanent rules of property by proclamation?" His most strenuous objection, he continued, was to the notion that "I as president shall expressly or impliedly seize and exercise the permanent legislative functions of the government."

Despite his personal convictions, he was bombarded by abolitionists with petitions and delegations during the spring and early summer of 1862. Immediate emancipation was urged by the *Anti-Slavery Standard*, whose editors labeled the chief executive "utterly ignorant and misled." Frederick Douglass made speech after speech in which he proclaimed emancipation to be the ultimate goal of the war. Henry Ward Beecher called Lincoln a good man but considered him to be totally without "a spark of genius, an element for leadership, one particle of heroic enthusiasm."

Abroad, diplomats underscored warnings that Britain and France were likely to become more sympathetic to the Confederacy unless Lincoln took a much stronger stance against slavery. Some northern governors threatened that their young men would cease to volunteer for service in "an army that does not demolish slavery." In many

Federal units, more and more soldiers who sang "The Battle Hymn of the Republic" pulled out all stops when they reached the phrase, "Let us die to make men free!"

Reporting on a visit to the capital by Progressive Friends of Longwood, Pennsylvania, the New York *Times* said the president was adamant. Even if he were to issue an emancipation proclamation, he told his visitors, "It could not be more binding upon the South than the Constitution, and that cannot be enforced in that part of the country now."

Abraham Lincoln said as little as possible and kept a keen eye upon the Radical Republicans who were his avowed foes in Congress. In March they succeeded in passing legislation under whose terms military leaders were no longer required to return runaway slaves to their masters. Thirty days later they abolished slavery in the District of Columbia, which was under direct congressional authority.

Meanwhile, the president begged lawmakers to support a plan of his own. Opposed by both northern Democrats and Union men from border states, it promised U.S. cooperation "with any state which may adopt gradual abolishment of slavery." Signed into law on April 10, it offered financial aid to participating states. No state ever took the steps necessary to get such aid. Reflecting upon his own course during the five months that began with March, Lincoln said, "I made earnest and successive appeals to the border States to favor compensated emancipation."

For years, anyone willing to listen or to read could easily have discovered Lincoln's personal position concerning slavery. It was "the only thing that has ever threatened the perpetuity of the Union," he told Illinois voters. Slavery was wrong, he emphasized, but "we can yet afford to let it alone where it is." In spite of this belief, unlike Stephen A. Douglas, he insisted, "The Negro is included in the word *men* in the Declaration of Independence."

As president-elect, he believed he was winning support in the South when he promised that he had no thought of abolishing slavery in the nation's capital. Neither did he plan to try to do away with the slave trade or the existing Fugitive Slave Law. "I hold it a paramount duty to let the slavery of the other states alone," he said repeatedly—firmly convinced that if let alone, the institution would die a natural death.

Strongly opposed to territorial extension of it, he said that under "the Republican view" slavery was an evil "to be tolerated and protected" where it already existed. Both the Constitution and the legal system made such toleration necessary, he pointed out.

Writing to Alexander H. Stephens in late December 1860, he assured the Georgian that the South had nothing to fear from the incoming Republican administration. It would not tamper with the slaves where they were, he wrote; hence, states leaning toward secession were "in no more danger than in the days of Washington."

In his March 1861 inaugural address, the man about to take the oath of office quoted from the Republican campaign platform adopted in Chicago in order to stress, "I have no purpose directly or indirectly to interfere with the institution of slavery in the States where it exists. I believe I have no lawful right to do so, and I have no inclination to do so."

He promised that as chief executive he would uphold the Fugitive Slave Law. Then he added that he would not object to a constitutional amendment requiring the federal government to observe a hands-off policy concerning "the domestic institutions of the states, including that of persons held to service."

It is no wonder that fiery abolitionist Wendell Phillips labeled his new president "the slave-hound from Illinois" or that some Radical Republicans sneered when they pronounced his name.

Goaded by Massachusetts senator Charles Sumner and his radical allies, Congress took drastic action on July 17, 1862, the last day of its session. A Confiscation Act was passed that day, the second such piece of legislation to originate on Capitol Hill. Under its terms, property belonging to military and civil leaders of the Confederacy became subject to immediate seizure. Rank and file Confederates were given sixty days' warning and invited to return to loyalty. If they did not, the measure specified, their property, too, would be liable to seizure—without the opportunity to defend themselves in court.

Slaves taking refuge with Union forces, who belonged to persons in rebellion, "shall be deemed captives of war, and shall be forever free," the Confiscation Act continued. Though there was no firm stipulation, it was suggested that such free slaves should immediately be put into Federal uniforms as soldiers.

Under the act, slave-owning Unionists in border states and the rebellious South were not affected. This concession is believed to have stemmed from Lincoln's insistence that while Congress could deal with individuals, lawmakers lacked the power to abolish the institution of slavery. Abolition could come about, he seems to have believed at that time, only by means of a constitutional amendment.

Before the Confiscation Act reached final form, Abraham Lincoln read and re-read its text. He threatened to veto it on the ground that seizure of slaves or any other property without a court appearance was unconstitutional. When Congress responded by limiting the length of forfeiture to the life of the offender involved, he reluctantly signed the measure. Orville Browning strongly opposed the modified statute and urged his friend to veto it, considering it to be a test as to whether the United States would be controlled by the Radical Republicans or by the president. Though it became law, it was never enforced; neither Attorney General Edward Bates nor Lincoln made a serious effort to implement the statute.

At least as late as early 1862, Lincoln never wavered in his insistence that neither his generals nor he had the authority to order emancipation. But the war he had expected to be small and short had become huge and long. Confederates were winning so many battlefield victories that the peace movement was growing rapidly in the North. The failure of Gen. George McClellan's long-awaited spring Peninsular campaign in Virginia added to the president's growing conviction that it would take something really extraordinary to bring the war to a successful conclusion. To make matters worse, leaders of border states went on record as formally rejecting Lincoln's offer of voluntary emancipation followed by compensation to owners.

On July 13 the harried chief executive put other duties aside to attend the funeral of one of Secretary of War Edwin M. Stanton's children. He rode in a carriage with Gideon Welles and William H. Seward. Later admitting his recognition that "things had gone from bad to worse," requiring that Unionists change their tactics or lose the game, he broached the subject of emancipation to his two advisers. It had become "a military necessity absolutely essential for the salvation of the Union," he suggested.

On July 21 he hinted to the full cabinet that he was almost ready "to take some definitive steps in respect to military action and slavery." The next day he opened a cabinet meeting by reading a chapter from a new book by humorist Artemus Ward. Then he shared with his advisers a personally prepared document dealing with emancipation. Having worked on it since June, he strongly urged gradual emancipation, with compensation of owners and colonization of freed slaves. But he believed states in rebellion that didn't adopt that course should be given a grace period in which to return to the Union fold—or see all of their slaves freed by presidential proclamation.

Startled cabinet members, whose reactions were reported by Welles but not by Secretary John Hay, didn't hesitate to speak. Stanton said, "The measure goes beyond anything I have recommended." Seward opposed it, believing that such action would bring foreign intervention in a move to protect the cotton supply. Montgomery Blair was positive that it would damage or perhaps even ruin the chances of Republican candidates in upcoming elections. Salmon P. Chase feared it would produce financial instability.

Only Bates strongly supported the president, who had already let it be known that he objected to putting Negroes into uniform. Sensing that their arguments were falling on deaf ears, Seward suggested that they support the chief executive but urged that there be no

Abolitionist Wendell Phillips labeled Lincoln the "slavehound from Illinois."
[NATIONAL ARCHIVES]

public announcement until Federal forces won a decisive victory. Otherwise, he pointed out, the proposed proclamation would be seen as "our last shriek on the retreat." Other cabinet members said they would endorse the course upon which Lincoln had already decided. He, in turn, told them he would welcome suggestions concerning language and minor details of his proclamation.

According to Welles, Lincoln told cabinet members that Seward's suggested timing was strangely in accord with his own ideas. He had made a vow—a solemn covenant—that "if God gave us the victory in the approaching battle, he would consider it an indication of Divine will, and that it was his duty to move forward in the cause of emancipation." According to Welles's terse summary, the crucial question facing the president had been submitted to divine disposal, and "God had decided this question in favor of the slaves."

At least as well as anyone else in the nation, Abraham Lincoln knew his proposal involved a personal turn about of 180 degrees. If implemented, it would mean that the Civil War would no longer be fought solely to save the Union. While that goal would remain central, the new objective of freeing all slaves in rebel territory would be equally significant.

To Seward and Welles he confided that emancipation "was a military necessity absolutely essential for the salvation of the Union."

Later he described himself as having been "driven to it." As late as 1864 he said, "I am naturally anti-slavery. Yet I have never understood that the presidency conferred upon me an unrestricted right to act officially upon this judgment and feeling."

So it was in his role of commander in chief that he was forced to accept emancipation as a goal of the Civil War whose outcome was still far from determined.

Since the new objective was not immediately made public, many in the North became increasingly impatient. Perhaps the most dramatic of all critical assessments of Lincoln's leadership came from Horace Greeley. Bewildered that there were no signs that the Confiscation Act would be enforced, the editor used pages of the New York *Tribune* as a forum. In an open letter to Lincoln written in the name of every slave, he made a passionate nine-point plea for immediate emancipation.

When "The Prayer of Twenty Millions" reached the Executive Mansion, Lincoln pondered for a full day before reaching for his pen. On August 22 he responded to Greeley with a telegram whose text was simultaneously released to the capital's *National Intelligencer*. A fervent central passage revealed what some readers called "the naked Lincoln," who informed the editor and the nation:

> My paramount object in this struggle is to save the Union, and it is not either to save or to destroy slavery—If I could save the Union without freeing any slave I would do it, and if I could save it by freeing all the slaves I would do it; and if I could save it by freeing some and leaving others alone I would also do that—
> What I do about slavery and the colored race, I do because I believe it helps to save the Union; and what I forbear, I forbear because I do not believe it would help to save the Union—

Though his open letter has much of the literary power that later made the Gettysburg Address immortal, it was not warmly received in some quarters. At a public rally on August 1, the commander in chief had been criticized for permitting his generals to use "Negroes for work in the army camps" but not as fighting men. Now the *Anti-Slavery Standard* condemned him as "utterly ignorant and misled."

Was the mystic who had been born in obscurity angry during this period? His surviving letters and papers give no clue. Perhaps he fumed and stormed, saying things his discreet secretaries did not record. Maybe he bit his tongue and bided his time, eagerly watching for a sign or an omen that would reveal to him—if to no one else—what course Providence directed him to take.

As later described by Lincoln to artist F. B. Carpenter, Wednesday,

Henry Ward Beecher considered Lincoln to be a dullard, without a single spark of genius. [AUTHOR'S COLLECTION]

September 17, brought to the believer in portents a message that "the advantage was on our side." At Sharpsburg, Maryland, where the Boonsborough Turnpike crossed Antietam Creek, McClellan had stopped the Army of Northern Virginia in its tracks. Bitter fighting left nearly 6,000 dead, 16,000 wounded men, and 2,000 missing. Casualties were almost evenly divided. But in the aftermath, Gen. Robert E. Lee recrossed the Potomac and abandoned his invasion of Maryland. A token Federal force sent in pursuit was repulsed by troops under the command of Stonewall Jackson.

Measured by military standards, Antietam was a drawn battle. But because Lee retreated afterward, Abraham Lincoln interpreted the bloodiest single day of the war to mean that he should go forward with tentative plans. Until now, he had made no irrevocable commitment; he had drafted and could issue a proclamation, or he could put it aside.

Five days after the battle he considered to have conveyed a dispatch from God, now knowing that it had not been a great victory, he issued the most explosive proclamation of his presidency. Under terms of his September 22 pronouncement, on January 1, 1863, all slaves in states then still in rebellion would be considered free. Earlier, he had not hesitated to act as he saw fit and to seek congressional approval afterward. This time he treated his preliminary proclamation as having been issued in order to enforce Confiscation Acts passed by lawmakers.

Since slave owners who lived in states not in rebellion were not to be affected by the forthcoming final version of the Emancipation

Proclamation, he promised on New Year's Day to define the regions affected. "All persons engaged in the military and naval service of the United States" were called upon to observe the Confiscation Acts.

Precisely one hundred days would pass before emancipation would be made final. By warning of his intentions more than three months in advance, the president and commander in chief gave insurgents an opportunity to consider his offer of "restoration of the constitutional relation." He hoped some states would voluntarily adopt emancipation measures, also taking steps to send freed slaves to colonies abroad. By giving insurgents one hundred days in which to change their loyalty, he also gave himself one hundred days in which to pursue other plans aimed at effecting the goal of the not-yet-issued Emancipation Proclamation.

Two days after having made public the preliminary proclamation, Abraham Lincoln suspended the writ of *habeas corpus* throughout the United States. This launched actions later labeled "catastrophic for American civil liberties." Throughout the North and the South, Americans paid little heed to the edict; they were too busy trying to decide precisely what Lincoln had promised—or threatened—to do on January 1.

In Harrisburg, Pennsylvania, the *Union* called his actions "an outrage upon the humanity and good sense of the country, to say nothing of its gross unconstitutionality." Editors of the New York *World* commented, accurately, that "President Lincoln has swung loose from the constitutional moorings of his inaugural address." Indiana legislators proclaimed that their government was for white men, not black men. Henry J. Raymond of the New York *Times* was sure that this attempt to make the war "subservient to abolition" would destroy the Union. According to the New York *Journal of Commerce*, the preliminary proclamation could be described in a single word: *disastrous.*

Many legal scholars voiced opinions that if issued, the forthcoming final proclamation would be unconstitutional even as a war measure. Vice President Hannibal Hamlin reported to Lincoln that stocks had declined and that troops were coming forward more slowly than ever. David Davis, who had directed the Chicago campaign that won the Republican nomination, urged his long-time friend to modify his views and his language.

Readers of the Richmond, Virginia, *Inquirer* were told that "'MURDER' is a term of honor compared to Lincoln's crime." Members of the Confederate Senate called his proclamation "a gross violation of the usages of civilized warfare" and suggested automatic death sentences for captured white commanders of Negroes or mulattoes.

But the author of "The Prayer of Twenty Millions" used his boldest type to proclaim, "God Bless Abraham Lincoln." Greeley wanted the commander in chief to know that "everywhere through the land he is hailed as wisest and best." Foreshadowing the wave of adulation that would follow Lincoln's assassination, the editor insisted, "So splendid a vision has hardly shone upon the world since the days of the Messiah."

At the *Anti-Slavery Standard*, editors were less jubilant. They considered the September 22 proclamation "not all that the exigencies of the times require." Still, they labeled it "a step in the right direction." William Lloyd Garrison's *Liberator* expressed fear that the one-hundred-day interval might give the C.S.A. time to win foreign recognition. At the same time, Lincoln's "overture to the slave states to sell their slave system at a bargain" was condemned.

An even worse aspect of the document, according to Garrison, was "its mean and absurd device to expatriate the colored population from this their native land."

Dire warnings seemed to have been fulfilled when votes were counted after the 1862 elections. Antiadministration governors captured the State House in New York and New Jersey. The five most populous northern states—all of which went for Lincoln in 1860—sent Democratic majorities to Capitol Hill. Republicans lost twenty-one congressional seats, giving Democrats a majority among national lawmakers representing Ohio, Pennsylvania, Michigan, Iowa, Illinois, Indiana, and Minnesota.

When the political debacle suffered by the administration became generally known, weeks still lay ahead before the announced deadline of January 1, 1863, would be reached. Abraham Lincoln's habitual secrecy was not abandoned during this period in which he experienced the dark night of the soul brought about by political and military reverses. Even his most intimate aides knew little, if anything, of what he thought.

26

A Racist by Today's Standards,
How Did He Become

THE GREAT EMANCIPATOR: A CRUSADER FOR RACIAL EQUALITY?

■

WHEN EDWARD M. THOMAS, president of the Anglo-African Institution, led four companions to the Executive Mansion on August 15, 1862, history was about to be made. For the first time, black citizens had been invited to the mansion to meet the president. Though not yet made public, the preliminary draft of the Emancipation Proclamation was familiar to cabinet members and aides to the chief executive.

Abraham Lincoln welcomed his invited guests warmly, then moved directly to the reason for their presence. They would encounter discrimination in the North as well as in the South, he said. Racial barriers were as high and as strong as ever; there really was no place in the nation for Negroes. "You and we are different races," he insisted. "We have between us a broader difference than exists between almost any other two races."

Members of the black delegation must have shown their surprise when the president stressed that freedom would not prove a cure-all for social ills of Negroes. There was a remedy, however, Lincoln added as he urged them to lead their people to accept it. "The practical thing I want to ascertain is whether I can get a number of able-bodied men, with their wives and children, who are willing to go to Central America."

During his debates with Stephen A. Douglas and his lecture tour of the Northeast, Lincoln had made his personal racial views clear. At Jonesboro, Illinois, his rival for the vacant U.S. Senate seat ac-

Lincoln and his cabinet reading the final version of the Emancipation Proclamation. [LIBRARY OF CONGRESS]

cused him of favoring racial equality. Lincoln said nothing then but three days later at Charleston he put his own ideas on record: "The proposition that there is a struggle between the white man and the Negro contains a falsehood. There is no struggle. If there was, I should be for the white man."

Four years earlier, speaking in Peoria, he admitted that he could offer no solution to the problem of "existing slavery." He would be strongly inclined to free all slaves and ship them to Liberia, he said. Insisting that the government was made for white people and not for Negroes, he posed a question and immediately answered it: "Free them and make them politically and socially our equals? My own feelings will not admit of this. We cannot make them equals."

He was, of course, speaking to an all-white audience of potential voters. At least as well as anyone else who was in touch with public opinion, he knew that in Illinois it would have been political suicide to be branded as an abolitionist. His partner, William H. Herndon, was outspokenly in favor of immediate and universal abolition; even in their private conversations, Lincoln never endorsed such a view. He developed hatred for slavery very early but repeatedly told audiences how he felt about Negroes.

Douglas, he noted, had expressed himself as being horrified at the notion of mixing white blood with black. "Agreed for once!" cried the future Great Emancipator. "A thousand times agreed! There are white men enough to marry all the white women, and black men enough to marry all the black women; and so let them be married."

At Columbus, Ohio, on September 16, 1859, Republicans of the Buckeye State listened intently as he expressed his racial views in some detail:

> Anything that argues me into the idea of a perfect social and political equality with the Negro is but a specious and fantastic arrangement of words, by which a man can prove a horse chestnut to be a chestnut horse. I agree with Judge Douglas that the Negro is not my equal in many respects— certainly not in color, perhaps not in moral or intellectual endowments.
>
> I am not, nor ever have been, in favor of making voters or jurors of Negroes, nor of qualifying them to hold office. There is a physical difference between the white and black races, which, I believe, will forever forbid the two races living to- gether on terms of social and political equality. I, as much as any other man, am in favor of having the superior position assigned to the white race.

Did his racial outlook undergo radical change when he found that black soldiers might be decisive in bringing Union victory during the Civil War? If so, he never made his modified views public. Writ- ing on March 13, 1864, to Gov. Michael Hahn of Louisiana about voting in the state, he wondered "whether some of the colored people may not be let in—the very intelligent, and especially those who have fought gallantly in our ranks." Careful to avoid being interpreted as having given the governor a directive, he ended by saying, "This is only a suggestion, not to the public, but to you alone."

More than a year later, calling for a national day of thanksgiving in celebration of Union victory, he delivered his last public address. Indicating that he had received complaints that "the elective fran- chise is not given to the colored man," he made public his own preference. If his personal wish were followed, he said, the privilege of voting would be "now conferred on the very intelligent, and on those who serve our cause as soldiers."

Employment of blacks as fighting men—to say nothing of permit- ting them to vote—was endorsed reluctantly by Lincoln. However, use of one-time slaves as laborers for the Union cause was another matter entirely. In 1862 the commander in chief authorized his gen- erals who occupied regions within states claiming to have seceded to "employ as laborers, so many persons of African descent as can be advantageously used." Eleven months after the final draft of the Emancipation Proclamation was issued, in his annual message to Congress he noted that about 100,000 Negroes were in U.S. military

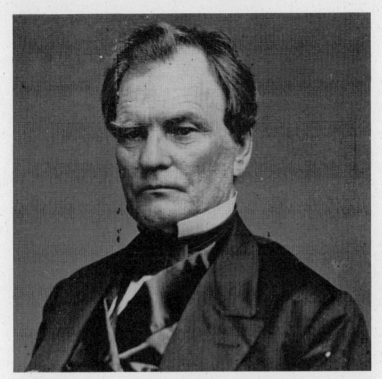

"Black Republican" Sen. Benjamin F. Wade was unrelenting in his demand for emancipation of all slaves. [LIBRARY OF CONGRESS]

service. Only half of them were in uniform in December 1863; the rest were working as laborers.

Still referring to Negroes in that message, he informed lawmakers, "So far as tested, it is difficult to say they are not as good soldiers as any." Earlier, he had reached a point of view made articulate in a letter to slaveholder Andrew Johnson, military governor of Tennessee. "The colored population is the great available and yet unavailed-of force for restoring the Union," he pointed out. "The bare sight of fifty thousand armed and drilled on the banks of the Mississippi, would end the rebellion at once."

Time proved that verdict to be wrong. Blacks eventually made up a significant part of the Federal fighting force, but Confederates who faced them did not throw down their weapons and surrender.

Enlistment of blacks as soldiers was urged by Frederick Douglass in the immediate aftermath of the surrender at Fort Sumter. Levi Tilmon of New York City wrote to the president at that time, offering to provide colored volunteers. There is no record that his proposal evoked a response of any sort.

At least as early as October 1861, senators Charles Sumner, Benjamin Wade, and their allies added their influence to that of Douglass. In 1863 enrollment of black soldiers was twice that authorized by Congress. Terms of the second Confiscation Act urged military leaders immediately to make use of them. Yet the same legislation stipulated that cash pay of a black soldier would be seven dollars per month, just over half of the thirteen dollars per month received by each of his white comrades who fought as privates.

After eighteen months, Commander in Chief Lincoln asked Attorney General Edward Bates for his opinion on "what pay, bounty, and clothing are allowed by law" to free persons of color who enlisted between December 1861 and June 24 of the current year. When Bates ruled that they should begin to get equal pay, the paymaster general directed his staff to conform to that opinion.

Total enlistment in the U.S. Colored Troops—as units of black fighting men were called—probably exceeded 180,000. Of these men, perhaps five one-hundredths of 1 percent, or about one hundred, became commissioned officers. Even after having proved their valor in some of the fiercest fighting of the Civil War, almost all units that included black soldiers were led by white officers.

For months, Abraham Lincoln hesitated to permit the enlistment of blacks as privates. He confessed he was not sure they would be assets to the Union cause. If arms were placed in their hands, "it would be a serious matter if they should go over to the rebels," he pointed out.

Senator Sumner of Massachusetts is generally believed to have persuaded his chief to adopt a different view. During the last week of 1862, he visited the Executive Mansion at least three times. Undocumented tradition asserts that it was then that he persuaded Lincoln to amend the forthcoming Emancipation Proclamation to make it possible for ex-slaves to become Union soldiers. Nearly a year later, Gen. Henry W. Halleck insisted that "Every slave withdrawn from the enemy is the equivalent of a white soldier withdrawn from combat." In spite of this reasoning, Lincoln temporarily suspended enlistment of blacks in Maryland and urged recruitment officers not to accept slaves of loyalists without the consent of their owners.

Perhaps he was looking back upon developments that had led him to change his ideas about black fighting men when in 1864 the commander in chief admitted: "I claim not to have controlled events, but confess plainly that events have controlled me."

Had Lincoln fully succeeded in controlling events, it is unlikely that any blacks would have entered the military force. Nor is it certain than anything resembling the Emancipation Proclamation of January 1, 1863, would have been issued by him had he not felt himself moved by forces beyond his control. Just thirty days before

*News of the preliminary proclamation produced a
pro–South cartoon depicting Lincoln and Davis playing
cards, with Lincoln's document being the president's last,
desperate card.* [Punch of London]

his pledge of September seemed to require him to sign the most
radical edict of his administration, he worked feverishly for a different course of action.

On December 1, 1862, the annual presidential message was transmitted to Congress. In printed form, with small type, it occupies
twenty pages. Much of it is of standard nature, even perfunctory. But
buried in the lengthy report is a discussion of the United States as
constituting a family that "demands union and abhors separation."
This situation, he said, led him to recommend that Congress launch
a move for adoption of three amendments to the U.S. Constitution.
As a preface to his arguments for favorable action upon the proposed
amendments, he cited his preliminary emancipation proclamation
of July 22. Yet he made no mention of the anxiously awaited final
Emancipation Proclamation of January 1, 1863. Summarized, the
president's plan for solving the slavery problem was:

1. Provide for compensation in U.S. bonds to every state that
would abolish slavery before January 1, 1900.

2. Give permanent freedom to all slaves who had escaped from
bondage "by the chances of war before the end of the rebellion," with
Unionist owners of such persons to be compensated.

3. Authorize congressional appropriation of funds "for colonizing free colored persons, with their own consent, at any place or places without the United States."

In language as vivid and forceful as he ever used, Abraham Lincoln urged lawmakers to sponsor his package of constitutional amendments: "Fellow citizens, we cannot escape history. We of this Congress and this administration will be remembered in spite of ourselves. No personal significance or insignificance can spare one or another of us. The fiery trial through which we pass will light us down, in honor or dishonor, to the latest generation."

Pondered out of context, these singing sentences by the author of the Emancipation Proclamation seem to have come from an impassioned crusader for change in social conditions. But they take on a different connotation when placed with succeeding lines that underscore the reason for the writer's passion:

> We say we are for the Union. The world will not forget that we say this. We know how to save the Union. The world knows we do know how to save it. We—even we here—hold the power, and bear the responsibility. In giving freedom to the slave, we assure freedom to the *free*—honorable alike in what we give, and what we preserve. We shall nobly save, or meanly lose, the last, best hope of earth. Other means may succeed; this could not fail. The way is plain, peaceful, generous, just—a way which, if followed, the world will forever applaud, and God must forever bless.

No clarion call for support of the not-yet-issued Emancipation Proclamation, this impassioned plea was framed in support of constitutional amendments that would have made the proclamation unnecessary.

Was emancipation the "last, best hope of earth" of which Lincoln wrote? Clearly not!

His shining hope was restoration of the Union, the institutional guardian of American freedom that he regarded as being unique in the world, a fruit of wisdom by the Founding Fathers of the Republic.

Douglass saw the clear implications of the president's position. "Abraham Lincoln was pre-eminently the white man's president," he later wrote. "We are at best only his step-children. Union was to him more than our freedom or our future." Horace Greeley summarized his own reaction to the December proposal in four words: "Gradualism, Compensation, Negro Exportation." Confident that neither Congress nor the general public would support the amendments drafted by the president, Greeley snorted, "If these tubs amuse the whale, let him have them."

Closing lines of the most radical and far-sweeping document from the hand of Abraham Lincoln. [NATIONAL ARCHIVES]

As a giant step toward preserving the Union and its freedom, the Emancipation Proclamation was a war measure—not an edict issued in a dramatic move to better the lives of blacks. No one knew this better than the author of the proclamation. Nine months after it was issued, he told Salmon P. Chase, "The original proclamation has no constitutional or legal justification, except as a military measure."

Earlier countermanding the edict of Gen. David Hunter, Lincoln had told his subordinate that "as commander in chief of the army and navy" he reserved for himself the right to declare slaves to be free. Such a declaration, he noted only weeks before beginning to draft his order of July 22, 1862, would be forthcoming only if it should become "a necessity indispensable to the maintenance of the Government."

Wholly consistent in both his reasoning and his decisions, Abraham Lincoln held that Congress "has no constitutional power over slavery in the states." Hence he issued the Emancipation Proclamation "by virtue of the power in me vested as commander in chief of

Cartoonist Adalbert Volck depicted Lincoln's edict as the "work of a demonic mind." [LIBRARY OF CONGRESS]

the army and navy in time of actual rebellion, and as a fit and necessary war measure for suppressing said rebellion."

Confident that the preliminary proclamation would become a presidential edict as scheduled, Jefferson Davis reacted to it a week in advance of its release. Since Gen. Benjamin F. Butler had been the first Union commander to refuse to return runaway slaves, whom he listed as "contraband," Davis ordered that upon Butler's capture, he should be hanged without a trial. Captured Negro soldiers and their officers, said the president of the C.S.A., should now be turned over to the states instead of being held as prisoners for exchange.

Once Lincoln issued the proclamation, many Democrats of the North were almost as furious as were Confederate leaders. Scores of them denounced the proclamation of January 1 as "clearly unconstitutional"—thereby hinting that should it lead to civil disorder, its author might be subject to impeachment proceedings. Cartoonist Adalbert Volck mocked the proclamation as being "the work of a demonic mind."

Many conservative Republicans expressed fears that the proclamation would wreck their party, but the Radical Republicans felt that it did not go far enough. Gen. George B. McClellan stuck firmly to his announced position, according to which the sole object of the war was the preservation of the Union and the Constitution.

*   *   *

Perhaps the most widely condemned aspect of the Emancipation Proclamation was the stipulation that it applied only to regions "in a state of rebellion." Slave owners in the four border states of Maryland, Delaware, Kentucky, and Missouri were not affected. Neither were slave owners in the northern states that constituted the heart of the Union. In addition, the commander in chief listed sections under Union military control, in which citizens could retain their slaves. Seven enumerated counties of Virginia and all of the section in the process of becoming West Virginia were exempted from provisions of the proclamation. So were thirteen named Louisiana parishes.

Outspoken foes of Lincoln castigated his edict as "leaving the slaves of his Unionist supporters in chains, while taking the shackles from the slaves of his rebellious foes." Douglass considered the Emancipation Proclamation to be "tardy, cold, dull, and indifferent" when viewed from what he called "the genuine abolition" point of view. Still, he conceded that the highly unpopular action by a man soon to make a bid for re-election was "swift, zealous, radical, and determined."

Even to his most zealous opponents, Lincoln conceded that he did not consider his Emancipation Proclamation to constitute the final word. It would cease to be operative the moment insurgents gave up their cause, he believed. Great numbers of blacks, perhaps hundreds of thousands, might be trapped in slavery when opposing forces agreed upon terms of surrender.

Complex and sometimes seemingly inconsistent, the battle-born Emancipation Proclamation was clearly seen by Abraham Lincoln as his most memorable edict. It was ultraradical, of doubtful legality, and less than wholly consistent. Yet it brought an end to Confederate bids for European recognition and was viewed as a beacon of hope by multitudes of slaves. Growing acceptance of black soldiers meant that the strength of Union fighting forces was boosted mightily, just when generals who led armies of insurgents found themselves unable to replace their battle casualties. In many respects, the crucial turning point of the Civil War came in the Executive Mansion rather than before the defenses of Vicksburg or on the hills of Gettysburg.

Yet the impact of the Emancipation Proclamation upon the outcome of the four-year struggle did not exhaust its effects. Soon editors of *Nation* magazine told readers, "The first real breach in the Constitution was made by the invention of the *war power* to enable President Lincoln to abolish slavery. No one would now say that this was not at that time necessary, but it made it possible for any President practically to suspend the Constitution by getting up a war anywhere."

According to this view, Lincoln's decision to offer freedom to slaves in rebel territory set the stage for continuous expansion of presi-

Abraham Lincoln was among those who supported the building of Hoffman Mission Station in Liberia—colonized by ex-slaves.
[National Archives]

dential power. More than any action by a chief executive prior to the Vietnam War, promulgation of the Emancipation Proclamation established a precedent for development of what has come to be known as "the imperial presidency." Thus, a document framed from military necessity, which brought freedom to multitudes, has had the long-range effect of reducing the personal freedom of every American who is subject to the still-expanding power of the chief executive.

By today's standards, words spoken and written by Lincoln brand him as an out-and-out racist. That being the case, how did he come to be venerated throughout the world as a champion of racial equality?

Most textbooks of American history treat the Emancipation Proclamation briefly, sometimes in a few paragraphs, often in just one. Almost without exception, they point out that it gave immediate freedom to only a handful of slaves but was among the most masterful wartime propaganda tools ever devised. It achieved its primary purpose with incredible effectiveness—that purpose being the military subjugation of "so-called seceded states." In the process of mightily boosting Union military strength, hope and freedom given to slaves and ex-slaves were almost incidental.

PART FOUR

■

*Unanswered Questions
Lurk in the
Shadow of the
Executive Mansion*

Frederick Douglass was among black leaders who had gone on record as having nothing but scorn for plans of colonization.
[NATIONAL ARCHIVES]

27

Did He Ever Lose Faith in

A BORROWED PLAN TO SOLVE THE SLAVERY QUESTION?

■

The dogmas of the quiet past are inadequate to the stormy present. The occasion is piled high with difficulty, and we must rise with the occasion. . . . Fellow citizens, we cannot escape history. We of this Congress and this administration will be remembered in spite of ourselves. No personal significance or insignificance can spare one or another of us. The fiery trial through which we pass will light us down in honor or dishonor to the last generation. . . .

In giving freedom to the slave, we assure freedom to the free. . . . We shall nobly save or meanly lose the last, best hope of earth. Other means may succeed; this could not fail. The way is plain, peaceful, generous, just—a way which if followed the world will forever applaud and God must forever bless.

ABRAHAM LINCOLN
December 1, 1862

Although Abraham Lincoln was a master of words, few of his passages are more powerful than these lines from his annual message to Congress in the second year of the war. Made public precisely one month before the promised final draft of the Emancipation Proclamation was due, they seem almost to have come from a life-long ardent abolitionist.

Not so.

This passage is the president's final argument to Congress, urging the adoption of three proposed amendments to the Constitution. Collectively, the amendments incorporate basic features of his borrowed plan for solution of the slavery problem: abolition by individual states, with compensation to owners, and colonization of black

Americans "with their own consent, at any place or places without the United States."

Had lawmakers been sufficiently inspired by Abraham Lincoln's winged words to act promptly upon his recommendations, the Emancipation Proclamation would not have been issued. Speedy adoption of his proposed amendments would have made the document obsolete before it could take effect.

Lincoln's close-to-final push for emancipation with compensation, plus colonization, rested upon ideas he espoused and made public in prepresidential years.

His papers do not reveal when he became interested in schemes aimed at removing free blacks from the nation. Neither do they indicate what person or factor led him to espouse that plan. Since Henry Clay was one of his idols when he entered politics in 1832, probability suggests that he may have been influenced by his fellow Kentuckian. Clay, in turn, acknowledged intellectual indebtedness to Thomas Jefferson and John Quincy Adams—both of whom were pioneers in the colonization movement.

National organization of the American Colonization Society was completed in 1816. Illinois soon had an active chapter whose membership included Abraham Lincoln. His first conspicuous involvement may have come on July 6, 1852. Clay having died at Washington a week earlier, Lincoln was selected to deliver a eulogy in the Hall of Representatives. He quoted at length from an 1827 speech made to the colonization society by Clay, long its president. Orator Lincoln stressed his personal support of Clay's views according to which "There is a moral fitness in the idea of returning to Africa her children."

Lawmakers and members of the general public must have heartily approved of sentiments expressed in the Clay eulogy, for on August 30, 1853, attorney Lincoln spoke on "colonization" in Springfield's First Presbyterian Church. In the aftermath of that appearance, he was invited to speak at the 1854 annual meeting of the state society. Illness in the family forced him to ask for a delay, as a result of which he was the featured speaker in January 1855. Two years later, his friend Orville H. Browning became president of the Illinois chapter, and Lincoln was elected to serve as one of its eleven managers.

In an 1854 speech at Peoria, Lincoln spelled out his personal position: His first impulse would be to free all slaves and send them to Liberia. That would be very difficult to accomplish. But he doubted the wisdom of any process that would "free them all, and keep them among us as underlings."

"What next?" came his rhetorical question. "Free them and make them politically and socially our equals? My own feelings will not admit of this, and if mine would we well know that those of the great mass of whites will not. We cannot make them our equals." With the nation facing so complex a dilemma, he suggested that "systems of

Abraham Lincoln told a Peoria audience that his first impulse would be to send all free slaves to the tiny republic of Liberia, which by then had its own tiny army. [ILLUSTRATED LONDON NEWS]

gradual emancipation might be adopted" but warned listeners not to judge "our brethren of the South" for tardiness in pursuing such a course.

Speaking at Springfield in 1857, he reminded listeners that "I have said that the separation of the races is the only perfect preventive of amalgamation." He insisted that most Republicans favored separation, then pointed out, "Such separation, if ever effected at all, must be effected by colonization." Because that would be "a difficult enterprise," what it needed most was "a hearty will." Such an attitude, said he, would develop only when masses of whites realized that it would be to their interest "to transfer the African to his native clime."

Among those who heartily espoused this view was Congressman Frank P. Blair of Missouri. According to him, "the idea of liberating the slaves and allowing them to remain in this country is one that never will be tolerated."

By the time the ex-congressman became president-elect, support for gradual emancipation with compensation, followed by colonization, had gained significant support. Discussed in Congress on the heels of Lincoln's victory, the plan was reported by the New York *Daily Tribune* to "meet with much favor from all but the fanatical devotees of slavery in the North."

Editors of the powerful newspaper thought that Delaware, Maryland, Missouri, Arkansas, Texas, and Louisiana included about 600,000 slaves. At a recent auction the average price of slaves sold was $437, suggesting that $240,000,000 would compensate for all slaves in the six states listed. Gradual emancipation, to be completed in 1876, could be followed by "removal to Central America, or to Hayti [sic] or Jamaica." Such a course, according to the *Daily Tribune*, would "in time rid us of an odious and formidable evil" and make it unnecessary to adopt some more drastic remedy that would "Africanize one-half of the continent."

In the light of such sentiments as these, it was not surprising that President Abraham Lincoln, in office barely five weeks, found time to meet with Ambrose W. Thompson of the Chiriqui Improvement Co. It owned large tracts of land in Panama, and officials of the company had insisted that its holdings would be suitable for colonies of ex-slaves. Listening intently to Thompson's presentation, the chief executive was gratified to learn that the Chiriqui land was also a potential source of coal for U.S. naval vessels.

Several more conferences during a period of eighteen months led to an agreement between the private for-profit corporation and the United States of America. Sen. Samuel C. Pomeroy of Kansas was selected by Lincoln to serve as his special agent in implementing the contract. Only a handful of blacks went to the colony, and most soon regretted having left the United States. Yet fifteen months after the Emancipation Proclamation went into effect, the Senate had to pass a resolution to get from the president a report concerning his Chiriqui scheme.

On the heels of launching the Central American experiment, Abraham Lincoln took bold political steps much closer to the nation's capital. His annual message to Congress, dated December 3, 1861, focused upon the recent Confiscation Act. Terms of the legislation dealt with slaves of rebels, whom the president called "property used for insurrectionary purposes." Plans should be immediately made for colonizing some such property, said he. At the same time, it would be well to inquire whether "the free colored people already in the United States" could be offered an opportunity to take part in "such colonization."

Congress did not immediately respond to this guarded overture, so the chief executive acted. A few weeks earlier he had personally drafted a bill providing for abolition in Delaware. Under terms of his plan, the nation would reward the state with $23,200 per annum for thirty-one years if the legislature would free Delaware's estimated 2,000 slaves in a graduated series of steps. Circulated among lawmakers of the state, it found a few supporters—and many angry opponents. Since it clearly had no chance of being passed, the bill never reached the floor.

Still, it had been the means of drafting a specific set of proposals rather than endorsing vague and general ones. William H. Herndon vowed that "Mr. Lincoln always contended that the cheapest way of getting rid of slavery was for the nation to buy the slaves and set them free." With a price tag and a timetable attached to the plan long favored by the American Colonization Society, the president would soon revise it. A new condition was embodied in a March 6, 1862, message to Congress in which he asked for the adoption of a joint resolution:

> Resolved that the United States ought to cooperate with any state which may adopt gradual abolishment of slavery, giving to such state pecuniary aid, to be used by such state in its discretion, to compensate for the inconveniences, public and private, produced by such change of system.

In support of his proposal, the president urged that "very soon the current expenditures of this war would purchase, at fair valuation," all the slaves in "border states" where slavery existed without secession. Strong interest evoked by publication of his proposal prompted the president to ask Henry J. Raymond of the New York *Times* to reconsider compensated emancipation. It would be highly desirable, said Lincoln, for the newspaper to stress that "one half-day's cost of this war would pay for all the slaves in Delaware, at four hundred dollars per head."

Usually compliant despite the noise made by Democrats and Radical Republicans, lawmakers incorporated Lincoln's resolution in a House-initiated bill that provided for gradual emancipation. Approved by the Senate, it went to the president who signed it on April 10 in conjunction with a proclamation of thanksgiving to Almighty God for having vouchsafed "signal victories to the land and naval forces engaged in suppressing an internal rebellion."

Any and all states in which slavery was legal were cordially invited to accept the process designed by the president and now enacted into law. Strangely, in the view of the chief executive, there was no flurry of activity in response to his generous initiative.

His patience exhausted, he called senators and congressmen from all "border states" to the Executive Mansion on July 12. When they assembled, he pointed out that Congress would soon adjourn. Considering lawmakers before him to "hold more power for good than any other equal number of members," he made a fervent appeal to them. Had his March plan for gradual emancipation been sup-

Thaddeus Stevens, carried in a chair to vote for the impeachment of Andrew Johnson, earlier denounced Lincoln's plan for resolving the slavery issue as "milk and water twaddle."
[LIBRARY OF CONGRESS]

ported, he insisted, "the war would now be substantially ended." According to him, once the states "which are in rebellion" see that the border states would never join them, "they can not much longer maintain the contest." Urging that they return to their states and push for gradual emancipation followed by colonization, he made a fervent appeal to them as "patriots and statesmen."

Though no official response was made that day, attitudes must have made clear what it would be. On July 15 a majority reply signed by twenty senators and congressmen dismissed the presidential plan as impractical. On July 16 a minority reply in support of Lincoln's proposal was signed by eight lawmakers, including three from Tennessee and one from the new state of West Virginia.

Always practical, Lincoln had anticipated just such a reaction and had prepared for it by drafting a presidential proclamation aimed at effecting emancipation. Vice President Hannibal Hamlin saw an early version of it on June 18 and was told that it would be used if all other measures failed. On the day following his appeal to border state lawmakers, while waiting for the reply whose nature he anticipated, the president shared with William H. Seward and Gideon Welles his plan to emancipate by proclamation "if the war is not soon brought to an end."

Once the negative response of border state representatives was official, he waited one week before sharing with the entire cabinet what he described as the first draft of an emancipation proclamation.

Battlefield reverses and the upcoming congressional election persuaded him to delay releasing an announcement. It came on the heels of "a divine signal" conveyed through what Union commanders claimed to be a victory at Antietam. As made public in the aftermath of that battle, emancipation would take place on January 1, 1863. Slave owners loyal to the Union would be compensated for their losses. But long-cherished plans for a gradual process were not mentioned; neither was colonization. Just two days later, however, the president's chief advisers were asked to give their opinions concerning treaties with nations whose leaders wished to establish colonies of Americans of African descent.

By then, it was widely known that the first blacks invited to the Executive Mansion went there to hear the president urge them to support colonization. Such a course of action on their part, said he, was not designed simply to benefit the black race or the white race. Rather, it was "one of the things, if successfully managed," that could redound "for the good of mankind" not simply in the present, but from age to age.

E. M. Thomas, chairman of the black delegation, promised to consult others and render a reply soon. There is no record that a formal response was ever made, however. Frederick Douglass and other black leaders had long ago gone on record as scorning colonization. On Capitol Hill, Congressman Thaddeus Stevens of Pennsylvania, a spokesman for Radical Republicans and ardent abolitionists in general, had earlier denounced the presidential plan as "diluted milk-and-water twaddle."

Faced with overwhelming opposition from every quarter, the president held steadily to his course. His 1862 annual message to Congress was dated December 1, precisely one month before the still-inoperative Emancipation Proclamation was due to take effect. To "Fellow citizens of the Senate and House of Representatives," Abraham Lincoln suggested adoption of resolutions supporting three constitutional amendments he had prepared. Under terms of these revisions, any state abolishing slavery before January 1, 1900, would receive compensation in the form of U.S. bonds. All slave owners who remained loyal to the Union would be reimbursed for their property losses. Congress would be authorized to appropriate money and to establish systems "for colonizing free colored persons, with their own consent, at any place or places without the United States."

As part of his lengthy argument in support of these plans, Abraham Lincoln penned the singing words of challenge at the beginning of this chapter.

The eloquence of the gifted orator-writer was wasted this time.

Congress having shown no signs of supporting his plan for a trio of amendments, the president called a special cabinet meeting at 10:00 A.M. on December 31. He listened to suggestions and promised to take them into consideration in making final revisions to the Emancipation Proclamation due to be issued within twenty-four hours.

Soon after the last cabinet member left the Executive Mansion, Lincoln had a private meeting with Bernard Kock. After discussing details, both men signed a contract calling for the establishment of a colony of freedmen on Haiti's Île à Vache.

"Governor Kock" and the project he promoted received presidential attention on at least half a dozen other occasions. Thirteen months after having issued the Emancipation Proclamation, Abraham Lincoln concluded that the Île à Vache experiment had failed. Hence he directed the War Department to transport from "the colored colony established by the United States" all persons who wished to return. He directed that these colonists be brought to Washington to "be employed and provided for at the colored camps around that city."

While watching his plan for colonization disintegrate despite his proclamation, the president clung desperately to the concept of gradual emancipation. To Gen. John M. Schofield, military governor of Missouri, he sent a June 22, 1863, message stressing his conviction that "*gradual* emancipation can be made better than *immediate* for both black and white, except where military necessity changes the case." After having ruled that the Emancipation Proclamation applied to Arkansas, on July 31, 1863, he indicated that for slaves who had not "tasted actual freedom," he continued to believe that "gradual emancipation would be better for both white and black."

Abraham Lincoln's own words and actions strongly suggest that the Emancipation Proclamation was issued against his wishes. He labeled it as a war measure, pure and simple. Lacking any emphasis upon racial justice or equality, it was made effective solely because it was considered the best—perhaps the only—course that would lead to military victory and re-establishment of the cherished Union.

After January 1, 1863, the president continued to favor gradual emancipation. He made no more public references to colonization but in private continued to pursue the idea until experiments proved it to be hopeless.

All of this leaves unanswered the question, "Did he ever lose faith in a borrowed plan to solve the slavery question?"

Clearly, he lost hope that it would become operative. Clearly, he capitulated but whether he lost faith remains an enigma.

Only Abraham Lincoln knew whether the shaking hand with which he signed on January 1, 1863, stemmed, at least in part, from conviction that the program adapted from that of colonization societies would have served the nation better than the Emancipation Proclamation that military concerns forced him to issue.

28

How Did He Reconcile
"No Secession" with

CARVING A NEW STATE FROM VIRGINIA?

■

WRITING TO SEN. CHARLES SUMNER on December 21, 1860, Edward Everett labeled his message as having been written on the first day of "the Disunited States." Like the vast majority in both North and South, Hale took secession to be an accomplished fact as soon as it was voted by the South Carolina convention. Not so the man who said hardly anything about this or any other issue between his nomination and his departure for Washington.

Abraham Lincoln's First Inaugural Address outlined his position: "No state upon its own mere motion can lawfully get out of the Union." This meant that "resolves and ordinances to that effect are legally void . . . . In view of the Constitution and the laws, the Union is unbroken," he insisted.

So-called secessionists, he argued in his July 4, 1861, message to Congress, "have invented an ingenious sophism" according to which a state may withdraw from the Union on its own initiative. "With rebellion thus sugar-coated," he said, these folk "have been drugging the public mind of their section for more than thirty years." Eventually they and their followers "enacted the farcical pretense of taking their state out of the Union."

According to Lincoln, all citizens, including slave owners in so-called seceded states, had equal protection under the Constitution. His goal was to restore regions "in a state of rebellion" to their "proper practical relation." Hence he took steps that made civil war inevitable and pursued it for four blood-soaked years. Yet he avoided use of the word *war*, even when pondering a statistical summary of carnage at Shiloh or Gettysburg. To the president, all of his military measures were designed "to suppress an insurrection existing within the United States."

At no time was public opinion in the North unanimous in accepting this position. Analyzing the First Inaugural Address, the New York *Journal of Commerce* said on March 5, 1861, that "he commits the practical error of setting up the theory of *an unbroken Union*, against the stubborn fact of a divided and dissevered one."

Yet the president never wavered. As he saw the matter at the time of his last public address on April 11, 1865, "the seceded states, so-called, are out of their proper practical relation with the Union." Actions regarded as having led to secession involved legal fictions, he said. No state had withdrawn from the indissoluble Union that came into existence before the Constitution. It was not necessary to restore so-called seceded states to their proper relation; they had never left it!

In July 1864 hasty congressional action was taken upon a bill whose preamble stated that seceded states were not in the Union. When it reached the Executive Mansion, the president exercised power he rarely used and subjected the measure to a pocket veto because of the reference to "seceded" states.

In reality, Lincoln had taken a paradoxical position on secession. Theoretically, there was no secession and hence no war. In practice, the Civil War was waged between independent political entities. This was despite the fact that the most influential figure in the entire conflict never admitted that lights burning very late in the Executive Mansion signaled anything more than "a domestic disturbance."

Disturbance was an extremely mild term with which to label events in Virginia. Lawmakers signed "a convention between the Commonwealth of Virginia and the Confederate States of America" on April 24, 1861. Yet the Old Dominion theoretically remained in the Union without congressional representation. In May self-appointed pro–Union "delegates" from twenty-six counties came together in Wheeling to discuss forming forty or fifty counties of the mountain region into a new state. Led by Ohio-born Archibald W. Campbell of the Wheeling *Intelligencer*, the rump body reassembled on June 11 and disavowed all allegiance to the C.S.A. Six days later, fifty-six persons from about two-thirds of the counties involved signed "a declaration of independence" from the old government of Virginia. When a provisional government was formed, a legislature was established and Francis H. Pierpont was elected governor.

Meeting at Wheeling on July 1, the new legislature selected John S. Carlile and Waitman T. Willy to represent "the restored commonwealth" in the U.S. Senate. An ordinance establishing the new state of Kanawha was enacted in August; three months later, the suggested name was shelved in favor of West Virginia. By then, troops led by George B. McClellan had effectively gained control of western Virginia—from which Robert E. Lee's men withdrew after a humiliating encounter at Cheat Mountain on September 15. When a new

Guarded by a battery on Shutter's Hill in Washington,
Alexandria was recognized as the capital of Virginia.

constitution was submitted to citizens, it was approved by a majority of 18,348 votes, a victory won by an average voter turnout of 404
persons in each of forty-eight counties.

With a brand-new political unit in Wheeling, Unionists in eastern
Virginia transferred their "restored government" to Alexandria. Only
Alexandria plus Norfolk and its environs were obedient to men oper-
ating from the state's newest "capital." Yet for two years beginning in
1861, men chosen there represented Virginia in both houses of the
national Congress.

Virginia—to whose leaders Abraham Lincoln had made a solemn
promise of no invasion—now had three capitals: Richmond for Confederates, Wheeling for citizens of western counties, and Alexandria
for a tiny group of Unionists who claimed jurisdiction over about
fifty eastern counties. While the Wheeling government was recognized in Washington, the Alexandria government had the greatest
influence there.

Federal acceptance of a new state hinged upon approval by the
state from which it came. Clearly, Richmond had no intention of
endorsing the formation of West Virginia. It would be less than legal
for Wheeling to endorse itself. So the federal administration turned

to Alexandria, whose leaders represented less than 5 percent of the people of the Old Dominion. Nevertheless, endorsement of the formation of West Virginia in Alexandria sent the matter to Capitol Hill.

Effectively partitioned into three parts, did actions in the region once famous as "the mother of presidents" represent democracy at work? Or was divided Virginia a sorry fruit of political expedience and eagerness to do anything whatever to weaken the enemy?

Regardless of how this central question is answered, the existence of a new entity was welcomed by some in Washington. Soon after the partition of Virginia was approved in Alexandria, statehood was sponsored in Congress. Numerous members of both houses expressed strong doubts concerning the constitutionality of actions taken, but debate ended when a bill aimed at admitting West Virginia into the Union was passed.

There is no indication that Lincoln studied the constitution in order to arrive at a decision concerning West Virginia. Instead of poring over law books, he told each of his cabinet members to render a written opinion on the advisability of admitting West Virginia into the Union.

William H. Seward insisted that the Wheeling government was "incontestably the state of Virginia." Salmon P. Chase and Edwin M. Stanton supported recognition, but were not so vocal as Seward. With the size of the cabinet reduced to six members as a result of resignations, Attorney General Edward Bates was emphatically opposed to the suggested action. In his diary he confided feelings that labeled the Wheeling government as made up of "a few reckless Radicals, who manage those helpless puppets as a gamester manages his marked cards." Gideon Welles and Montgomery Blair joined in judging the creation and admission of West Virginia to rest upon unconstitutional actions.

To his long-time intimate friend Orville H. Browning, the president had already confided that he was greatly distressed. Faced with an evenly divided cabinet, he said that he pondered the issue at length. Eventually he elevated expedience above legality, saying that:

> We can scarcely dispense with the aid of West Virginia in
> this struggle; much less can we afford to have her against us
> in Congress and in the field. Her brave and good men regard
> her admission into the Union as a matter of life and death.
> We cannot fully retain their confidence and cooperation if we
> seem to break faith with them.

Less than twenty-four hours before the public ceremony in which he signed the Emancipation Proclamation—December 31, 1862—the president signed into law the bill that would make West Virginia a state.

Harpers Ferry, situated at the dividing line between Virginia and the new state of West Virginia, held a Federal arsenal that was of great importance. [THE EPIC OF AMERICA]

* * *

West Virginia became the thirty-fifth state of the Union on July 20, 1863. Since the new state was exempted from provisions of the Emancipation Proclamation, its constitution provided for a system of gradual emancipation of the handful of slaves within the region.

About 15,000 men from West Virginia fought in Confederate gray. Only about 25,000 from the same region wore Union blue, so the state's contribution to Union victory "in the field" was not significant. Quite a different impact was felt in the realm that master politician Lincoln delicately described as "in Congress." There the two senators from West Virginia and the two from the Alexandria government were of major importance. With statehood having come less than four months before November 1864, twenty-one or more electoral votes from Wheeling and Alexandria were sure to be vital in a presidential race most experts considered to be a tossup.

How did an astute student of the Constitution reconcile views that seem to be far apart: no secession under any circumstances and the creation of a new state supported by votes of a tiny fraction of Virginia's citizens?

There is no solid evidence that Abraham Lincoln wrestled with this issue. This time, the man of mystery broke his self-imposed code of silence. He had sworn to make upholding of the Constitution a primary obligation, but in the case of West Virginia, expedience became the ruling factor.

29

*Why Did the World Leader of
Democracy Approve of*

PUNISHMENTS FAVORED BY KINGS AND DICTATORS?

■

> Long experience has shown that armies can not be maintained unless desertion shall be punished by the severe penalty of death. Must I shoot a simple-minded soldier boy who deserts, while I must not touch a hair of a wiley agitator who induces him to desert? I think that in such a case, to silence the agitator, and save the boy, is not only constitutional, but, withal, a great mercy.

Incorporated in a lengthy letter of June 1863, when seen out of context the president's argument appears to be logical and perhaps reasonable despite his recognition of constitutional problems. Examined in detail, unanswerable questions arise.

Nothing in the record indicates that evidence was produced to show that "wiley agitator" Clement L. Vallandigham persuaded a single Union soldier to desert. Lincoln's defense of his own actions seems to have hinged upon a hypothetical, rather than a real, offense.

Did the skilled master of words simply draw a red herring across a complex trail of charges, countercharges, and sentences? Or did he arrive at a verdict of guilt by equating probability with proof that the culprit had weakened Union fighting forces by persuading specific individuals to desert?

This insoluble question, intriguing as it is, is secondary to another. From the start of his tenure in the Executive Mansion to the time of his death, Abraham Lincoln considered the undeclared war to involve much more than the survival of the Union. Upon the outcome of the regional struggle, he repeatedly said, the fate of democracy rested—for the Union represented the world's best hope that democracy would survive and thrive.

As elected leader of this all-important political experiment, Lincoln resorted to banishment as a punishment. Though he did not personally order deportations, he approved such actions by his commanders.

Why were punishments linked with kings and dictators part of the military effort aimed at saving democracy?

Gen. Ambrose Burnside precipitated the controversial Vallandigham case. Angry at prosecessionists in his Department of the Ohio, he issued General Order No. 38 on April 19, 1863. In it he declared that he would no long tolerate "the habit of declaring sympathy for the enemy." Persons who ignored that warning, he said, would be arrested and tried as spies or traitors—or banished "into the lines of their friends."

Vallandigham of Dayton, Ohio, editor of a newspaper and a former member of Congress, reacted angrily to the warning issued by Burnside. At Dayton on May 4 before a crowd estimated at twenty thousand, he shouted that he spit upon the military order, "trampled it under his feet and despised it." Before yielding the platform, he demanded an armistice aimed at bringing "wicked, cruel, and unnecessary" sectional fighting to an end. Had the administration in Washington wished, he cried, the conflict could have been ended long ago. A war that Lincoln claimed to be leading for the sake of the Union was actually "for the purpose of crushing liberty and erecting a despotism," he charged as soldiers out of uniform recorded what he said.

At approximately 2:30 A.M. on the following morning, uniformed soldiers armed with bayonets broke down the door of the editor's home and arrested him. Within hours he was found guilty of having publicly voiced ideas "designed to hinder suppression of the rebellion" and was ordered to prison for a term that would end only after Confederate capitulation.

Secretary of the Navy Gideon Welles considered that "The proceedings were arbitrary and injudicious. Good men, who wish to support the administration, find it difficult to defend these acts." Sen. John Sherman, brother of Gen. William T. Sherman, was outraged. Gov. Oliver Morton of Indiana warned that the matter served to increase "the extent and intensity of Democratic opposition to the war." These and other vocal critics of Lincoln's action protested what they regarded as infringement upon civil liberties. So central was this issue that the constitutionality of banishment received little or no attention.

Presiding over courts of a federal district, Judge Humphrey H. Leavitt consented to hear a motion for release of the prisoner upon a writ of *habeas corpus*. He pondered the issue, then issued a lengthy decision. Burnside, he pointed out, acted as an agent for the president of the United States; therefore, he was authorized both to arrest and to hold the opponent of the war effort. When Lincoln learned that Leavitt had denied *habeas corpus* to the former congressman, he termed the verdict of the judge "equal to three victories in the field."

Though he had nothing to do with initiating actions taken by Gen. Ambrose Burnside in May, the president endorsed decisions of his commander. Soon, however, criticism from high levels forced him to change his position. Unwilling to repudiate the verdict of a military tribunal, he seized upon the alternative proposed by Burnside and ordered that Vallandigham be shipped to headquarters of Gen. William S. Rosecrans at Murfreesboro, Tennessee. From that point, Lincoln directed, Valladingham was to be conveyed into Confederate lines and set free. Should he return to Union territory, the prior sentence of imprisonment would become operative.

Duly escorted to Confederate lines, Vallandigham stayed in the South only a few weeks. He proceeded to Canada, where he established residence at Windsor, Ontario. Later he waged from Canada an unsuccessful campaign for the governorship of Ohio.

Though the C.S.A. was not recognized by Lincoln as an independent nation, Vallandigham's expulsion from the region of his birth was for all practical purposes a clear case of banishment—equivalent to exile.

This punishment was frequently used by rulers of ancient Greece and Rome. Absolute monarchs of later periods, claiming their thrones by divine right, often employed the same device. So did military conquerors and dictators.

Nothing in the Constitution of the United States or in acts of Congress made banishment legal. Burnside's listing of it as an option seems to have resulted from a whim that would have attracted little or no attention had it not been for an opponent of the war.

Did attorney Lincoln ponder the complex legal issue and his role in it as a prelude to modifying his position concerning imprisonment of the Ohio leader? Apparently not.

Responding to protests from Democrats of the Buckeye State, he explained that "military arrests and detentions" were made not as a form of punishment, but as preventive measures. There being no evidence that Vallandigham had committed any crime, the original sentence in his case was handed down "to prevent injury to the military service."

Writing at great length to protesting Democrats of New York State, the president relied upon the same set of arguments. Some arrests, he said, "are made, not so much for what has been done, as for what probably would be done." Such preventive detentions were designed to deal with "the man who stands by and says nothing when the peril of his government is discussed."

Arrested in the middle of the night, Clement L. Vallandigham was the first notable to be banished from Federal territory.
[HARPER'S WEEKLY]

When the rebellion began, according to Lincoln, "Gen. John C. Breckenridge, Gen. Robert E. Lee, Gen. Joseph E. Johnston, Gen. John B. Magruder, Gen. William B. Preston, Gen. Simon B. Buckner, and Commodore Franklin Buchanan were all within the power of the government and were nearly as well known to be traitors then as now." It was a mistake, he wrote, not to have arrested these men while they were still in Federal service—in order to weaken the insurgent cause. "In view of these and similar cases," he insisted, "I think the time not unlikely to come when I shall be blamed for having made too few arrests rather than too many."

When preparing a written opinion upon the legality of military conscription in September 1863, the president conferred with his secretary of the navy. According to Welles, in an Executive Mansion conversation Lincoln said that if Chief Justice Walter H. Lowrie of the Pennsylvania Supreme Court and others "continued to interfere and interrupt the draft, he would send them after Vallandigham." Only four months earlier, he had banished Clarence Prentice, not simply from Union territory but from the entire United States.

Vallandigham owned and edited a newspaper. Perhaps as a result of his banishment, at least five other journalists were made to leave their country. John W. Basughman of the Baltimore *Republican Citizen* was sent beyond Federal lines by Gen. David Hunter. Gen. Stephen G. Burbridge ordered Paul R. Shipman of the *Louisville*

Any person in the North who showed
sympathy for the South was derided as a
Copperhead—here mocked as offering
"peace soup" for sale. [LIBRARY OF CONGRESS]

Journal into Confederate lines. In Baltimore three staff members of
the *Republican* were banished by Gen. Robert C. Schenck: Beale H.
Richardson, Francis Richardson, and Stephen J. Joyce.

World War II internment of American citizens descended from
Japanese ancestors led to Supreme Court decisions that produced
formal apologies and compensation. In the heated climate of the
Civil War, a docile Supreme Court accepted arguments of Judge Advocate General Joseph Holt according to which it could not hear
appeals from verdicts rendered by military tribunals. There is no
record that a case concerning forcible deportation was argued before
the high court.

Abraham Lincoln never released a personal order requiring civilians to evacuate their homes and relocate elsewhere. But he never
directed one of his military commanders to revoke such an order,
despite the promptness with which he did so when emancipation
proclamations were issued by John C. Frémont and David Hunter.

Deportation seems to have been launched about the time Vallandigham decided to risk imprisonment by returning to Ohio. Commanding the District of the Border in the West, Gen. Thomas Ewing, Jr., became determined to get rid of pro—Confederate guerrillas of Kansas and Missouri. As a move in that direction, his General Order No. 11 of August 25, 1863, gave residents of four counties just fifteen days in which to evacuate the region. There were no hearings of any sort; believing the fifteen thousand or so citizens of these counties included Southerners who sympathized with William C. Quantrill, Ewing simply ordered men, women, and children to pack up and leave. A subsequent directive warned that any who violated the deportation order would be subject to summary execution.

Four days before General Order No. 11 was made public, Quantrill's guerrillas sacked Lawrence, Kansas, in one of the most brutal atrocities of the war. Clearly, mass punishment without trial was not a guarantee that the level of violence would be reduced. Yet on October 1, 1863, the president told Gen. John M. Schofield, "With the matter of removing the inhabitants of certain counties en masse, I am not now interfering, but am leaving to your own discretion."

There was no interference from the president when Gen. William T. Sherman issued a special directive concerning a key southern city. As the Union commander remembered the matter in later years, "I peremptorily required that all the citizens and families resident in Atlanta should go away, giving to each the option to go south or north. I was resolved to make Atlanta a pure military garrison or depot, with no civil population." Expecting to be severely criticized for having ordered the mass deportation of civilians, Sherman gave an advance answer to his critics: "I will answer that war is war, and not popularity-seeking."

Instead of rebuking Atlanta's conqueror or treating him as he had Frémont and Hunter, the president was so overjoyed at Sherman's victory that he ordered the nation to observe a day of thanksgiving.

30

By What Exercise in Logic
Did He Decide That

10 PERCENT OF THE ELECTORATE COULD CONSTITUTE A GOVERNING MAJORITY?

■

MASTERY OF CONFEDERATE territory by Federal forces, slow as it was during the spring of 1862, created new situations. After the battle of Shiloh, part of Tennessee came under the control of Union forces. The battle of Pea Ridge served, in the language of the president, to "liberate" sections of Arkansas. A Union victory at Roanoke Island meant that North Carolina was no longer wholly Confederate. Above all, the capture of New Orleans put the city into Federal hands.

Fresh administrative problems arose, but these were linked with opportunities for the president to make political progress. Always, the ultimate stated goal was full restoration of states to the Union. Since this could not be accomplished in a single sweeping step, a series of smaller movements took place. Andrew Johnson became military governor of Tennessee in March 1862. Two months later, Edward Stanley was named to the same office in North Carolina and was simultaneously designated as head of the civil government.

Lincoln's secretaries who later became his biographers initially avoided speaking of "reconstruction." Echoing views of their chief, they dealt with "the reorganization of loyal State governments," a task initially seen as falling within the province of a military governor.

Louisiana was a special case. A few months after the fall of New Orleans in April, one-time Democrat Gen. Nathaniel P. Banks be-

Maj. Gen. Nathaniel P. Banks supervised a Louisiana made up of only a tiny fraction of the state's inhabitants. [J. C. BUTTRE ENGRAVING]

came commander of the Department of the Gulf. He quickly aligned himself with pro–Union leaders and forces, including "Gov. G. F. Shepley," who claimed to represent loyalists.

Writing to Shepley on November 21, the president said, "I wish election for congressmen to take place in Louisiana, but I wish it to be a movement of the people of the district, and not a movement of our military and quasi-military authorities." Urging Shepley not to waste a day in opening the polls, he stressed that he wanted results by New Year's Day 1863.

Only the city of New Orleans and its immediate environs were firmly under Federal control. Yet this region constituted two prewar congressional districts. When voters cast their ballots on December 3, the election was reported as having been held "in perfect order and quiet." B. F. Flanders having received 2,643 votes and Michael Hahn having received 2,799, both were declared elected and were seated in the House of Representatives.

Louisiana's two-district election represented a giant step above earlier establishment in Alexandria of "the loyalist government of Virginia." Yet the skeleton system in the port city returned only a portion of the state to the Union. Probably influenced by events in New Orleans, Abraham Lincoln redoubled his efforts to devise a workable plan by which so-called seceded regions could be returned to the fold of loyalty.

December 8, 1863, was a special day for the nation. With his annual message to Congress signed and delivered, the president made last-minute changes in a Proclamation of Amnesty and Reconstruction. Directed to citizens and to states having engaged in "rebellion and treason," it offered a full pardon to persons willing to take a prescribed oath.

By this time it was clear that the Emancipation Proclamation had proved to be a war measure far more potent than anyone anticipated. More than any other single action taken by Lincoln, it turned the tide with respect to attitudes in England and Europe. At the same time, it led black soldiers to enlist in far greater numbers than expected. As a result, the president, who for so long had fought for gradual emancipation with compensation and subsequent colonization, had adopted a new position.

Henceforth, Lincoln made it clear, he would require emancipation at the state level as a prerequisite to restoration of civil government in southern states. His oath of amnesty published on December 8 required individuals to swear that they would "abide by and faithfully support all proclamations of the President made during the existing rebellion having references to slaves." Elected officials of "the so-called Confederate government" were barred from gaining amnesty by means of the oath. So were Confederate diplomats and military officers above the rank of colonel and naval officers above the rank of lieutenant.

With most of his conditions having been prescribed, Abraham Lincoln continued:

> I do further proclaim, declare, and make known, that whenever, in any of the states of Arkansas, Texas, Louisiana, Mississippi, Tennessee, Alabama, Georgia, Florida, South Carolina, and North Carolina, a number of persons, not less than one-tenth in number of the votes cast in such State at the Presidential election of 1860 . . . shall re-establish a State government which shall be republican and shall be recognized as the true government of the State.

Any provision made by these voters concerning the "freed people of such state" must declare their freedom and provide for their education, the proclamation stipulated. Temporary arrangements for this "laboring landless, and homeless class" would be acceptable to "the national executive," he said.

"Reconstitution of state governments" was offered by the proclamation. It would come, not when the majority of citizens accepted it through democratic processes, but as a result of votes cast by a tiny minority of loyalists. This government would of course be supported

Andrew Johnson's appointment as military governor of Tennessee constituted a first step toward "restoration of the full Union." [AUTHOR'S COLLECTION]

by Federal troops. It would be represented in both houses of Congress—and at the time of the 1864 election would send delegates to the electoral college.

According to John G. Nicolay and John Hay, who were close to Abraham Lincoln during his entire time in the Executive Mansion, his primary goal with respect to new governments was "to awaken and crystallize dormant Union sentiment, with a view as much as possible to detach captured localities and generally insurrectionary states from their military support to the rebellion."

Preservation of the Union was still the president's dominant goal. Secondary considerations focused upon the future of the conquered South and political factors. That the latter were never ignored is indicated by a September 11, 1863, message sent to Johnson of Tennessee. "Not a moment must be lost," in re-establishing "a loyal state government." Such "reinauguration must not be such as to give control of the state, and its representation in Congress, to the enemies of the Union."

Use only trusted Union men, the president insisted. "Exclude all others; and trust that your government so organized will be recognized here." Then the wartime decision-maker who never forgot political processes added, "It is something on the question of time to remember that it cannot be known who is next to occupy the position I now hold nor what he will do." That was an oblique way of stressing that Tennessee's electoral votes could be significant or even decisive in 1864.

Part of Tennessee came under Federal control in the aftermath of the battle of Shiloh, where Grant and Sherman conferred while on horseback. [LESLIE'S ILLUSTRATED NEWSPAPER]

Obedient to these orders, Johnson held an election on March 5, 1864. Few persons went to the polls, and the results were far from decisive. Unionists therefore soon met at Knoxville, then moved to Nashville and "made provision for taking part in the approaching presidential election." Conditions remained so unsettled that in a September election, voters cast ballots only for electors of the president and vice president.

Subsequent Union victories on the battlefield paved the way for still another state convention to assemble in January 1865. "Fifty-eight counties and some regiments" being represented, delegates denounced the state's secession as having been "an act of treason and usurpation, unconstitutional, null, and void." Confederate debts were repudiated, along with all laws enacted by the secessionist government. On February 25 William G. Brownlow, a belligerent Unionist, was made governor of Tennessee. Shortly after a Union legislature was elected, its members ratified the Thirteenth Amendment to the Constitution of the United States. U.S. senators were chosen, and members of the U.S. House of Representatives were named.

* * *

In Arkansas and Louisiana the pattern of "re-constitution of governments" differed from that in Tennessee. An expedition under Gen. Frederick Steele captured Little Rock on September 10, 1863. By the time Unionists were ready to organize, Lincoln's proclamation of amnesty and reconstruction was in their hands. Under the supervision of Steele, voter registration followed the taking of the amnesty oath. Instructions from Washington directed the military commander that "when 5,406 votes should have been cast" in a bid to alter the constitution by banning slavery, he should "ascertain and announce the result."

Polls opened on March 24, 1864, and remained open for three days during which 12,179 persons voted for the new constitution and 226 voted against it. On April 11 the new Unionist government, whose legislature included representatives of forty of the state's fifty-five counties, was inaugurated.

By the time new senators and congressmen from Arkansas reached Washington, Radical Republicans had decided not to accept governments formed under Lincoln's plan. They decided that at least half of all voters—not a mere one-tenth—should participate in a legitimate election. No longer in a mood to conciliate the president, Congress refused to seat men elected by fractional votes. In Louisiana a statewide voter turnout of 11,411 was considered by Lincoln to be highly gratifying—nearly twice the minimum response he had stipulated. Yet Congress treated men chosen there precisely as it had those from Arkansas.

Abraham Lincoln formally recognized the reconstituted governments of the two states, but Congress refused to acknowledge them. In July 1864 lawmakers enacted the Wade-Davis Bill whose provisions for reconstruction were much more stringent than those of the chief executive. When the measure reached the Executive Mansion, it was killed by a pocket veto just as Radical Republicans launched a major campaign to deny renomination to Lincoln. His victory at the Republican convention and in the general election, followed by his assassination in April 1865, removed his firm hand from the reconstruction process.

31

How Did He Succeed in Winning

THE ELECTION OF 1864?

■

AS CABINET MEMBERS arrived for their meeting of August 23, 1864, according to presidential secretary John Hay, Lincoln showed each man a folded sheet of paper. Edges securely pasted, it displayed no message. "Write your name across the back," he instructed each man in turn. Once all had signed, the president deposited the endorsed document in his desk, without giving a hint as to its nature.

When his key advisers assembled on November 11, he pulled out the mysterious paper and remarked, "Gentlemen, do you remember last summer when I asked you all to sign your names to the back of a paper of which I did not show you the inside? This is it. Now, Mr. Hay, see if you can get this open without tearing it?"

Though it was pasted in such fashion that Hay said it required some cutting to get it open, he did not damage the hidden message. Having reminded his key advisers that they signed blindly, six days before a political convention convened in Chicago, he read to them the commitment they had made:

> Executive Mansion
> Washington, Aug. 23, 1864
> This morning, as for some days past, it seems exceedingly probable that this administration will not be re-elected. Then it will be my duty to so cooperate with the president-elect, as to save the Union between the election and the inauguration; as he will have secured his election on such ground that he can not possibly save it afterwards.
>
> A. LINCOLN

One of the most unusual political documents on record, the secret pledge demanded by Lincoln underscores the dominant goal of his

Veteran political analyst and leader Thurlow Weed informed Lincoln that he could not possibly be re-elected. [NICOLAY & HAY, ABRAHAM LINCOLN]

presidency—preservation of the Union. At the same time, it reveals the apparent desperation of his bid for re-election.

Obstacles to a second term seemed to be insuperable.

No president had won re-election during the previous thirty years; only Martin Van Buren had succeeded in winning renomination by his party as a prelude to an overwhelming defeat.

With the military movement to quell rebellion going badly, hordes of people in the North were literally screaming for peace. Bloody riots to halt conscription had not persuaded the president to change his course; on February 1, 1864, he sternly called for 500,000 additional men—to serve for three years or the duration of the conflict. Six weeks later he ordered an additional draft of 200,000. Yet in every region, Federal forces experienced defeat or stalemate: Texas's Red River country, Virginia's Wilderness area, New Market in the Shenandoah Valley, Drewry's Bluff, Cold Harbor, Petersburg, Richmond . . .

Key political leader Thurlow Weed of New York wrote to Lincoln early in August, telling him that re-election was impossible. Almost simultaneously, Henry J. Raymond decided he could keep quiet no longer. As head of the Republican National Executive Committee, he felt it essential that the president be informed that his following had shrunk in every part of the country. Wendell Phillips had gone on record as labeling the president "a more unlimited despot than the world knows this side of China." Multitudes in the North agreed with that assessment.

At the battle of Cold Harbor, Federal artillery blasted attacking Confederates, but lack of a clear victory diminished Lincoln's chances at the polls. [HARPER'S WEEKLY]

Veterans of many campaigns took the congressional election of 1862 as an omen. Democrats scored such impressive gains that some immediately began boasting that they would win the Executive Mansion in 1864. Radical Republicans, who had as little use for any Democrat as for Abraham Lincoln, were sure that their hour had come. They negotiated with Salmon P. Chase and secured his pledge to seek the presidency, if nominated. An open letter circulated over the signature of Kansas Sen. Samuel C. Pomeroy advocated dropping Lincoln in favor of Chase. When it became public, the secretary of the treasury offered his resignation. When Lincoln successfully urged him to remain in the cabinet, the possibility of a Chase nomination vanished.

Far from defeated, Radical Republicans called a convention at Cleveland. There they turned to Gen. John C. Frémont, the man who had been the Republican nominee in 1856, whose fame—or notoriety—had since been boosted by Lincoln's countermand of his Missouri emancipation proclamation. As the running mate for Frémont, the Cleveland body chose Gen. John Cochrane of New York.

Democrats were equally eager for a nominee with a well-known war record. Under the influence of Clement L. Vallandigham, they adopted a peace platform and offered Gen. George B. McClellan for the Executive Mansion. George M. Pendleton, who had won a following by his opposition to Lincoln's institution of paper currency, was selected as McClellan's running mate.

Some Democrats boasted that their candidate, earlier famous as the Pathfinder of the West, "would carry the country by storm." Other analysts were not so sure of this outcome, believing that neither Frémont nor McClellan could win a majority in the November election. But their combined influence was believed sufficient to thwart Lincoln's bid for re-election.

Even Lincoln's most outspoken foes failed to take into account the acumen of the man they hoped to defeat. Long before delegates to his party's convention assembled at Baltimore on June 7, 1864, the president was quietly at work. Careful allocations of federal patronage, and firm promises of more to come after November, had his renomination secured before Republicans convened. Delegates, gloated John G. Nicolay and John Hay, "had less to do than any other convention in our political history."

Once Lincoln was renominated on the first ballot, delegates listened to persuasive speeches and agreed to change their party's name. So it was as the nominee of the National Union party that Abraham Lincoln set out to do battle with Frémont and McClellan. It would be far easier to deal with the leader of Radical Republicans than with the Democrat who was idolized by thousands of soldiers who had served under him.

Michigan Sen. Zachariah Chandler surveyed the situation and

Adm. David Farragut, shown here in the main rigging of a warship, boosted Lincoln's chances by his August victory at Mobile Bay.
[AUTHOR'S COLLECTION]

confided to intimates, "Abe Lincoln may look like a farmer, but he's as smart as a fox. Knowing he has to get Frémont out of the way, he's looking for bait with which to tempt him." That bait was found, according to Chandler, in the cabinet. Everyone in the capital knew that Frémont had long hated Montgomery Blair, whose family for decades had made the key political decisions in Missouri. When it was learned that Blair had resigned as postmaster general late in September, Chandler and other analysts immediately concluded that "a swap was made."

Whether a secret agreement was actually reached is unknown, but Blair's resignation was timed to coincide with Frémont's withdrawal from the presidential contest. The mood of the North had already undergone a dramatic shift. Adm. David Farragut's victory at Mobile Bay boosted hope that the Confederacy would be conquered or would collapse, and Gen. William T. Sherman's capture of Atlanta triggered wild celebrations in the streets of many cities.

Capitalizing upon the sudden shift in military fortunes, the president issued yet another proclamation to the nation. In it he called for observance of a day of "thanksgiving and praise to Almighty God the beneficient Creator and Ruler of the Universe" on the last Thursday of November:

> And I do farther recommend to my fellow citizens aforesaid that on that occasion they do reverently humble themselves in the dust and from thence offer up penitent and fervent prayers and supplications to the Great Disposer of events for a return of *the inestimable blessings of peace, union and harmony throughout the land*, which it has pleased him to assign as a dwelling place for ourselves and for our posterity throughout all generations.

Preparations for an elaborate thanksgiving celebration were sure to sway many voters, but nothing was left to chance. Commanders in the field were instructed to take care that their men were allowed to vote in their camps, or to return to states that did not permit this practice. Surely the Virginia government conducted from Alexandria could be counted upon, as well as Tennessee and "reconstituted" Arkansas and Louisiana.

When popular votes were tallied, the candidate of the National Union party received 2,213,635—an astonishing 347,183 more than given to the candidate of the Republican party four years earlier. Abraham Lincoln this time won 55 percent of the popular vote, against just under 40 percent in 1860. McClellan's popular vote of 1,805,237 was impressive—but meaningless.

Wary of the electoral college process because some Confederate states were believed ready to demand seats, Congress took charge. A

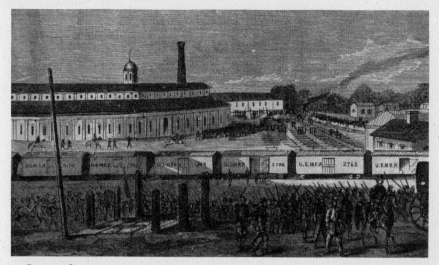

Soon after conquered Atlanta began to fill with cars of the U.S. Military Railroad, a few optimistic followers declared that Lincoln was now sure to win in November. [HARPER'S WEEKLY]

joint resolution enumerated states in rebellion and stipulated that they were not "entitled to representation in the electoral college for the choice of president and vice-president." To the chagrin of Abraham Lincoln, this meant that votes of Louisiana and Texas and the loyalist government in Alexandria, Virginia, would not be counted.

This loss was balanced by certainty that electoral votes of new states would go into the Republican column. West Virginia, Kansas, and Nevada were assured before the November popular election.

When the crucial votes were counted, National Union party candidate Abraham Lincoln received 233 from twenty-five states—91 percent of those cast. McClellan received only 21 votes from three states, giving him a bare 9 percent of the total. Eleven Confederate states, formerly entitled to eighty electoral votes, were barred from participation.

Sitting in the office of the U.S. Military Telegraph, where he spent so many wartime days, the president estimated on October 13 that he was sure of at least 120 electoral votes. On election night he learned that Maryland had given him more than twice the support he received there in 1860. Other good news followed; Ohio, Indiana, and Pennsylvania were firmly in the National Union column. Boosting his estimate, Lincoln that night calculated that he would win by a huge margin.

Few political upsets have been more surprising than the November landslide victory of a man whose campaign was in August considered to be hopeless. For decades, analysts have tried to determine precisely how Lincoln won in 1864; few agree about anything other than very broad details.

New states supported him, but he would have won without them; loss of votes expected to come from Louisiana and Tennessee proved to be inconsequential.

He used the power of patronage with unmatched skill. He appealed for and received much of the soldier vote, though it was not decisive in any state. By elevating the concept of national union and taking it to the polls, he may have secured thousands of otherwise doubtful votes. He persuaded the North to move toward a mood of thanksgiving that credited battlefield victories—not to the president or to his generals—to "Almighty God the beneficent Creator and Ruler of the Universe."

No factor was decisive. When all elements were combined, their cumulative effect gave the nation its first second-term president since Andrew Jackson in 1832. He was returned to the Executive Mansion despite hunger for peace and widespread understanding that, more than any other individual, he made the crucial decisions in the domestic conflict he preferred not to label as a war.

How Did He Plan to Secure

32

RATIFICATION OF THE THIRTEENTH AMENDMENT?

∎

ISSUED AFTER LONG hesitation and with apparent reluctance, the war measure known as the Emancipation Proclamation proved to be far more potent than expected. Influence upon England and Europe was immediate and dramatic; all fear that some governments might give diplomatic recognition to the Confederate States of America vanished. Blacks enlisted in far greater numbers than had been anticipated; more than any other group, they helped to overcome problems caused by draft resistance. Although the measure seems to have led to little or no civil unrest in the C.S.A., it added greatly to the anger and frustration of Jefferson Davis, his aides, and his generals.

By the time the president abandoned his long-cherished plan to colonize freed slaves outside the United States, his personal attitude toward emancipation had undergone dramatic change. Support for it was adopted in desperation as a possible means of bringing unconditional surrender by the enemy. Once seen as a military measure likely to weaken the enemy, it evolved into a separate war aim. This meant that while battles were still being fought "for the preservation of the Union," war also began to be waged for the abolition of slavery.

By the time this late-coming goal emerged, Abraham Lincoln was increasingly doubtful that the Emancipation Proclamation was adequate. He had successfully defied the Supreme Court concerning civil rights, but now he worried that once hostilities ceased the court might declare his proclamation null and void. Mulling over this issue, he concluded that his critics might decide that "it only aided those that came into our lines, that it was inoperative as to those who did not give themselves up, or that it would have no effect upon children of slaves born hereafter."

Lincoln customarily worked alone in drafting documents. In this instance, he consulted Senator Lyman Trumbull concerning its language. [NICOLAY & HAY, *ABRAHAM LINCOLN*]

Still another ominous possibility was envisioned. All so-called seceded states might suddenly seek and gain full restoration to the Union. If they did so, the Emancipation Proclamation would have no more effect in these states than in those exempted from its provisions because of loyalty. Congress, he declared in a July 1864 proclamation, lacked constitutional competency to abolish slavery. This could be done, he had always insisted, only by individual states, including those in so-called secession who were fighting to preserve slavery.

Facing this dilemma, the master strategist residing in the Executive Mansion changed his mind concerning a key issue. Years earlier, he had gone on record as opposing all attempts to amend the Constitution, last altered five years before he was born. Now he concluded that only a constitutional amendment would bring victory in the new military goal of abolition.

To become effective, a proposed amendment must pass both houses of Congress by a two-thirds majority. Then it must be ratified by three-fourths of the individual states.

With strong support from the president, late in 1863 Republicans drafted a proposed amendment. Aimed at ending slavery—not simply in rebellious southern states but throughout the nation—it stipulated that lifetime bondage would cease "except as a punishment for crime." Working chiefly with Sen. Lyman Trumbull of Illinois, Lincoln helped to frame the final language of the measure. Having pointed out that most northern states did not yet permit blacks to vote, he insisted that abolition not be linked with the franchise. In the Senate, this "emasculated" proposal was denounced by Radical Republicans as not nearly strong enough; yet it won easy passage on April 8, 1864. In the heavily Democratic House of Representatives, the measure went down to defeat on June 15.

Weeks before final action in the House, Radical Republicans met at Cleveland. Once they had nominated John C. Frémont for the presidency, they shaped a platform whose key plank was a proposed Thirteenth Amendment aimed at abolition throughout the nation.

Frémont and his backers had stolen a march upon Lincoln, but he refused to be swayed by their actions. Before former Republicans came together for the National Union convention in June, the president conferred at the Executive Mansion with Sen. E. D. Morgan. Scheduled to give the opening speech in Baltimore, Morgan agreed to stress as "a keystone" a platform plank concerning slavery. Having denounced slavery as the cause of the rebellion, the document would give a clarion call for a constitutional amendment designed to "terminate and forever prohibit" what was often called the "peculiar institution."

As expected, Lincoln won renomination by acclamation. Exuberant delegates then shaped a party platform calling slavery "hostile to the principles of republican government." This social evil, delegates agreed, must be utterly extirpated "from the soil of the republic."

Informed of his renomination by a committee, the president ex-

Some Republicans mocked John C. Frémont as "riding an abolition nag"—yet he advocated a Thirteenth Amendment before it gained the backing of the president. [FRÉMONT AND '49]

pressed his gratitude to "the Union people." He had no reason to think he would refuse the nomination, he said. Yet he hesitated to accept "before reading and considering what is called the platform." Even before doing this, he said, he gave his approval to "the declaration in favor of so amending the Constitution as to prohibit slavery throughout the nation."

Few if any intimates misunderstood the ceremonial invitation and Lincoln's response to it. Better than anyone else, those close to him knew he was responsible for the abolition plank—and that after having worked for months to secure his renomination, he had no thought of refusing it.

Overwhelming victory by Republicans who briefly called themselves National Unionists brought quick change in the climate of the capital. When the Thirty-eighth Congress assembled for its last session in December 1864, many Democrats in the House of Representatives knew that they would not return. Some of them seem to have made it known that they might now be ready to consider supporting the proposed Thirteenth Amendment.

Never slow to act upon an opportunity, the president issued a stirring call for passage of the joint congressional resolution in his fourth annual message to lawmakers. Then he invited Moses F. Odell of New York to the Executive Mansion. As a result of their confidential session, the congressman who had earlier voted against the amendment now became an outspoken proponent of it. Shortly after Congress adjourned, he won appointment to New York City as navy agent of the federal government. Congressman James S. Rollins of Missouri, a slave owner, also saw the president in private and apparently reached an agreement with him.

On Capitol Hill, Congressman Thaddeus Stevens made what many admirers called his most persuasive speech. "We have suffered for slavery more than all the plagues of Egypt," he cried. "I verily believe that the amendment will serve to stay the sword of the destroying angel, so that this people may be reunited."

Numerous other speeches were made, and Abraham Lincoln seems to have made other political bargains. On January 21, 1865, sixteen other Democrats joined with Odell in voting to submit the Thirteenth Amendment to the states. That day, the joint resolution of Congress passed the House by 119 to 56—supported by three votes beyond the required two-thirds majority. When Speaker Schuyler Colfax announced the result in a trembling voice, he insisted that his own aye also be recorded.

Announcement of the tally led to a one-hundred-gun salute that roared the message throughout the capital and far beyond. Lincoln affixed his signature, though it was not required. This action, somewhat reminiscent of his having hired a substitute soldier whom he

Voting on the Thirteenth Amendment in the House of Representatives, January 31, 1865. [LESLIE'S ILLUSTRATED NEWSPAPER]

did not need, brought a formal rebuke from the Senate. Still, all that was needed to make the amendment effective was the support of three-fourths of the states.

Surely the Constitution must be interpreted to mean that three-fourths of the loyal states could ratify, Radical Republicans insisted. Not so, according to the president. Here the meaning of the nation's charter was clear; it would take three-fourths of all the states, including those claiming to have seceded. That was one reason he had been adamant in insisting upon acceptance of the "10 percent governments" he had created, he explained.

On February 1, Illinois became the first state to ratify. Before the month ended, Lincoln's adopted state was joined by sixteen others, including West Virginia, Virginia, and Louisiana. Yet the measure designed to abolish slavery throughout the United States did not become effective during the life of the president. At the time of his assassination, only twenty-one of the necessary twenty-seven states had ratified the Thirteenth Amendment.

Sixteenth among those twenty-one was the new state of Nevada, whose positive vote was recorded on February 16. When its admission had been debated in October 1864, the legality of the territory's case was highly doubtful since it did not have the population required for statehood. Lincoln probably worked harder for Nevada than for West Virginia, reputedly basing his activity on a verdict that "it is better to admit Nevada than to have to raise another million men" for the war.

Arkansas, last to ratify during the life of Lincoln, registered its support of the amendment on April 14, 1865.

William H. Seward, who remained as secretary of state in the cabinet of Andrew Johnson, had repeatedly labeled the amendment as "another war measure." Ratification might be blocked by seceded states, he hinted, if they surrendered immediately. Since they did not, he announced ratification on December 18, 1865. According to his formal statement, "Legislatures of twenty-seven states, constituting three-fourths of the thirty-six states of the Union," had acted favorably. As a result, the amendment became "valid as a part of the Constitution."

Secretary Seward failed to point out that states "in rebellion" until conquered were included in the twenty-seven-state total, along with Nevada. Had he mentioned this factor, hordes of citizens would have recognized that ratification was effected as a result of support from Virginia's rump government in Alexandria and "10 percent governments" in three states that earlier fought to remain out of the Union.

Four of the states counted as joining in ratification had not even put Lincoln's "10 percent governments" into effect. South Carolina, Alabama, and North Carolina were members of the C.S.A., subdued by military force and barely started on the road to "reconstruction." Georgia was in the same category, but a favorable vote by a segment of that state's citizens on December 9 made it the decisive twenty-seventh state.

Texas waited until 1870, long after the amendment became effective, to endorse it. Stubborn Delaware rejected the proposal in February 1865 and did not change its stance until Lincoln's birthday in 1901.

No one knew better than Abraham Lincoln that if and when slavery was abolished, that would not confer full rights of citizenship upon black Americans. He saw the Thirteenth Amendment as the most that could be accomplished in 1864–65, so he worked mightily to achieve this late-conceived war goal.

PART FIVE

■

Nancy Hanks's Son Was a Cluster of Unsolved Riddles

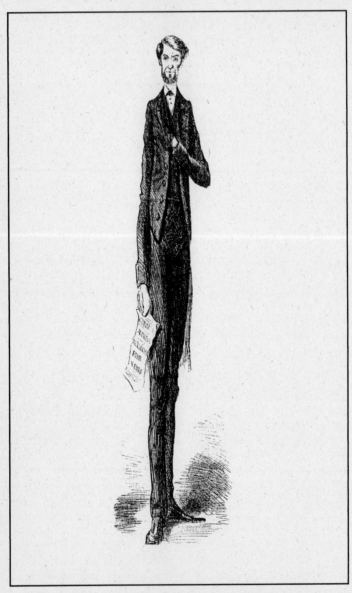

Cartoonists made fun of Lincoln's height—so great that he said his body needed frequent "oiling" to supplement poor circulation of his blood. [LIBRARY OF CONGRESS]

Why Is He Remembered As

THE MERRIEST OF ALL CHIEF EXECUTIVES?

■

"ALL MEMBERS OF THE CABINET were present," Salmon P. Chase noted in his diary for September 22, 1862. If a few were ignorant of the vital issue to be discussed, the secretary of the treasury was not. He was among the first to be taken into confidence by their secretive chief. Part of his terse account of the all-important session tells us that:

> There was some general talk, and the president mentioned that Artemus Ward had sent him his book. Proposed to read a chapter which he thought very funny. Read it and seemed to enjoy it very much; the heads also (except Stanton). The chapter was "High-Handed Outrage at Utica."
> The president then took a graver tone and said: "Gentlemen, I have as you are aware, thought a great deal about the relation of this war to slavery.
> "I have got you together to hear what I have written down."

Secretary of War Edwin M. Stanton, according to his colleague's record of the momentous session, did not pretend to be amused. Like everyone else in the room, he knew that Ward was the pen name of self-taught humorist and lecturer Charles F. Browne. Even in 1862, some Americans did not laugh at his ridiculous spellings and grammatical usages; today, they are all but unintelligible.

A chapter from a book of humor served as a prelude to the first intimate reading of the Emancipation Proclamation! Broad jokes preceded discussion of one of the most deadly serious documents ever issued by an American chief executive! Why this seemingly incongruous and (to Stanton at least) inappropriate prelude to sharing ideas destined to work radical change in the life of the nation?

Abraham Lincoln's voluminous papers give no hint concerning his reasoning on the morning he prepared to reveal to his cabinet the specifics of the preliminary Emancipation Proclamation. One thing is clear, however. Even in times of great tension—perhaps especially then—the chief executive was prone to crack jokes and guffaw at them as though there was not a cloud on the horizon.

On March 28, 1861, the Lincolns held their first state dinner in the Executive Mansion. Cabinet members had already rendered written opinions advising against attempting to resupply Fort Sumter. Secessionists had threatened to resort to force if such a move was made. Better than anyone else, Nancy Hanks's son knew that his decisions about the confrontation in Charleston Harbor could trigger civil war. Yet to a puzzled guest he seemed to be "in his usual jolly mood, telling stories as if he had not a care in the world."

As a boy on the western frontier, Lincoln participated in horseplay and practical jokes. He even tried his hand at writing and produced a broad satire about life in a neighboring cabin. Mrs. Elizabeth Crawford, who knew young Lincoln well, memorized twelve lines of Abe's poetry in which he described how a fellow named Billy went through a marriage ceremony—only to find himself husband of a male. According to the poem, Betsy had earlier rejected Billy on the grounds that "your low crotch proclaims you a botch."

Abe's cousin Dennis Hanks later attested that when tired of work at a house-raising or corn-shucking, "instantly he would commence his pranks, tricks, jokes, and stories. Sure enough, all would stop,

Judge David Davis considered Lincoln's use of humor a "device to whistle down sadness." [Author's collection]

gather around Abe and listen, sometimes crying and sometimes bursting their sides with laughter."

By the time he began spending months each year on the legal circuit, his colleagues admired him as the best storyteller they knew. Their testimony indicates that had Lincoln been born a century later he could have been a howling success in vaudeville.

Many signs indicate that he would have enjoyed such a role tremendously. For he not only remembered, adapted, and told jokes and stories, he seemed to get even more pleasure from them than did many of his listeners. Newspaper reporter Henry Villard jotted down notes describing a period of merrymaking:

> A high-pitched laughter lighted up his otherwise melancholy countenance with thorough merriment. His body shook all over, and when he felt particularly good over his performance, he followed his habit of drawing his knees, with his arms around them, up to his very face.

Ward Hill Lamon said that as his chief approached the punch line of a yarn, laughter bottled up inside him "seemed to diffuse itself all over him, like a spontaneous tickle." William H. Herndon echoed that description by commenting that "his frame quivered with suppressed excitement; and when the point—or 'nub' of the story, as he called it—came, no one's laugh was heartier than his." According to his partner, the storyteller was sometimes so amused at his own tales that he would punch out the crown of his hat "by running his hand through it."

Since most of Lincoln's humor was vocal, it depended heavily upon gestures, intonations, and mimicry. A yarn that threw his listeners into spasms of laughter is likely to seem awkward and lifeless when preserved in printed form.

Long before he reached the Executive Mansion, the Republican from Illinois was known and admired as a storyteller among his circle of friends. Newsmen picked up this facet of his life and some wrote about it during the months between election and inauguration, when he said little or nothing on national issues. Printers and publishers saw an opportunity, and so they began putting out little books such as *The Humors of Uncle Abe* and *Old Abe's Jokes*. New Yorker Robert DeWitt issued a ten-cent pamphlet packed with *Wit at the White House* that became a steady seller at railway stations of major cities. Few if any yarns and quips in such compilations actually came from Lincoln. Dozens or hundreds of others, attributed to him but having no link with him, circulated orally as early as 1862.

Some later collections have been put together with care. *Presidential Anecdotes*, with only twenty-three pages devoted to Lincoln, is a notable example. Most others, including *Anecdotes By & About*

Abraham Lincoln (312 pages) and *Lincoln Talks* (698 pages), almost certainly include jokes and stories he never heard—despite the fact that the latter was compiled by faithful Lincoln devotee Emanuel Hertz.

Only that humor which appears in the president's papers can be regarded as his own, without question—though probably borrowed and adapted. Allusions, puns, and others types of word play are sprinkled through letters and documents at random. Even the laugh-inducing tales that appear in them are almost always very short—and are not certain to be recognized as humorous by modern readers.

Although he clearly got great pleasure from telling stories and reacting to them, his use of humor was also highly utilitarian. He used jokes and quips as weapons in verbal fray. Sometimes he made a memorable point by means of an illustrative yarn. Many, many times humor was a protective device. By introducing a funny story that had little or nothing to do with the subject being discussed, he often diverted attention or dismissed callers.

Addressing the Illinois legislature in 1841, he told of an old gentleman who repeatedly fired at what he thought to be squirrels. When his brother examined the marksman carefully, he found a big louse on one of his eyelashes. Opponents of legislation he favored, said Lincoln, "imagined they could see squirrels every day, when they were nothing but lice."

He pretended to praise the facial appearance of Stephen A. Douglas, then got a hearty laugh by saying, "Nobody has ever expected me to be president. In my poor, lean, lank face, nobody has ever seen any cabbages sprouting out."

On his journey from Springfield to Washington early in 1861, at Utica, New York, and other stops the president-elect laughed at himself as a way of sidestepping public yearning for a speech. Having informed an eager crowd that he would say only a few words, on February 18 he continued:

> I appear before you that I may see you, and that you may see me; and I am willing to admit, that so far as the ladies are concerned, I have the best of the bargain, though I wish it to be understood that I do not make the same acknowledgement concerning the men.

Besieged by office seekers once he reached the Executive Mansion, he often seemed not to hear requests. "Your remark reminds me of a little story," he was likely to begin. Having told it in some detail, he was likely to laugh heartily while slapping his own thighs—as a prelude to gesturing that the visitor's time was up.

*   *   *

William H. Herndon reported that his law partner's brain was warmed by action in telling a story and the reactions of his listeners. [AUTHOR'S COLLECTION]

Some who heard a sampling of Lincoln jokes were offended by them. As early as 1839, the *Illinois State Register* complained that his buffoonery was "assumed—assumed for effect, rather than being genuine." Before his first inauguration, *Harper's Weekly* told readers that the president-elect was a prankster who seemed to have no inkling of the nation's serious plight. Villard of the New York *Herald* found many of the president's yarns so coarse that he said he was disgusted at having to listen to them. Among cabinet members, only Lincoln's second secretary of war, Stanton, dared openly to reveal his dislike for presidential humor.

Hosts of his countrymen who never laid eyes upon the Rail-Splitter paid indirect tribute by laughing at stories said to have been told by him. In modern times, many Americans seem to feel that Lincoln stories tend to lower barriers. As a result, the perceived gulf between the chief executive and ordinary citizens is perhaps shortest in the case of the sixteenth president.

William H. Herndon and others who knew Abraham Lincoln intimately felt they knew why he spent so much time and energy joking. This exercise, several close acquaintances agreed, served to break Lincoln's frequent and deep periods of melancholy.

Since his partner's body was subject to poor circulation, said Herndon, he was in constant need of "oiling." When he told a story and reacted vigorously to it, more blood sent to the brain "aroused the whole man to an active condition." Judge David Davis, who played a key role in the momentous Republican nomination of 1860, went on record as being certain that "Lincoln's stories were merely devices to whistle down sadness." Artist Francis B. Carpenter, who was Lincoln's house guest for six months during 1864, concluded that laughter was "the president's life-preserver." Charles A. Dana pondered the enigma of hearty laughter in times of crisis and decided that it relieved both "the strain of mind under which Lincoln had so long been living" and "the natural gloom of a melancholy and desponding temperament."

If the judgment of Dana is correct, the moody and often melancholy man reared on farms might have lost his sanity had he not deliberately cultivated laughter.

Lincoln himself said little about his indulgence in humor, but in a contemplative moment once observed, "I laugh because I must not weep—that's all, that's all."

Several factors, rather than one, probably contributed to his indulgence in jokes and stories. Hence no firm explanation for this habitual practice can be offered. Were he alive and subjected to a modern press conference, perhaps the Civil War leader could explain what motivated his actions. Since he never did more than hint at some reasons for his use of humor, every analyst must weigh conjectures and arrive at what seems a reasonable explanation of conduct that often appears to have been bizarre.

34

What Accounts for Lincoln's
Rapid and Radical Changes?

OPPORTUNISM? CAPACITY FOR COMPROMISE? OR DRAMATIC PERSONAL GROWTH?

■

EVERY CHIEF EXECUTIVE has modified his positions and goals during his tenure in office. Abraham Lincoln's changes were frequent, often dramatic, and sometimes so sweeping that they constituted complete reversals.

Although it proved to be the decision that launched the Civil War, his dispatch of relief to Fort Sumter did not result from a modification of views. His firm inaugural promise to repossess forts and other installations signaled his intentions, despite the fact that multitudes failed to interpret them properly.

Treatment of captured sailors was a different matter. In a May 21, 1861, diplomatic dispatch, he summarized his policy toward such belligerents in one sentence: "We treat them as pirates." That was precisely what he had said he would do in his April 19 proclamation. But secessionists responded by selecting Federal officers captured at First Bull Run and making them hostages for the safety of their seamen. Abruptly, without explanation, the issue of piracy was dropped and was never revived. Clearly, events over which Lincoln had no control forced his hand.

An equally abrupt reversal of position centered upon dealings with elected officials of Maryland. Gen. Benjamin Butler was hardly established on Baltimore's Federal Hill before he advocated wholesale arrests. Orders from the president prevented him from pursuing his announced course. Yet less than half a year later Lincoln quietly assented to plans that led to the arrest of nineteen members of the legislature and the mayor of Baltimore. In the chief executive's judgment, rapid acceleration of hostilities required him to alter his stance.

Lincoln had no long-standing views, made public through speeches and letters, concerning piracy or the arrest of elected officials suspected of aiding insurrection.

In the case of war powers of the president, he had staked his political future on his convictions. President James K. Polk, he asserted, had far exceeded his constitutional authority by launching a war against Mexico. Only Congress, said the representative from Illinois, had power to declare war.

By what authority, then, did Lincoln call for 75,000 militia for three months of Federal service?

Troops designed to serve at his direction, said Lincoln, would not be engaged in warfare. They would act quickly to quell a domestic insurrection. Here, he clearly responded to changed circumstances by reasoning along lines that, in practice, led to alteration of his own principles.

The outbreak of war frequently persuaded him to break promises and pledges, often abandoning stated goals as well.

To the man who challenged Stephen A. Douglas at Peoria on October 16, 1854, a clause of the Declaration of Independence was seen as vital. All governments derive "their just powers from the consent of the governed!" Lincoln thundered that day. But to the sixteenth president, consent by citizens in so-called seceded states was not needed; unless these folk gave up their ways, military force must persuade them to follow Federal dictates.

When he was a notable spokesman against presidential actions leading to the Mexican War, Congressman Lincoln said he was positive that all peoples have a right to wage revolutions:

> Any people anywhere being inclined and having the power have the right to rise up and shake off the existing government, and form a new one that suits them better. This is a most valuable, a most sacred right—a right which we hope and believe is to liberate the world.

Yet in 1860–61 the author of these impassioned lines was convinced that persons in South Carolina, Alabama, Georgia, and other states of the South must be subdued by armed troops unless they accepted the government as it existed in Washington.

Lincoln firmly assured Garret Davis of Kentucky that the state could remain neutral unless processes of law and order were resisted. Soon, however, his subordinates were preparing shipments

Senator John J. Crittenden received shipments of weapons from Lincoln's agents during a time when the president was promising that Kentucky could maintain its neutrality. [NICOLAY & HAY, *ABRAHAM LINCOLN*]

of weapons designed for use by followers of Sen. John J. Crittenden and other staunch Unionists of Kentucky.

In his inaugural address he promised that there would be no invasion and stressed his adherence to this principle in later negotiations with Virginians. But on May 24, barely five weeks after the surrender of Fort Sumter, long lines of Federal troops marched across bridges of the Potomac into Virginia. They occupied Alexandria and seized the Arlington estate of Mrs. Robert E. Lee—moves explained as being purely defensive.

Six months later the chief executive's message to Congress stressed moderation in suppressing the insurrection. "I have been anxious and careful," he wrote, "that the inevitable conflict shall not degenerate into a violent and remorseless revolutionary struggle." Yet, more than any other American, it was Lincoln whose long-range goals and day-to-day decisions turned the Civil War into the nation's most bloody and deadly military conflict.

In early stages of the conflict, he promised the North as well as the South that Federal forces would "avoid any devastation, any destruction of, or interference with, property." But the rape of the Shenandoah Valley and the burning of Columbia, South Carolina, were among scores of military operations that involved destruction of civilian property on a colossal scale.

Lincoln solemnly assured the nation that property rights of so-called secessionists, including their ownership of slaves, would be

Arlington Mansion, owned by the wife of Robert E. Lee, was seized by Federal troops a few weeks after the president had pledged there would be no invasion of states claiming to have seceded. [LIBRARY OF CONGRESS]

respected. Partly in order to guarantee these rights, he told citizens everywhere that the Fugitive Slave Law would be rigidly enforced. But it was only a matter of months before runaway slaves were being called "contraband of war," a label that provided an excuse for refusing to return a fugitive to his owner. On New Year's Day 1863, this usage became obsolete; persons in Confederate-held regions were suddenly declared to have lost all property rights in slaves.

At age twenty-nine, with many of his life-shaping principles already firmly fixed, Lincoln spoke at the Springfield Lyceum. He saw potential for mass discontent, he warned, then gave his formula for "fortifying against it":

> Let every American, every lover of liberty, every well-wisher to his posterity swear by the blood of the Revolution never to violate in the least particular the laws of the country, and never to tolerate their violation by others. As the patriots of '76 did to the support of the Declaration of Independence, so to the support of the Constitution and laws let every American pledge his life, his property, and his sacred honor.

Much more than a product of youthful exuberance, this principle was embodied in Lincoln's First Inaugural Address. Noting that maintenance of all constitutional rights was calculated to bring universal contentment, he asserted that no constitutional right had been denied anyone. He then declared:

> Happily, the human mind is so constituted that no party can reach to the audacity of doing this. Think, if you can, of a single instance in which a plainly written provision of the Constitution has ever been denied.

Within weeks a presidential order—eventually extended to apply to the entire nation—denied the right of *habeas corpus* to persons living in the Washington-to-Baltimore military zone.

That was just the start, of course. Before the conflict was over, constitutional rights of multitudes in the North as well as in the South were flagrantly violated as a result of presidential actions taken in the name of wartime necessity.

Some of Lincoln's many changes in attitude stemmed from an evolution of his concept of his role as chief executive. Initially, he was scrupulous to consult his cabinet members, even when he had no intention of being guided by them. His early letters and telegrams to his generals are almost diffident in tone. They included numerous suggestions but few orders.

Soon he was writing, "You must remember that Abraham Lincoln

is president of the United States." To cabinet members he said in
1864, "My wish is that on this subject no remark be made nor question asked by any of you, here or elsewhere, now or hereafter." Within
weeks after appointing a general, he began telling him precisely
what he was expected to do. Without using the language of direct
threat, the president made it clear that any commander who failed to
win victories faced removal. Formal documents identified their author as "president of the United States, acting as the Commander in
Chief of the Army of the United States in time of actual rebellion and
war against the United States."

It was in this dual role that he expressed dismay at Gen. John C.
Frémont's proclamation freeing some of Missouri's slaves. Future
condition of persons in bondage, he informed the Pathfinder, "must
be settled according to laws made by lawmakers, and not by military
proclamations. The proclamation in the point in question is simply
'dictatorship.'" Yet he never regarded his own Emancipation Proclamation as dictatorial; it was an essential war measure and nothing
more.

Right of states, and states alone, to emancipate slaves within their
borders . . . Gradual emancipation with compensation and colonization . . . Property rights of slave owners in the District of Columbia
. . . Federal creation of new territories, leaving their citizens to determine whether or not slavery would be legal in them . . . Enlistment
and recruitment of blacks for military service . . .

On each of these issues, the man whose boyhood years were
largely spent in the Indiana wilderness modified, revised, or completely altered stated positions sometimes held for years.

A December 15, 1860, letter of the president-elect to John A.
Gilmer is headed "Strictly confidential." In it he assured his correspondent that he had never even thought of "employing slaves in
arsenals and dockyards" until he saw Gilmer's letter. Having been
presented with this idea, he continued, he had no thought of recom-
mending that it be adopted. Yet it was only a matter of months before
he not only sanctioned but actively encouraged use of runaway
slaves as laborers.

Even his views concerning suffrage for blacks did not remain un-
changed. In 1858 he was publicly opposed to "making voters or
jurors of Negroes." He then doubted that any man, woman, or child
favored "equality, social and political, between Negroes and white
men." Yet in his last public address he admitted to a personal preference. "The very intelligent Negroes and those who serve our cause as
soldiers" should be permitted to cast votes whose impact would be
the same as those cast by whites, he said.

Some of Abraham Lincoln's many sweeping changes in attitudes
and goals may have resulted from opportunism. Others suggest that

Some residents of Columbia, South Carolina, remembered that Abraham Lincoln had pledged that if war should come, there would be no destruction of property. [LIBRARY OF CONGRESS]

he experienced what was, from some perspectives, significant personal growth. Many broken promises and modified objectives can be attributed to a surprisingly flexible mental outlook that fostered compromise.

Yet in one respect he did not waver a hair's breadth.

He never explained why, very early, he became passionately devoted to preservation of the Union. Origin of that passion is a riddle whose answer is concealed in the life of a man who was scrupulously secretive about personal matters.

Although its roots remain mysterious, effects of that passion are known to the entire world; for it was his unswerving commitment to the mystical pre-existent Union of states that caused him to wage a relentless war that ceased only upon unconditional surrender of the enemy.

In his three-volume narrative of *The Civil War,* Shelby Foote ponders the relationship between Lincoln and McClellan and concludes of the president that:

> Some might praise him for being flexible, while others called
> him slippery, when in truth they were both two words for just
> one thing. To argue the point was to insist on a distinction

that did not exist. Lincoln was out to win the war; and that
was all he was out to do . . . he would keep his word to any
man only so long as keeping it would help to win the war. If
keeping it meant otherwise, he broke it.*

Many—perhaps all but a few—of Lincoln's personal changes were
made in response to his all-encompassing goal of military victory as
a means of preserving the Union. Over and over, the man who was
the chief guiding spirit of the Civil War said he did not control
events. Rather, he said, he was himself controlled by events.

---

*Shelby Foote, *The Civil War.* Vol. 1, *Fort Sumter to Perryville* (New York:
Random House, 1958), 247ff.

35

*Why Was the Declaration of
Independence Seen As*

THE CORNERSTONE OF THE INDISSOLUBLE UNION?

■

AT OTTAWAY, ILLINOIS, site of the first formal debate between Douglas and Lincoln, the crowd far exceeded the expectations of either candidate for the U.S. Senate. Congressman William Kellogg introduced Lincoln, who spoke with great passion, soon captivating the vast audience.

Only the Chicago *Press and Tribune* claimed to give readers a verbatim transcription of a brief segment of Lincoln's lengthy speech. Having denounced Steven A. Douglas's views concerning slavery, he made what a Chicago reporter considered "one of the finest efforts of public speaking I ever listened to."

Speaking of the Declaration of Independence, Lincoln conceded that of the thirteen states that adopted it, twelve permitted slavery. Without exception, these dozen states "greatly deplored the evil," he said. As a result, they later included in the Constitution a provision designed to bring the domestic evil to an end by abolition of the slave trade.

Having pointed out that Douglas and others supported "doctrines conflicting with the great landmarks of the Declaration of Independence," the would-be senator thundered a challenge:

> If you have been inclined to believe that all men were not created equal in those inalienable rights enumerated by our chart of liberty, let me entreat you to come back.
> Return to the fountain whose waters spring close by the blood of the Revolution! Think nothing of me—take no thought for the political fate of any man whomsoever—

but come back to the truths that are in the Declaration of
Independence.

I charge you to drop every paltry and insignificant
thought about any man's success. It is nothing; I am
nothing; Judge Douglas is nothing. But do not destroy
that immortal emblem of Humanity—the Declaration of
American Independence.

An undated memorandum of the same period, probably written in
preparation for a speech, begins with what appears to have been
Abraham Lincoln's personal credo: "I believe the declaration that 'all
men are created equal' is the great fundamental principle upon
which our free institutions rest."

Among the voluminous Lincoln papers, William H. Herndon found
a notebook about four inches by six inches in size. Originally blank,
it was filled with clippings pasted between occasional scribbled sentences. Containing about 185 items, this workbook prepared for
Lincoln's debates with Douglas is headed by a copy of the second
paragraph of the Declaration of Independence.

At Chicago on July 10, 1858, the aspirant for the U.S. Senate
termed the Declaration "the electric cord . . . that links the hearts of
patriotic and liberty-loving men together." He repeatedly said that he
saw the phrase concerning equality as having been included, not for
1776, but for the future. In Philadelphia, only days away from becoming chief executive of the nation, he described that "sentiment"
as having given liberty "not alone to the people of this country, but
hope to all the world, for all future time."

"I have never had a feeling politically that did not spring from the
sentiments embodied in the Declaration of Independence," he said.
Shortly afterward he vowed that he "would rather be assassinated on
this spot than surrender" this principle.

Words alone cannot convey the depth of Lincoln's emotional involvement. According to a frequent listener, when eulogizing the
Declaration of Independence, Lincoln "extended out his arms, palms
of his hands upward somewhat at about the same degree as if ap-
pealing to some superior power for assistance and support; or that
he might embrace the spirit of that which he so dearly loved." At
least briefly transformed when he assumed this posture, "he seemed
inspired, fresh, from the hands of his Creator."

Though seldom recognized as such, the Gettysburg Address is a
fervent eulogy to the Declaration of Independence. In it the birth of
the nation is linked, not to the year the Constitution was ratified,
but to 1776, the year of the Declaration.

Total fidelity to the spirit of the Declaration, Lincoln insisted repeatedly, required a return to the spirit of the Founding Fathers who

Norman P. Judd heard Lincoln denounce the Fugitive Slave Law as ungodly—while insisting that since it was the law, it must be upheld. [NICOLAY & HAY, *ABRAHAM LINCOLN*]

framed it. Such a course of action would constitute a second American Revolution, for much that Americans sanctioned—slavery in particular—was far from "the pure fresh, free breath of the revolution."

"Whenever any form of government becomes destructive" of life, liberty, and the pursuit of happiness, he said, "it is the right of the people to alter or abolish it, and to institute new government." At Peoria on October 4, 1854, he warned, "Our republican robe is soiled and trailed in the dust." Then he challenged, "Let us turn and wash it white, in the spirit, if not the blood, of the Revolution." Only by readoption of the Declaration of Independence, he said, would it be possible again to declare that "all men are created equal."

In the last of his debates with Douglas, the man from Springfield asserted that the nature of liberty was the real issue. "Let us readopt the Declaration of Independence," he pleaded, "and with it, the practices, and policy, which harmonize with it." Such a course of action would do more than simply save the Union, he asserted. It would "so save it as to make and to keep it forever worthy of the saving."

Far more was involved than mere saving of the Union. "German, Irish, French, and Scandinavian" Americans who had come since 1776 had a stake in the document prepared that year. "They have a right to claim it as though they were blood of the blood, and flesh of the flesh, of the men who wrote that Declaration, and so they are!" As "the standard maxim for free society," the Declaration was "constantly spreading and deepening its influence, and augmenting the happiness and value of life to all people of all colors everywhere."

Thomas Jefferson's document, said Lincoln, appeared on the surface to be merely revolutionary. But it was based upon "an abstract truth, applicable to all men and all times." Hence the struggle to preserve the Declaration as envisioned by the Founding Fathers would affect "the whole great family of man" now and hereafter, throughout the world.

Despite the fervor with which he stressed the "equality" of the Declaration, Lincoln was aware that some persons did not accept his views concerning this cardinal principle. Douglas's Kansas-Nebraska Bill had potential for extending slavery into new regions. This factor, said Lincoln, put the senator "into an open war with the very fundamental principles of civil liberty, criticizing the Declaration of Independence."

By "his example and vast influence," he charged, Douglas was muzzling the July 4 cannon that thundered the "annual joyous return" of equality, for Douglas denied that the principle applied to Negroes. Such a view, said Lincoln, made "a mere wreck—a mangled ruin—of our glorious Declaration!" Years later, President Lincoln conceded that Douglas may not have been the first person to suggest this idea. Perhaps he learned of this idea earlier from U.S. Supreme Court Chief Justice Roger B. Taney, Lincoln declared.

Actually, John C. Calhoun of South Carolina may have been responsible for new national debate concerning the meaning of the liberty cherished by the Founding Fathers. In 1848 he denounced the clause concerning freedom and equality. Calling it "the most false and dangerous of all political errors," Calhoun declared that "there is not a word of truth in it."

Denunciation of the nearsightedness of those who interpreted the vital clause to mean "all men are created equal, except Negroes" was a frequent emphasis in Lincoln's prepresidential speeches.

He was aware of some contradictions in his own views, for he recognized he also qualified the concepts of freedom and equality. The authors of the Declaration, he admitted, did not intend to call all men equal in all respects. "Certainly the Negro is not our equal in color," he told a Springfield audience in 1858; "perhaps not in many other respects. Still, in the right to put into his mouth the bread that his own hands have earned, he is the equal of every other man, white or black. All I ask for the Negro is that if you do not like him, let him alone. If God gave him but little, that little let him enjoy."

Despite the primacy of the Declaration of Independence in Lincoln's thought, he simultaneously stressed the centrality of the U.S. Constitution and of laws based upon it. "To the support of the Constitution and laws let every American pledge his life, his property, and his sacred honor," he challenged listeners in 1838. Twenty years later, his attitude had not changed. "I do not propose to destroy, or alter, or disregard the Constitution," he told a Peoria audience. "I stand to it, fairly, fully, and firmly."

Lincoln found important new meaning in the words of the document adopted by Founding Fathers in Independence Hall. [HARPER'S ENCYCLOPEDIA OF U.S. HISTORY]

It was from this point of view that he stressed the importance of his 1861 oath of office. "It was in the oath I took," he said in retrospect, "that I would, to the best of my ability, preserve, protect, and defend the Constitution of the United States. I could not take the office without taking the oath." No sentence of the inaugural address—not even a clause within a sentence—suggests that on March 4, 1861, Abraham Lincoln expected to do anything except faithfully conform to the Constitution in dealing with problems of a divided nation.

To Norman B. Judd he once admitted that he saw the Fugitive Slave Law as being ungodly. "But it is the law of the land," he pointed out, "and we must obey it as we find it." One man he wanted in his cabinet, Gideon Welles, had expressed reservations concerning enforcement of the Fugitive Slave Law. Before admitting him into his inner circle, the new president exacted from him a pledge to support the law—even in Massachusetts.

As Lincoln saw the two documents, the Declaration and the Constitution were in conflict on a central issue; the Constitution included stipulations that protected interests of slave owners. That made the latter document flawed, he said.

According to Lincoln, our revered Founding Fathers permitted this apparently contradictory state of affairs because they confidently expected slavery to disappear. They deliberately avoided any mention of slavery in the Constitution, hiding the concept away "just as an afflicted man hides a wen or cancer which he dares not cut out at once, lest he bleed to death—with the promise, nevertheless that the cutting may begin at a certain time." Douglas's challenger said that "ambiguous, roundabout, and mystical" language was adopted by the Founding Fathers so that when slavery disappeared, "there should be nothing on the face of the great charter of liberty suggesting that such a thing had ever existed among us."

Since slavery had not disappeared—indeed, was in danger of spreading—the sacred Constitution was, in Lincoln's thought, subsidiary to the Declaration of Independence. It was the Declaration, rather than the Constitution, that he described as the source of his entire political outlook. Because it proclaimed freedom and equality, to him it constituted "a law higher than the Constitution."

Ultraradical from the perspective of the late twentieth century, Lincoln's doctrine was actually conservative from some points of view. Abolitionist William Lloyd Garrison addressed a meeting of the Anti-Slavery Society in 1854. After having denounced the Fugitive Slave Law, he read from the Constitution those clauses that sanctioned "the peculair institution." Shouting that the Constitution was no less than "a covenant with death and an agreement with hell," he publicly burned a copy of it.

Had he been present in Framingham Grove, Massachusetts, that momentous day, Abraham Lincoln would have been horrified at burning the Constitution. Over and over he insisted that he had sworn to uphold the entire compact, including those sections of which he did not approve. Yet when the war seemed to drag on endlessly, with no sure prospect of Union victory in sight, he adopted a working compromise.

According to his personal formula, the entire Constitution was sacred and must be obeyed, but it was all right under some circumstances to ignore a few of its details. Thus the president indicated willingness at times to violate a section of the Constitution in order to preserve the whole compact. On April 4, 1864, he expressed this principle in a letter to Albert G. Hodges:

> Often a limb must be amputated to save a life; but a life is never wisely given to save a limb. I felt that measures otherwise unconstitutional might become lawful by becoming indispensable to the preservation of the nation. Right or wrong, I assume this ground, and now avow it.

"Rebels," he once commented to Salmon P. Chase in a discussion over the legality of a fiscal proposal, "are violating the Constitution to destroy the Union. I will violate the Constitution, if necessary, to save the Union: and I suspect, Chase, that the Constitution is going to have a rough time of it before we get done with this row."

Denounced by former Supreme Court Justice Benjamin R. Curtis for having taking "extra-legal measures" against civil liberty, Lincoln borrowed from his famous store of wit to frame a reply. Contending that his wartime measures would be forgotten as soon as peace was restored, he argued, "I never heard of a patient acquiring a taste for emetics by being obliged to take one now and then." Turning to more conventional language, he insisted that his government could not stand "if it indulges constitutional constructions by which men in open rebellion against it are to be accounted, man for man, the equals of those who maintain their loyalty to it."

Even the U.S. Supreme Court could be ignored or defied under some circumstances, he believed: "If the policy of the government is to be irrevocably fixed by decision of the Supreme Court . . . the people will have ceased to be their own rulers, having resigned their government into the hands of that tribunal."

In Abraham Lincoln's view, the Mexican War had been "unnecessarily and unconstitutionally begun by the president of the United States." Yet his own decisions that affected the destiny of both the North and the South were defended as legitimate because of wartime necessity. Even the Emancipation Proclamation—*especially* the Emancipation Proclamation—was seen by President Lincoln as of doubtful constitutionality except as a temporary military measure.

Responding to public criticism in 1863, he outlined his position clearly:

> If I be wrong on this question of constitutional power, my error lies in believing that certain proceedings are constitutional when, in cases of rebellion or invasion, the public safety required them.
>
> In other words, the Constitution is not in its application in all respects the same in case of rebellion or invasion involving the public safety, as it is in times of profound peace and public security.

Liberty and equality were the foundation stones of the democratic experiment, Lincoln insisted, They produced both the Union and the Constitution. Hence the civil war waged to preserve the Union was made necessary by the Declaration of Independence. He never explicitly described the war in these terms; yet much that the president did and said was designed to bring about "a second American Revolution" that would elevate the Declaration into actual rather than theoretical supremacy.

36

*What Accounts for His
Interest in*

Signs, Omens, Portents, and Dreams?

■

SECRETARY OF THE NAVY Gideon Welles, who kept detailed notes, confided to his journal that the cabinet meeting of April 14, 1865, was "special." Victorious Gen. Ulysses S. Grant gave a personal account of the surrender of Gen. Robert E. Lee at Appomattox.

Prior to Grant's arrival, Welles and Salmon P. Chase were alone with the president for a few minutes. Abraham Lincoln took this opportunity to confide in the man whom he initially regarded with doubt but had come to trust implicitly. He commented that he had an unusually strange dream the previous night that "belongs to the Navy Department, since it dealt with water." According to Welles, the president then continued:

> I seemed to be in a singular and indescribable vessel that was moving with great rapidity toward a dark and indefinite shore.
>
> I had this same dream preceding the firing on Sumter, the battles of Bull Run, Antietam, Gettysburg, Stone's River, Vicksburg, Wilmington, and others.
>
> Though victory has not always followed it, some important event has. I have no doubt, this time, that a battle has taken place or is about to be fought and that Johnston will be beaten.
>
> My dream must relate to Sherman. My thoughts are in that direction, and I know of no other very important event which is very likely just now to occur.

Welles recorded these remarks by Lincoln on the evening of April 14, perhaps about the time of the "very important event" that followed after the president and his wife took their seats in Ford's Theater. A few days later Welles was startled to learn that other history had been made. Three days after he recorded his chief's strange dream, Joseph E. Johnston met with Gen. William T. Sherman near Durham's Station, North Carolina. There was no battle; instead, the two commanders conferred about terms under which the last significant Confederate army would surrender to Sherman.

Abraham Lincoln's letters and papers include no mention of his revelations to Welles. That was characteristic of the highly secretive man; documents produced by him or signed by him are silent concerning what seems to have been a compulsive interest in signs, omens, portents, and dreams.

Battles mentioned by Lincoln that Welles remembered to include in his list were not in chronological or alphabetical order. Instead, they represented a jumble that may have poured from the president's lips without advance thought. Except for Bull Run and Antietam, military encounters noted by Welles resulted in Federal victories. Since Lincoln stipulated that such an outcome did not always follow

To the chief executive who admitted being superstitious, the drawn battle at Antietam was a sign that he should issue the preliminary Emancipation Proclamation. [LESLIE'S ILLUSTRATED NEWSPAPER]

one of his repetitive dreams about moving over water, he implied that the list of battles cited was only partial.

In the case of Antietam, fought on September 17, 1862, Lincoln found meaning so special that he discussed it with members of his cabinet. Again, the diary of Welles is the most detailed source of information concerning symbolic potency of the battle. It is, however, confirmed by recollections of Chase.

According to the secretary of the navy, when cabinet members assembled on the morning of Monday, September 22, 1862, Lincoln turned to the subject of emancipation. He read his draft of a proposed proclamation, and vigorous discussion ensued. Welles then noted that:

> In the course of the discussion on this paper, which was long, earnest, and, on the general principle involved, harmonious, he remarked that he had made a vow, a covenant, that if God gave us the victory in the approaching battle, he would consider it an indication of Divine will, and that it was his duty to move forward in the cause of emancipation.

Revelation of the fashion in which Lincoln was led to proceed in a matter about which he had long hesitated caused Welles to comment to himself, "God decided this question in favor of the slaves."

Judged by military standards, Antietam was a drawn battle. Combined casualties of the two armies made their meeting near Sharpsburg, Maryland, on September 17, 1862, the bloodiest single day of the Civil War. Both Federal and Confederate forces were totally exhausted and debilitated at the end of the day; neither was in any condition to resume the conflict. During the night, Lee's forces withdrew from the field and recrossed the Potomac in the process of withdrawing from Maryland. Only in the sense that Gen. George B. McClellan's Army of the Potomac remained at the site of battle could Antietam be considered a Union victory.

Yet Lincoln decided to proceed with the Emancipation Proclamation because he chose to see Antietam as a sign that Providence approved of his tentative plans.

Two years prior to Antietam, Abraham Lincoln stretched out on a horse hair sofa in his Springfield home. He was weary but exultant. Telegrams of November 6 had dissipated all doubts; now he really was president-elect of the United States!

On the verge of dropping off to sleep, he glanced into a mirror across the room, tilted at just the right angle to show him his reflection. To his astonishment, he clearly saw his own torso—surmounted by two faces instead of one. Puzzled and concerned, he tried to re-create the circumstances and at least twice more saw "a Lincoln with two faces, one of them very pale."

*Confederate general Joseph
E. Johnston surrendered to
Sherman without a fight, in
spite of Lincoln's having
deemed that Sherman
would be engaged in a
mighty battle.* [HARPER'S
ENCYCLOPEDIA OF U.S.
HISTORY]

After discussing the bizarre phenomenon with Mary Todd Lincoln,
he and she may have agreed that the strange image in the mirror
was an omen. It meant that the man from Springfield would be
elected to two terms as president; but since one face was much paler
than the other, it seemed to warn that he would not live to complete
his second four-year stint in the Executive Mansion.

To many persons, so strange an optical effect might have been
discussed and analyzed—only to be forgotten immediately. Not so in
the case of the attorney reared on the frontier. He was so impressed
by his experience that he never forgot it. On the evening of June 8,
1864, when his renomination was official, he told F. B. Carpenter
and John Hay about the "very singular occurrence" of 1860. So vivid
was the experience, he confessed, that in the Executive Mansion he
had tried to re-create the situation by arranging a couch and a mirror as he remembered them to have been in Springfield. Since he did
not get the same result, he told Carpenter and Hay that he believed
the image could have been "the result of some principle of refraction
or optics which I did not understand."

Shortly afterward, he repeated his story to Noah Brooks. Hay, who
later became U.S. secretary of the interior, was so mystified by the
Springfield incident that he described it for *Harper's Weekly* only
three months after the assassination of his chief.

On March 4, 1861, the day on which he took the oath of office in a
wing of the U.S. Capitol, the new president looked about himself. For

So long as work continued on the unfinished Capitol, said the chief executive, he would remain at the helm of the nation. [NATIONAL ARCHIVES]

the first time, said those who stood close to him that day, he fully realized that the building used for the ceremony was far from finished. He surveyed it solemnly, then commented that he was glad that gangs of laborers would spend many months there. "I take it as a sign that so long as work continues on the Capitol, the Union will continue," he reputedly commented.

With work on the Capitol still far from completed, in June 1863 Mary Todd Lincoln and their son Tad departed for a shopping expedition in Philadelphia. They had been in the city only a few hours before a June 9 telegram was dispatched by Abraham Lincoln: "THINK YOU BETTER PUT TAD'S PISTOL AWAY. I HAD AN UGLY DREAM ABOUT HIM."

Perhaps somewhat mentally retarded and hyperactive, little Tad was obsessed with the idea of becoming a soldier in his father's army. He delighted in wearing a uniform tailored for him and insisted upon carrying a regulation weapon. When his mother took it away from him after receiving a warning from his father, Tad sulked. Still, the pistol was left behind in the hotel when they returned to Washington. They had been back for only a few hours before the boy's father relented and sent a second telegram to Philadelphia, directed this time to the owner of the hotel: "TAD IS TEASING ME TO HAVE YOU FORWARD HIS PISTOL TO HIM."

Months later, another premonition so troubled the president that he was unable to sleep in his City Point, Virginia, quarters. According to his widow, he had a vivid dream in which he saw the Executive Mansion consumed by flames. He was so troubled by this dream, said she, that he "sent me up the river." Only when she met Secretary of War Edwin M. Stanton and was escorted to the undamaged Executive Mansion was she able to send reassuring word to her troubled husband.

Lincoln's best-known dream does not focus upon structures such as the Capitol and the Executive Mansion, or even upon major battles. Instead, it is highly personal—interpreted by him to presage his own death.

Discussing dreams and their nature with his wife and Ward H. Lamon during the second week of April 1865, Lincoln described a recent experience. He had worked late and began to dream almost as soon as he was prone, he explained. Muffled sobs heard in the dream state drew him to the East Room. He said that in his dream he entered it, then continued:

> Before me was a catafalque, on which rested a corpse wrapped in funeral vestments. Around it were stationed sol-

Little Tad Lincoln was inordinately fond of his pistol, but after having had "an ugly dream," his father took it away from him.
[NICOLAY & HAY, *ABRAHAM LINCOLN*]

diers who were acting as guards; and there was a throng of people, some gazing mournfully upon the corpse, whose face was covered, others weeping pitifully.

"Who is dead?" I demanded of one of the soldiers.

"The president," was his answer. "He was killed by an assassin."

Then came a loud burst of grief from the crowd, which awoke me from my dream. I slept no more that night; and although it was only a dream, I have been strangely annoyed by it ever since.

Lamon, who venerated Lincoln and spent much of his time as a volunteer bodyguard, made the story public almost as soon as the bullet of John Wilkes Booth caused the dream to seem to have been prophetic. W. H. Crook, an official Executive Mansion bodyguard, vowed that the president had told him about having dreamed three nights, hand-running, of his assassination.

Life on the edge of the expanding nation, in frontier Indiana and Illinois, was a significant factor in shaping Abraham Lincoln's beliefs and outlook. When a well in the community went dry, the homesteader did not seek a geologist; he sent for a dowser who used a forked wand to locate the site to dig a new well. When a child was bitten by a rabid dog, parents did not try to get a doctor; there was none. Their only hope was to find the owner of a mad stone and persuade him to place it upon the broken skin "in order to suck out the poison."

Though his fertile mind soon took him far away in imagination, frontier incidents and beliefs may have persuaded Lincoln to give more than ordinary credence to signs and portents. In a letter of July 4, he discussed with his friend Joshua Speed the fears both had about the marriage of Speed. "I was drawn to it as by fate," wrote Lincoln, who continued, "I always was superstitious and as part of my superstition, I believed God made me one of the instruments of bringing your Fanny and you together."

John T. Stuart, once Lincoln's law partner and long an intimate friend, had a different explanation. According to him, the future president suffered from digestive abnormalities. "His liver failed to work properly—did not secrete bile—and his bowels were equally as inactive."

If the role of digestive disturbances is debatable, that of visions in literature is not. A vivid passage in one of the few books owned by young Lincoln, Mason Weems's *Life of Washington*, deals with a dream that haunted the Washington family. According to the imaginative biographer—whose influence upon Lincoln is believed to have been significant—a dream about the burning of the Washington home meant that the nation he founded would experience civil war.

More important and influential even than the Weems biography was the Bible, over which young Lincoln pored in order to memorize many passages and to absorb numerous figures of speech. As president of the United States, he told Lamon that dreams are prominent in sixteen chapters of the Old Testament plus four or five in the New Testament. On the night after he first dreamed of assassination, he said to Lamon, he opened the Bible at random and found himself reading of Jacob's wonderful dream, as described in Genesis, chapter 28. Everywhere he turned in the sacred book that night, he recalled, it seemed that his eyes fell upon an account of a vision, a dream, or a supernatural visitation.

Frontier life in which superstition was one of the basic ingredients . . . Bouts of acute depression that may or may not have been rooted in malfunction of bodily organs . . . Weems's account of a Washington dream about a burning house . . . Story after vivid story in the Bible . . .

All these factors doubtless affected the way in which the man whose boyhood was spent in Indiana interpreted and reacted to dreams and portents. Yet another influence may have been at work.

Is it possible that a man who was convinced that he had been selected to do the work of Providence, or fate, was continually looking for signs and signals that would direct that work? If that was the case, the degree to which reliance upon omens and dreams affected crucial wartime decisions is a matter for conjecture only.

In the case of concluding to proceed with the Emancipation Proclamation, Lincoln is his own clear witness that when a dream directed him to look for a sign, he found it in bloody confrontation on the banks of Antietam Creek. As a result, he issued a preliminary draft of the most significant and far-reaching edict of the Civil War.

37

Why Was He Casual When
Constantly Confronted by

ASSASSINATION THREATS AND OTHER DANGERS?

■

Directly after the Lincoln and Douglas campaign in 1858, soon after it was over, he, Lincoln, commenced receiving through the post office all manner of odd pictures cut out of newspapers, expressive of pain, starvation, sorrow, grief, etc.

Frequently threatening letters were received by him through the post office, all of which he burned at the time. He said to me once, "I feel as if I should meet with some terrible end," and so this great man felt through time and space instinctively his coming doom.

Writing to Lincoln biographer Jesse Weik in 1885, William H. Herndon relied upon his memory in describing the aftermath of the famous debates. But at age sixty-seven his memory was remarkably keen and focused; since the 1860 Republican nomination of his one-time partner, the story of Lincoln's life had been his all-absorbing passion.

Once the man from Springfield became a candidate for the presidency, everyone closely associated with him learned that he was constantly subjected to threats, mostly anonymous. Recalling this period, Lincoln told artist Francis B. Carpenter in 1864:

Soon after I was nominated at Chicago, I began to receive letters threatening my life. The first one or two made me uncomfortable, but I came at length to look for a regular installment of this kind of correspondence in every week's mail. It is no uncommon thing to receive them even now, but

A broken glass negative prepared by Alexander Gardner four days before the assassination, shows a president who was war-weary but still unconcerned about his personal safety. [LIBRARY OF CONGRESS]

they have ceased to give me any apprehension. There is nothing like getting used to things.

Secession of one Cotton Belt state after another caused Lincoln's intimates and key national leaders of the Republican party to fear violence. Hence they tried to arrange for strict security during the trip of the president-elect from Springfield to the nation's capital. Norman B. Judd may have been responsible for putting detective Allan Pinkerton aboard the special train, whose armed guards included Ward Hill Lamon. Officials of the Great Western Railroad Company issued a special time card for use on February 11, 1861:

It is very important that this train should pass over the road in safety. Red is the signal for danger, but any signal apparently intended to indicate alarm must be regarded, the train stopped, and the meaning of it ascertained.

On the roundabout journey that included numerous stops made to greet admirers or to deliver speeches, railroad crews met nothing that appeared to pose unusual danger. But in Philadelphia, Frederick Seward came to the presidential party with dire warnings. Threat of violence in Baltimore was great, reported the son of the Republican leader chosen to serve as secretary of state. At his fa-

President-elect Lincoln reached Washington from Springfield in safety, regretting that aides had persuaded him to change his schedule because of threats of assassination. [ALLAN PINKERTON, THE SPY OF THE REBELLION]

ther's insistence, young Seward begged the president-elect to alter his announced route.

At first Abraham Lincoln shook his head in refusal. But under the insistent demands of Judd, Pinkerton, and Lamon, he reluctantly agreed to pass through the troubled city half a day ahead of schedule. Later, he grumbled at having made such a concession to fear— for the clandestine journey evoked a stream of cartoons that mocked him as having traveled in disguise.

Plans for his inauguration were made by the out-going Buchanan administration, so he had no control over them. Soldiers were stationed on roof tops of buildings along the parade route. Elite squadrons guarded vehicles in their ceremonial trip along Pennsylvania Avenue. At the unfinished Capitol, riflemen were stationed in every window that overlooked the platform erected for ceremonies. To the surprise of many, there was no attempt by Virginia secessionists or anyone else to assassinate Lincoln or even to disrupt ceremonies.

That closely guarded inaugural was the last occasion on which the new president permitted elaborate and highly visible security precautions.

At the Executive Mansion, there were no guards until the Civil War had dragged on for three weary years. Visitors could and sometimes did walk into the place, heavily armed. Often they wandered about the big building at will. On many occasions, the president greeted two thousand or more members of the public. No attempt was made to check identities or to search for concealed weapons.

Gen. Henry Halleck frequently used an aide, Col. Charles G. Halpine, as a messenger. During one of his frequent encounters with Lincoln, something was said about security. "It would never do," said the chief executive, "for a president to have guards with drawn sabres at his door—as if he fancied he were, or were trying to be, or were assuming to be, an emperor."

Halpine was aghast. Later he wrote that on his visits to the Executive Mansion he was troubled by "the utterly unprotected condition of the president's person." Doors leading into the building were open all day and well into the night, he remembered. "I have many times entered the mansion and walked up to the room of the two private secretaries, as late as nine or ten o'clock at night, without seeing or being challenged by a single soul."

The intensity of the Civil War reached such a peak that aides acted in November 1864 without consulting the president. Four officers selected by the Washington chief of police were stationed at the Executive Mansion. Two were on duty from 8:00 A.M. to 4:00 P.M.; for the remainder of the day, only one guard was present. This meant that the president made his well-known nightly visits to the telegraph office of the War Department with a single guard at his side. At his insistence, this man and his three comrades always wore plain clothes. If a policeman should be seen accompanying him, Lincoln directed, the officer must be dressed so he would appear to be "a casual friend, a petitioner, or a seeker after an office."

When he traveled about the capital, the president insisted that security—if any—had to be relaxed and casual. During the six months he lived at the Executive Mansion, artist Carpenter often strolled "at a late hour of the night with the president, without escort."

Gen. Benjamin Butler once confronted his chief with the question, "Is it known that you ride alone at night out to the Soldiers' Home?"

"Oh, yes," replied Lincoln, "when business detains me until late."

Pondering dangers of riding unguarded in an open carriage or on horseback to the site three miles beyond the city's limits, Butler spoke plainly, "I think you peril too much. We have tonight passed half a dozen places where a well-directed bullet might have taken you off."

Lincoln retorted casually: "Oh, assassination is not an American crime."

As late as Independence Day 1864, the president who knew that city streets included some secessionists, refused to travel with a guard of twenty men. "I believe I need no escort," he told a military commander. "Unless the secretary of war directs, none need attend me."

Any inventor who claimed to have developed a new weapon found it easy to get access to Lincoln and to be close to him for an hour or more. William H. Seward once made a caustic remark hinting that he considered his chief to be somewhat deranged. Only a lunatic, said the secretary of state, would frequently expose himself to possible death by an accidental explosion or deliberate use of a gun offered for demonstration.

But if potential danger was envisioned at testing grounds and on the lawn of the Executive Mansion, real danger was encountered in at least one battle. A strong Confederate force struck at the capital in 1864. Danger was so great that on July 10 the president was moved to telegraph to a Baltimore commitee: "I HOPE NEITHER BALTIMORE OR WASHINGTON WILL BE SACKED."

That night, he rode with Gen. James A. Hardie on a tour to inspect forts that ringed the city. Reluctantly, he agreed to abandon his summer abode, the Soldiers' Home, for the more secure Executive Mansion. On the following morning he rode to the front, then repaired to Fort Stevens.

From a parapet of the fort, he peered toward the direction from which enemy troops were expected to strike. Ordered by a soldier to climb down, he obeyed without revealing his identity. But back at the same spot about 4:00 P.M. on July 12, he again watched from a parapet. This time, Confederate minié balls were whizzing directly toward the installation. When a soldier standing near the president was hit, Gen. Horatio Wright suggested that the commander in chief should get out of danger. According to stories told by soldiers who were present, Lincoln did not respond to Wright's warning. Capt. Oliver Wendell Holmes, Jr., who saw what was happening, is said to have shouted, "Get down, you fool!" Only then did Lincoln move from the vulnerable spot.

Most aides stopped voicing warnings since they knew Lincoln would not heed them. Secretary of War Edwin M. Stanton was an exception. On July 9, 1864, he dispatched a special message reporting that a War Department watchman had seen a strange horseman following the presidential carriage. This warning came about the time that the New York *Tribune* reported discovery of a Confederate plot. A band of five hundred to one thousand men with headquarters in Richmond, said the newspaper, had made plans to abduct the president. Failing in that attempt, they were said to be sworn to give their lives to assassinate him.

Lamon never tired of stressing to his long-time friend that his life

Although he wept at news that Senator Edward D. Baker had been killed in action, Lincoln faced death so frequently that he shrugged off attempts to provide him with security. [NICOLAY & HAY, *ABRAHAM LINCOLN*]

was in constant danger. He should not walk alone at night, urged Lamon. Under no circumstances should he indulge in his favorite pastime—attending the theater—without being sure that veteran guards were on hand. "You know that your life is sought after," he insisted repeatedly. "It will be taken unless you are more cautious; you may have many enemies within our own lines."

Nothing that Lincoln heard from Stanton, Lamon, the *Tribune*, or any other voice led to a change in Lincoln's outlook and habits. Although every war zone was suspected of having been infiltrated by secessionists, the president made long trips through them. In May 1862 he spent four days at Fort Monroe. Five months later, he visited Harpers Ferry for seventy-two hours. He spent so much time at headquarters of Gen. George McClellan and Gen. Ulysses Grant that he was photographed at both sites.

On April 4, 1865, he brushed warnings aside and personally inspected just-captured Richmond, whose streets bristled with Confederate civilians and ex-soldiers. His "security detail," consisted of fifteen or more men and his pistol-packing eleven-year-old son, Tad. Often gesturing for guards to stay where they were, he abandoned them to sit in the chair used by Jefferson Davis. Later he rode through the streets—unguarded—in an army ambulance.

Having made plans to attend Ford's Theater ten days later, he ordered his most persistent bodyguard—Lamon—to Richmond. General and Mrs. Grant were invited to join the Lincolns for a performance of *Our American Cousin*. Probably because Julia Grant despised Mary Todd Lincoln, the guests of honor made a last-minute excuse.

A few hours after having told the cabinet of his recurring dream of a ship moving toward "a dark and indefinite shore," the president headed for the theater. He was accompanied by Mrs. Lincoln, Clara Harris, and Maj. Henry Rathbone. A single guard stationed outside the presidential box is believed to have left his post to watch the performance.

On the night he was fatally wounded, Abraham Lincoln was his usual fearless self. Despite at least five years of constant threats against his life and regardless of warnings repeatedly voiced by friends and aides, he refused to sanction anything other than the most perfunctory of security measures. Had Lincoln been more cautious, John Wilkes Booth would not have found it so easy to reach his mark.

A final mystery of the living Lincoln can be reduced to a single sentence: *Why was he casual when constantly confronted with assassination threats and other dangers?*

Firm answers to this riddle are suspect. At least four sets of conjectures may hint at a solution.

1. Familiarity with danger may have bred carelessness with regard to it. A major task of Secretary William O. Stoddard was the screening of incoming mail, which reached the Executive Mansion at the rate of two hundred to three hundred letters a day. Always, many of them contained threats; on some days, letters of this sort constituted a majority. Lincoln repeatedly emphasized his view that any threatening letter had to have been penned by a lunatic or a crank. Consequently, such a communication was categorized by Stoddard as "having no scare in it" and was tossed aside.

2. By 1865 the state of his health—which may or may not have been greatly affected by the Marfan syndrome—could have caused him to believe that the end of his life was near. At least since 1848, he had frequently and publicly described himself as being old. "My old withered dry eyes are full of tears," he said that year in the aftermath of a dramatic speech by Congressman Alexander H. Stephens. In a letter of the same year he called himself "one of the old men."

A decade later he apologized to a Chicago audience for delivering a tedious speech from "an old man that has to put on spectacles." At Ottawa, Illinois, in the same year he assured listeners, "I am no longer a young man."

On the day before his fifty-second birthday, the president-elect told Springfield admirers that among them he had "passed from a young to an old man." A few hours later in Indianapolis, he stressed his age when speaking to an immense crowd. In New York City on February 19 he termed himself "rather an old man."

Did these repeated references constitute platform rhetoric, or did the deteriorating body of the president-elect cause him actually to regard himself as "already old"? If the latter answer is correct, he may have felt himself so close to death from natural causes that he feared no violent act.

3. Lincoln's deep-rooted and life-long fatalistic philosophy, coupled with constant awareness of death and his own mortality, may have made him immune to fear. Nancy Hanks died of "milk sickness" when her son was just nine years old. One after another, he saw other relatives and loved ones precede him to the grave: his sister Sarah, his cousins Tom and Betsy Sparrow, his youthful sweetheart Ann Rutledge, his father, his stepmother, his sons Edward and William (Willie), his exuberant young protégé Elmer Ellsworth, his bosom friend Edward Baker, and the Confederate brother-in-law of his wife, Gen. Benjamin H. Helm . . .

At age thirty-seven he returned to his boyhood home and was inspired to write a poem that included a terse description of his mood:

> I range the fields with pensive tread,
> And pace the hollow rooms,
> And feel (companions of the dead)
> I'm living in the tombs.

Chatting with Francis Carpenter about possible assassination, he said of "the Richmond people" that "if they wanted to get at me, no vigilance could keep them out." Feeble attempts to thwart political plots, he said on another occasion, would be like "putting up the gaps in only one place, when the whole fence was down." To a female visitor who wondered whether or not a few cavalrymen could protect him, he mused, "I believe when my time comes, there is nothing that can prevent my going."

4. A few brief hints in surviving letters and speeches suggest that the man who remembered having carved pegs for his mother's coffin at age nine saw martydrom as a path leading to a special kind of immortality.

Until April 14, 1865, no American president had been assassinated. Yet in his famous Lyceum Address, young Lincoln noted that Founding Fathers had won "deathless names." Days before assuming the reins of the nation, in Philadelphia he fervently declared that he would choose assassination on the spot to surrender of principles embodied in the Declaration of Independence.

John Wilkes Booth fired his derringer on Good Friday—widely known as "crucifixion day"—April 14, 1865. On the following Sunday, many mourning clergymen dried their tears long enough to voice a conviction. It was no accident, they said, that martyrdom came to "the second Father of our nation" on the anniversary of the day Jesus Christ died on the cross.

Widespread oral tradition asserts that Abraham Lincoln earlier pondered the riddle of his existence and its end, then declared:

It appears that the Lord wants a sacrificial victim, as he did in the time of Moses. I must confess that I believe I have been chosen to be that victim. So many plots have been made against my life that it is a miracle that none has succeeded. But can we expect God to work a perpetual miracle in order to save my life? I believe not . . .

Whether or not the time and place were "written in the stars," his Good Friday martyrdom actually did help confer upon this man of mystery a special kind of immortality not matched in the annals of the nation.

38

*What Part of His Prodigious
Output Is*

LOST BEYOND
HOPE OF
RECOVERY?

■

AN ILLEGITIMATE DAUGHTER of the frontier, briefly
mistress of a one-room cabin with a dirt floor, never learned to read
or to write. Her only son, taught in "blab schools" for a few months,
became a consummate master of spoken and written words.

As edited by Roy P. Basler, Abraham Lincoln's *Collected Works* run
to 4,375 pages. Manuscripts held by the Library of Congress occupy
ninety-seven reels of microfilm. Every scrap of paper definitely known
to have been associated with the man who ran the Civil War is being
made public in a series of supplements to Basler's nine-volume compilation.

With so much that he said and wrote readily available, is it possible that anything of importance has been lost beyond hope of
recovery?

A listener-captivating political address made in Bloomington, Illinois, on May 29, 1856, is famous as "The Lost Speech." Oral tradition has it that the speaker so intrigued his audience that no one
turned his attention to the process of making notes. If Lincoln had a
manuscript, it was not preserved.

Decades later, a brief condensation of what the aspiring political
leader said that spring day was found in the Alton, Illinois, *Weekly
Courier.* Reprinted in the Basler collection, it occupies less than half
a page. At that time a formal address seldom lasted less than an hour
and was often much longer. Most of the ideas expressed at Alton by a
man who may already have had his eye upon the Executive Mansion
are not likely ever to be known.

At the first national convention of the new Republican party in

1856—organized by fusion of antislavery Whigs and Free Democrats—the man from Springfield was offered as a candidate for the vice presidency. He lost to William L. Dayton of New Jersey but entered the fray with zest. Years later, he told associates that in Illinois he delivered more than fifty speeches, not one of which was published except in greatly abbreviated form. He spoke in county seats throughout the state, but newspapers seldom devoted more than a paragraph to his message.

Having gone to Kalamazoo, Michigan, to deliver the keynote address at a rally, he was surprised to find that a reporter for the Detroit *Daily Advertiser* was in his audience since three other men were speaking from other stands at the same time. Perhaps because the visitor from Illinois was introduced by Hezekiah G. Well of the Republican executive committee, the Detroit newspaper published a substantial portion of his message.

At Kalamazoo, according to the only journalist who was present that day, Lincoln declared that the vice president resigned when "he got the job of making a slave state out of Kansas." Then he tossed a rhetorical question: "Was not that a great mistake?"

"(A voice—'He didn't mean that!')," continued the *Daily Advertiser* account.

Shortly afterward, said the newspaper, the speaker was interrupted by "(laughter and cheers)" and then by "(laughter)." His final sentence was followed by "(great cheering)."

Even with these memoranda concerning audience reactions included, the printed version—if reasonably accurate—does not even approximate the message heard and seen at Kalamazoo that day. Inflections, pauses, shouts, whispers, and other vocal changes were not captured by the reporter. He made no attempt to convey to readers what listeners saw: movements of the speaker's long torso, punctuation delivered by means of jabbing hand and bobbing head, sweeping movements of long arms, facial changes that included smiles, frowns, and grimaces.

Even when a manuscript of a Lincoln address has been preserved, readers who find it in print get only part of the message conveyed to listeners. Stunning as it is to modern eyes, when reduced to black marks upon white paper, the Gettysburg Address loses a significant part of its November 19, 1863, impact upon listeners who had assembled upon hallowed ground.

Written words, especially when in Abraham Lincoln's own handwriting, suffer far less than spoken words as interpreted by newspaper reporters. Yet these, too, have their shortcomings—and their vast voids.

Diligent search over a period of 150 years has failed to uncover a scrap of authentic documentary evidence concerning Lincoln's having broken an engagement with Mary Todd. Tradition has it that a wedding planned for January 1, 1841, was canceled when the bridegroom failed to appear.

More than a year later, a confidential letter to his intimate friend Joshua F. Speed referred to "that fatal first of Jany. '41." Yet there is no indisputable evidence that the attorney was referring to the day on which an understanding with Mary Todd was broken. Precisely what he meant by "the fatal first," and just what occurred on that momentous day, remains a matter for conjecture. If documentary evidence concerning it ever existed, it seems to have been destroyed or lost.

In the case of missing family letters, there is much more evidence. Mary Todd Lincoln clung firmly to most written messages sent to her by her husband. These were "too private in nature" ever to leave her hands, she insisted. Four letters written to his wife from Washington by Congressman Lincoln have been preserved; all are routine and perfunctory rather than being intimate. A handful of additional letters and several telegrams from the presidential years have been found. None shed significant light upon the husband-wife relationship that has been the subject of much speculation.

Late in 1835 or early in 1836, young Lincoln prepared material for a booklet. In it he challenged some ideas concerning historical accuracy of the Bible. When he showed it to Samuel Hill of New Salem, then his employer, Hill snatched the manuscript from him and stuffed it into a stove.

Later, when suffering from one of his recurrent spells of deep despondency, he wrote a brief poem he called "Suicide." It soon appeared in Springfield's *Sangamon Journal*. But when a friend went to look for it years afterward, he found that the morbid lines had been cut from the newspaper's file copy.

Preparing to leave the town for Washington, the president-elect scanned his papers and discarded many of them. A chance caller saw the floor littered with letters, picked up a few, and found that they had been written by the attorney to his wife.

Many or most items not destroyed at that time were stuffed into a carpetbag and turned over to his cousin by marriage, Elizabeth Todd Grimsley. She gave away several manuscript sheets as souvenirs; these were later discovered by Oliver R. Barrett. But most of the material consigned to the care of "Cousin Lizzie" went up in flames when a housemaid looked into the carpetbag and decided that it included only trash.

Alexander K. McClure, owner of a Pennsylvania newspaper and an early supporter of Lincoln at the 1860 Republic convention, accumulated a substantial quantity of Lincoln material. No one knows what was included in the collection, for it fell into the hands of Confederate general John McCausland, who burned it without revealing its nature.

After the tragic death of the president, Robert Todd Lincoln took possession of his father's papers. Immediately besieged by requests that they be made available to biographers, he was adamant in refusing. For years, boxes of documents reposed in a Bloomington, Illinois, bank.

Former secretaries John G. Nicolay and John Hay were not run-of-the-mill aspirants for production of a Lincoln biography. Both men were warmly regarded by Robert Todd Lincoln, president of the Pullman Company, because they had been intimately associated with his father during his entire time in the Executive Mansion. Furthermore, they solemnly pledged that if permitted to use the papers they would give Robert Todd Lincoln the privilege of striking out anything he found offensive.

It was on this basis that the immense collection of Lincoln papers was transferred to the Washington home of Nicolay. Articles prepared by Nicolay and Hay for *Century* magazine, beginning in 1885, formed the basis of their ten-volume biography that was published in 1890. Aware that they could use nothing that displeased the son of the president, the collaborators were cautious about inclusion of material they considered in any sense derogatory. Yet Robert Todd Lincoln followed their prepublication work closely and may have made free use of his editorial blue pencil. In at least one instance he struck out a rather long passage that described a boyhood incident in which Abraham Lincoln appeared to have been callous to the suffering of hogs.

As approved by Lincoln's son, the ten-volume biography prepared by his secretaries runs to more than 4,700 pages, 4,400 of which deal with the last sixteen years of his life. So little space is devoted to his first forty years that matters such as his ancestry and paternity, early romances, courtship and marriage receive only perfunctory treatment.

At the death of Nicolay in 1901, Hay took charge of the papers and separated manuscripts from letters. Then assistant secretary of state, he had access to vaults of the State Department; so he deposited the letters there. Presidential documents went to the National Capital Bank for storage.

Hay, who addressed Robert Todd Lincoln as "Dear Bob," died in 1905, so the president's son assumed physical possession of the all-important papers and took them to his Chicago office. Six years later he retired from the Pullman Company, moved to Washington, and took his father's papers with him. Annually he went to Hildene, his summer home in Manchester, Vermont—each time with eight trunks packed full of Abraham Lincoln's papers plus many letters and messages sent to him by other persons. Why he took them and what he did with them remains a matter of conjecture.

Later, Robert Todd Lincoln agreed to give his father's papers to the Library of Congress. He stipulated that they must remain sealed until twenty-one years after his own death. When opened on July 26, 1947, the collection of about eighteen thousand documents yielded no startling revelations.

Had Horace G. Young been alive, he would not have been surprised. According to his account, on the day he paid an unexpected visit to Robert Todd Lincoln, the president's son was busy destroying documentary evidence of treason on the part of a member of his father's cabinet.

Whether or not Young's observations and recollections are accurate is a matter of conjecture. But the record clearly indicates that on at least two occasions Robert Todd Lincoln threatened to destroy documents in his possession. He had been meticulous in striking from the Nicolay and Hay biography everything he considered damaging to his father's reputation. He subsequently refused the request of Senator Albert J. Beveridge for access to the collection.

During eight summers in Vermont the Lincoln papers must have been carefully scrutinized and sifted by the son of the president. If Robert Todd Lincoln destroyed letters and other papers, it is unlikely that their contents will ever be known.

Perhaps one or several mysteries concerning the life and deeds of Abraham Lincoln would be resolved, at least in part, if everything he said and wrote had survived. Since some of it did not, the question of what was lost or destroyed—and why—constitutes a final riddle concerning the deliberately enigmatic son of Nancy Hanks.

CONCLUSION

■

A casual conversation in Maggie Valley, North Carolina, brought the startling realization that there are unsolved mysteries concerning the life of Abraham Lincoln. In an almost matter-of-fact fashion, Granny Gaddy made an offer:

"Give me half an hour, and I'll take you to the spot on Jonathan Creek where Abraham Lincoln was born," she said.

Soon it was evident that she was not joking. When she was a girl, relatives and friends often pointed out to her the nearly destroyed cabin in which they said young Nancy Hanks bore the illegitimate son of Abraham Enloe and named him for his father before marrying Thomas Lincoln.

Reflection concerning the incredible tale that has retained its vitality through decades of oral transmission evoked related but almost forgotten memories. At Audubon Park in Kentucky, just south of the Ohio River, an eloquent conversationalist had insisted upon sharing a detailed account of events he believed led to the pregnancy of servant girl Nancy Hanks by wealthy Samuel Davis—father of Jefferson Davis. Anyone who has spent a few years in South Carolina is likely to have heard the tale according to which John C. Calhoun was Abraham's father.

Alex Haley's *Roots* brought new appreciation of the power of oral tradition. Preposterous as the North Carolina, Kentucky, and South Carolina tales appear to be, why have they survived so long? If these stories were created to disparage Lincoln, why did most of the reputed fathers move in social and economic circles far above that of Thomas Lincoln?

Soon it was discovered that paternity stories abound and that the accepted record of the marriage of Thomas Lincoln and Nancy Hanks rests upon three scrawled signatures on loose documents. These were found, not in Hardin County as expected, but in adjoin-

Since he did not know the name of his Virginia grandfather, young Lincoln may have imagined that ancestor to have been Thomas Jefferson. [LIBRARY OF CONGRESS]

ing Washington County—years after Lincoln's death. If so little is positively known about the paternity of Abraham Lincoln, perhaps other aspects of his life and thought warranted careful examination.

Once the search for answers to unsolved riddles was launched, twists and turns led in every direction. This volume is the result of that quest. Throughout, emphasis is upon unanswered questions, not clear-cut answers.

A unique series of events propelled a son of the western frontier into the Executive Mansion at a time when sectional and social tensions had reached their zenith. Shaped by biological influences, the psychology of the wilderness, and ceaseless hunger for knowledge and power, Abraham Lincoln saw himself as having been chosen by fate—or Providence—through "the mandate of the people."

To most of us today, it is a matter of no importance that Lincoln did not know the identity of his maternal grandfather, but to him this seems to have been of some significance as a source of frustration. However, ignorance also constituted an opportunity: he could imagine himself to be the grandson of anyone he chose. His reverence for the Declaration of Independence and his elevation of that document above the Constitution hint that he may have believed himself to be a grandson of Thomas Jefferson.

Whether he believed that or not, Lincoln's fascination with the words and deeds of the Founding Fathers shaped his consuming goal as chief executive. Preservation of the mystical pre-existent Union with whose fate he felt the entire world to be concerned took precedence over all other issues. Denying that the Union had been severed, he launched what he regarded as a campaign to quell insurrection, not a war upon a southern nation carved from the Union and most certainly not a war to get rid of slavery.

Asked to name the most influential figure in the Civil War, typical respondents are likely to reply: Robert E. Lee, Ulysses S. Grant, or even Stonewall Jackson. While these revered leaders had decisive impact upon battlefields, they and their subordinates acted largely in response to decisions made in the Executive Mansion on Pennsylvania Avenue.

Lacking extensive administrative experience at a high level, Abraham Lincoln functioned as a one-man executive branch while simultaneously directing the course of the U.S. War Department. He expressed reverence for the Constitution of the United States, but he did not hesitate to "bend it a little." For the most part, he reached decisions and acted upon them without asking for congressional approval. Some such endorsements were made after the fact, but in numerous instances he did not bother even to request *post facto* approval of his actions.

To a degree not generally recognized, Abraham Lincoln curtailed civil liberties and scoffed at the U.S. Supreme Court. Had that body exercised in 1860 the power it does today, the Civil War might well have ended in stalemate and permanent separation of regions, for in the name of preserving the Union, the president came perilously close to establishing a military dictatorship in the North. Doubting the loyalty of many in the established governmental structure, he entrusted early purchase of military goods to John A. Dix and two associates. Compared with the sixteenth president's delivery to them of $2 million from the U.S. Treasury in April 1861, the thirty-seventh president's involvement in the Watergate scandal was a minor abuse of power.

Because he generally interpreted the U.S. Constitution to suit his own purposes, the son of Nancy Hanks succeeded in vastly expanding the concept of "war powers of the president." Precedents he set led to the twentieth-century development of "the imperial presidency." Executive action in 1861 involved calling out militia to fight an undeclared war. By making that move, Lincoln established precedents that led to Viet Nam. Subsequently George Bush secretly spent months and millions of dollars preparing to launch Operation Desert Storm before seeking congressional approval.

Military considerations, not eagerness for social justice, led a frontiersman who today seems to have been bigoted to issue the Emancipation Proclamation.

Despite a never-ending toll of battlefield casualties, Abraham Lincoln refused to concede that the mystical Union had been severed. Had someone else been selected to head the nation in 1860, would efforts aimed at conciliation and compromise have succeeded? Had secession been accepted as a reality, would the dissident states soon have been forced by economic developments to return to the Union?

Very early, Lincoln indicated his certainty that the Founding Fathers expected slavery to die a natural death. Would that have happened had not war of his own choosing forced upon him the decision to issue the Emancipation Proclamation?

These and other major questions cannot be answered.

Such matters are as far beyond logical analysis as are many other aspects of the life and thought of the most mysterious man who ever headed the Union he revered.

Woodrow Wilson contemplated the most influential of all presidents and concluded that Lincoln was "a brooding spirit so constituted that he could not completely reveal himself." As Wilson saw it, "This strange child of the cabin kept company with invisible things."

Whatever those invisible things may have been, they shaped the life and thought of Abraham Lincoln. Once pushed into the presidency as—in his own eyes—an instrument of fate, he never wavered in his conviction that he knew his destiny and must reach it. Possessed of a vision and believing that many of his actions were predetermined, he followed a course that cost the lives of an estimated 623,000 Americans.

In doing so, he did much more than simply preserve the Union. From a group of strong states with a loose central government, he forged a nation in which Washington became the center of power. He established paper currency as the basis of commerce and initiated the practice of forcing Americans into military service by means of conscription.

Would any other American have been capable of preserving the Union at such cost? Had William H. Seward gone to the Executive Mansion as expected, would there be a United States of America today? What would the portion of North America that now includes forty-eight states be like had Booth or some other assassin struck early enough for Hannibal Hamlin to have become the great decision-maker?

Many who visit the awesome Lincoln Memorial in Washington are overcome by their emotions. Here it seems that ordinary folk must respond, not with logical analyses but with feelings.

In many respects the life of the Great Emancipator is like his memorial. It is beyond authoritative analysis, because there are many gaps in the record, but even so we can experience its power.

Not even George Washington in all his glory made a lasting impact upon the nation comparable to that of the inspired self-taught mystic who was all but obsessed with the notion of Union.

APPENDIXES

■

LINCOLN'S CABINET MEMBERS:
FIFTEEN MEN FOR SEVEN POSITIONS

Secretary of State	March 6, 1861—April 15, 1865	William H. Seward
Secretary of the Treasury	March 7, 1861—June 30, 1864	Salmon P. Chase
	July 1–4, 1864	George Harrington
	July 5, 1864—March 3, 1865	William P. Fessenden
	March 4–8, 1865	George Harrington (ad interim)
	March 9—April 15, 1865	Hugh McCulloch
Secretary of War	March 5, 1861—January 14, 1862	Simon Cameron
	January 15–19, 1862	(not filled)
	January 20, 1862—April 15, 1865	Edwin M. Stanton
Attorney General	March 5, 1861—November 24, 1864	Edward Bates
	November 25—December 4, 1864	(not filled)
	December 5, 1864—April 15, 1865	James Speed
Postmaster General	March 5–8, 1861	(not filled)
	March 9, 1861—September 23, 1864	Montgomery Blair
	September 24, 1864—April 15, 1865	William Dennison
Secretary of the Navy	March 5–6, 1861	(not filled)
	March 7, 1861—April 15, 1865	Gideon Welles
Secretary of the Interior	March 5, 1861—December 31, 1861	Caleb B. Smith
	January 1–8, 1863	John P. Usher (ad interim)
	January 8, 1863—April 15, 1865	John P. Usher

SOME SIGNIFICANT EVENTS DURING THE LIFE OF LINCOLN
AND THE NATION'S GREATEST CRISIS

1776 (?)	Thomas Lincoln is born in Rockingham County, Virginia.
1784	Nancy Hanks, probably illegitimate, is born somewhere in Virginia.
1802	Thomas Lincoln moves to Hardin County, Kentucky, and purchases a 238-acre farm.
1806	Thomas Lincoln and Nancy Hanks are married by Methodist circuit rider Jesse Head.
1807	Sarah, about whom little is known, is born to Thomas and Nancy Lincoln.
1809 February 12	Abraham is born to Thomas and Nancy Lincoln, now living on a 300-acre farm on Nolin Creek near present-day Hodginville.
1811	The Lincolns move a short distance to Knob Creek, where in 1815 Abraham briefly attends a "blab school" in which everyone talks at once.
1816	Late in the year, the Lincolns move to Spencer County, Illinois, where they build a log cabin of about 16 x 18 feet that has one window.
1818	Kicked in the head by a mule some time during the year; Abraham remains unconscious for many hours.
October 5	Having drunk milk from a cow that ate white snakeroot, Nancy Lincoln dies from milk sickness.
December 3	Illinois, the twenty-first state, is admitted to the Union.
1819 December 2	Thomas Lincoln marries illiterate Sarah Bush Johnston in Kentucky; she brings to Spencer County her three children: Elizabeth, 12; John, 9; Matilda, 8. Soon the tiny cabin accepts another resident, Abraham's twenty-year-old cousin, Dennis Hanks.
1820	Legislation known as the Missouri Compromise preserves the balance between slave and free states in the U.S. Senate by admitting Maine as a free state along with allowing slavery in the Missouri Territory.
1821	Dennis Hanks marries Elizabeth Johnston, age fifteen.
1826	Aaron Grigsby marries Sarah Lincoln, age nineteen.
	Squire Hall marries Elizabeth Johnston, age nineteen.
1828	Sarah Lincoln Grigsby dies in childbirth.

Abraham Lincoln uses a flatboat to take a load of farm produce down the Mississippi River to New Orleans. Rail-splitting and other farm work for his father is a daily requirement any time he is at home.

1829 Abraham works for James Gentry in his general store.

1830 Thomas Lincoln and family move to Macon County, Illinois; soon Thomas sells his farm for $125 and settles in Coles County. Abraham makes his first political speech.

1831 Now independent of his father, Abraham makes a second trip to New Orleans; soon after his return, he is hired as a storekeeper in New Salem where he boards at Rutledge's tavern and becomes acquainted with his landlord's daughter, four years his junior.

1832 Lincoln enlists for service in the Black Hawk War and is elected captain of a volunteer company, but he gains no combat experience. Upon his return from a few weeks of service, he opens his own store.

Having developed a yearning for political office, he runs for a seat in the legislature and is defeated.

1833 Failure of his store plunges Lincoln into debt, so he becomes postmaster at New Salem and deputy to county surveyor John Calhoun.

Mary Owens, age twenty-five, visits New Salem from Kentucky and becomes acquainted with Lincoln.

1834 Lincoln wins a seat in the Illinois General Assembly and begins self-study of law. During eight years as a state lawmaker, his salary plus travel allowance amounts to a total of $1,950.

1835 Ann Rutledge dies of fever, causing Abraham Lincoln to suffer a prolonged period of deep melancholy.

1836
March 1 Lincoln becomes a licensed attorney.

1837 Lincoln proposes marriage to Mary Owens, perhaps jokingly.

Having helped to move the capitol from Vandalia to Springfield, Lincoln seeks a residence there and finds storekeeper Joshua Speed willing to share his bed with him.

John T. Stuart, a fellow legislator who had encouraged Lincoln to begin the study of law, takes him into his Springfield office. At age twenty-eight, Lincoln's life is half over.

1839 Mary Todd of Lexington, Kentucky, visits her sister and brother-in-law in Springfield; despite great differences in background, she and Lincoln become interested in one another.

1841

January 1
Joshua Speed returns to his native Kentucky, leaving Lincoln disconsolate and troubled about whether either of them should ever marry.

August and September
Lincoln visits Joshua Speed at his home near Louisville.

1842

February 15
After much agonizing in correspondence with Lincoln, Joshua Speed marries Fanny Henning.

November 4
Lincoln marries Mary Todd of Lexington, Kentucky, after earlier having terminated their relationship.

1843

August 1
Abraham and Mary name their first child Robert Todd in honor of Mary's father.

1844
Lincoln forms a law partnership with William H. Herndon, a relationship destined to last for twenty years.

1846

March 10
A second son is born and is named Edward Baker in honor of a rising politician of that name.

1847

December 2
Lincoln reaches Washington as a Whig member of the U.S. House of Representatives. In a series of resolutions, he denounces President James K. Polk for having initiated war with Mexico. Friends tell him that this stance has ruined him as a politician, and he does not seek re-election.

1850
Young Edward ("Eddie") Lincoln dies.

1852

March 20
Publication in book form of *Uncle Tom's Cabin; or, Life Among the Lowly,* has an immediate and dramatic impact upon the movement for abolition of slavery.

1854

April 4
Abraham and Mary name their fourth and last child Thomas; they call him "Tad" because his father says he looks like a tadpole.

May 26
Passage of the Kansas–Nebraska Act by the U.S. Congress allows settlers in the West to determine for themselves whether or not slavery will be allowed.

Passionately opposed to territorial extension of slavery though willing to tolerate where it exists, Lincoln sees the measure as the "end of the Missouri Compromise." He voices unwavering opposition to it and to the Democrats who framed it.

Lincoln is again elected to the Illinois legislature but resigns to make an unsuccessful bid for nomination as a Whig candidate for the U.S. Senate.

Without Lincoln's knowledge, leaders of the fledgling Republican Party list him as a member of the state's central committee.

1855 Lincoln goes to Cincinnati as an attorney in the noted McCormick reaper case.

1856 Lincoln plays a key role in perfecting the organization of Illinois Republicans and gives more than fifty speeches in support of Republican presidential nominee John Charles Frémont.

1857
March 6 Members of the U.S. Supreme Court announce their decision that Dred Scott is not and never can be a citizen because Missouri law treats him as a slave.

1858 Nominated for the U.S. Senate by Republicans whose party he has now joined, Lincoln challenges nationally prominent Stephen A. Douglas to a series of debates.

Since election to the post is made by the legislature, which was controlled by Democrats, the outcome of the senatorial contest is never in doubt; Douglas is re-elected. But his seven verbal contests with Lincoln, centering upon possible extension of slavery into new western states, bring the "prairie lawyer" to the attention of Republicans throughout the state.

1859
August to November Lincoln makes political speeches in Missouri, Indiana, Wisconsin, Iowa, and the Kansas Territory.

October 18 At Harpers Ferry, Virginia, U.S. Marines led by Lt. Colonel Robert E. Lee subdue militant abolitionist John Brown. Found guilty of murder and treason, he is hanged at Charlestown on December 2.

1860 As a highly successful general purpose attorney, Lincoln is now earning about $5,000 a year, a large income at the time.

February 27 Lincoln delivers an address at Cooper Union Hall in New York City, then embarks upon a ten-day speaking tour of New England.

April and May Democratic quarrels over the slavery issue cause the party to split into three segments, virtually guaranteeing election to the presidency of any Republican who is nominated.

May 18 Although William H. Seward of New York is expected to win the Republican nomination easily, it goes instead to Lincoln, whose views on major issues offend few delegates to the nominating convention because they do not know where he stands.

November 6 Having won 39 percent of the nation's popular vote and 9 percent of the electoral votes of thirty-three states, Abraham Lincoln becomes president-elect.

December 20	By unanimous vote, a special convention meeting in South Carolina declares that the state has seceded from the Union.
December 26	Without authorization, Major Robert Anderson leads a contingent of U.S. troops to unfinished and never-garrisoned Fort Sumter in Charleston harbor.

1861

January 9	By 84 to 15, members of the Mississippi legislature vote to secede. Secessionists fire upon the relief ship *Star of the West*, sent to Fort Sumter with supplies. President James Buchanan wrings his hands and says he is powerless to do anything.
January 10	Florida secedes by a vote of 62 to 7.
January 11	Alabama secedes by a vote of 61 to 39.
January 19	Georgia secedes by a vote of 164 to 133.
January 26	Louisiana secedes by a vote of 113 to 17.
January 29	With slavery banned, Kansas becomes the thirty-fourth state in the Union.
February	Members of a Texas convention vote for secession by 166 to 8.
February 11	President-elect Lincoln leaves Springfield for Washington.
February 18	Jefferson Davis is inaugurated as provisional President of the Confederate States of America.
March 4	Lincoln is inaugurated as the eighteenth president of the United States.
March 29	Lincoln approves a secret plan to relieve Fort Sumter, plus Fort Pickens in Florida.
April 12	At 4:30 A.M., Confederate forces under P. T. G. Beauregard begin shelling Fort Sumter, which surrenders at 2:30 P.M. on the next day.
April 15	Lincoln announces the existence of a state of insurrection and invites 75,000 Union volunteers to serve for ninety days. He calls for a special session of Congress to convene on July 4.
April 17	By a vote of 88 to 55, members of a Virginia state convention vote to secede.
April 19	Lincoln proclaims a blockade of the entire Confederate coastline.
April 27	Lincoln authorizes suspension of *habeas corpus* along a military line that stretches from Washington to Philadelphia.
May 6	The Confederate Congress declares that a state of war exists between the C.S.A. and the U.S.A.
	Members of the Arkansas legislature vote for secession by 69 to 1.

May 13	Queen Victoria proclaims Britain's neutrality and brands both sides as belligerents.
May 20	Having reluctantly arrived at a firm decision, North Carolina becomes the eleventh state to secede.
June 8	A popular vote in Tennessee throws the state into the Confederacy.
June 11–25	Delegates from Virginia's western counties form a pro-Union "alternate government" for the state.
July 4	Lawmakers assemble for a special session of Congress and applaud Lincoln's assurance that the war will be short. Before adjournment they approve Lincoln's legally doubtful acts, orders, and proclamations taken while Congress was in recess.
July 16	General-in-chief Winfield Scott's plan for gradual conquest of rebels having been rejected, Federal troops cross the Potomac River and head for Richmond, now the capital of the C.S.A.
July 21	Anticipating easy victory, troops of Gen. Irvin McDowell meet Confederates in the region of Bull Run Creek and are decisively defeated.
November	Pro-slavery forces of Missouri cause the state to be recognized by rebels as members of the C.S.A.
November 8	James M. Mason and John Slidell, Confederate commissioners to Great Britain, are taken by force from the British packet *Trent*.
December 10	The Confederate Congress recognizes a minority government of Kentucky and admits the state as the thirteenth and last member of the C.S.A.
December 26	Facing the possibility of British intervention, Washington labels the seizure of Mason and Slidell as illegal and plans their release.

1862

January 27	Lincoln's General War Order #1—generally ignored by his commanders—sets February 22 as the day for a general advance by Union military and naval units.
February 5	Set to the tune of "John Brown's Body," Julia Ward Howe's "Battle Hymn of the Republic" is published in the *Atlantic Monthly* magazine.
February 20	William Wallace Lincoln, age twelve, dies in the White House of typhoid fever.
March 6	Lincoln urges Congress to establish a pattern of compensation for slave owners in loyal states that agree to a plan of gradual emancipation.
March 9	An epic drawn battle between the ironclad vessels USS

Monitor and CSS *Virginia* (or *Merrimac*) puts an end to the era of wooden warships.

June 19   Lincoln signs into law a congressional act that forbids the extension of slavery into U.S. territories.

July 22   Lincoln shares with his cabinet his first draft of an executive order designed to free all slaves in rebellious states.

August 14   For the first time, black Americans are received at the White House—to hear the president's request that they support his plan to colonize freed slaves in Central America.

September 22   Following an Antietam Creek, Maryland, battle that he interprets as a Federal victory, Lincoln announces that his Emancipation Proclamation will take effect on January 1, 1863.

December 1   In his State of the Union message to Congress, Lincoln urges compensation of owners whose slaves are free, plus colonization of blacks involved.

1863

January 1   Lincoln signs the Emancipation Proclamation, under whose terms slaves in rebellious areas are declared to be free. All free blacks are invited to join the U.S. Army.

March 3   Lincoln signs the first conscription act, making most males ages twenty to forty-six liable to enforced military service, provided they do not purchase exemption or hire substitutes.

April 20   Lincoln announces yet another war measure; the state of West Virginia will be formed from much of the mountainous region of western Virginia. On June 20 it becomes the thirty-fifth state of the Union.

July 11–18   In New York City popular resistance to conscription for military service erupts into "draft riots"—the war's worst civil disturbance.

September 22   Word reaches the Executive Mansion that C.S.A. Gen. Ben Hardin Helm, husband of Mary Todd Lincoln's half sister, has been killed in battle.

November 9   At the studio of Alexander Gardner, Lincoln poses for a group photograph with aides—secretaries Nicolay and Hay.

November 19   At Gettysburg, Pennsylvania, Lincoln delivers a brief but powerful message that confirms and amplifies his fame as a master of words.

December 8   Lincoln issues a Proclamation of Amnesty and Reconstruction. Under its terms most rebels become eligible for pardon and a new government may be established in a seceded state when 10 percent of those who voted in 1860 take an oath of allegiance and agree to bar slavery.

1864

February 1 — The president orders that 500,000 more men be drafted for three years or the duration of the war.

February 24 — Lincoln signs a measure that provides $300 compensation to owners in loyal states for each slave who volunteers to enlist in the U.S. Army.

March 2 — Having been nominated by the president, U. S. Grant is confirmed by the senate as the first full lieutenant general since George Washington; soon he assumes his role as General-in-Chief of Union armies.

March 14 — Lincoln calls for 200,000 additional fighting men, with any shortage to be filled by draftees.

June 7 — Calling themselves the National Union Party, Republicans meet in Baltimore to nominate Abraham Lincoln for a second term.

All federal employees learn that they are expected to contribute 5 percent of a year's pay to the Lincoln campaign.

July 2 — The Wade–Davis Bill, a package of congressional plans for reconstruction of seceded states, is passed by lawmakers. Lincoln, who has little use for the statute, subjects it to a pocket veto.

August 29–31 — Gen. George B. McClellan, running as a peace candidate, becomes the Democratic nominee for the presidency.

October 31 — Nebraska becomes the thirty-sixth state of the Union, readily admitted because its two votes in the Senate will help to gain passage of the Thirteenth Amendment.

November 8 — After having previously expressed to his cabinet his conviction that he will be defeated at the polls, Lincoln is elected for a second term.

1865

February 3 — Three C.S.A. peace commissioners come to a Hampton Roads, Virginia, peace conference led by Lincoln and Secretary of State Seward. Lincoln's demand for unconditional surrender, countered by Confederate insistence upon diplomatic recognition, brings talks to a speedy close.

March 11 — The president offers a full pardon to every military or naval deserter who will return within sixty days.

April 2–3 — President Davis and his chief aides flee from Richmond. On April 4 Lincoln visits the war-ravaged city.

April 9 — At Appomattox Court House, Virginia, Robert E. Lee surrenders the Army of North Virginia to Ulysses S. Grant.

April 11 — Speaking from the White House, Lincoln tells a crowd of citizens that he hopes for early return of all seceded states to the Union.

April 14	At Ford's Theater, the president receives a fatal bullet wound from the derringer of John Wilkes Booth at about 10:13 P.M.; he lingers near death until 7:22 the following morning.
April 15	Vice President Andrew Johnson of Tennessee takes the oath of office to become the seventeenth president of the United States.
April 16	Having been shot on Good Friday, in pulpits of the North the martyred president is lauded as a new incarnation of Jesus Christ.
April 19 to May 4	Funeral ceremonies for Abraham Lincoln are followed by a circuitous journey to Springfield for interment of the ex-president and his son Willie.
June 30	A military commission renders a guilty verdict for each of the eight conspirators accused of involvement in the assassination of Lincoln.
December 18	The House of Representatives awards Mary Todd Lincoln $25,000 in lieu of the $100,000 in salary her husband would have collected had he lived to complete his second term.
	Having been ratified by twenty-seven states (including several former members of the C.S.A. still under military rule), the Thirteenth Amendment is declared ratified and slavery becomes illegal throughout the country.
	Late in the year, Robert Todd Lincoln takes possession of his father's papers.
1882 July 16	Mary Todd Lincoln dies.
1890	Using papers held by Robert Todd Lincoln, former presidential secretaries John G. Nicolay and John Hay issue a ten-volume biography of Abraham Lincoln that is censored by his son before publication.
1892	William H. Herndon and Jesse W. Weik publish a two-volume biography of Lincoln. Long scorned, this work and the documents upon which it rests is now being studied with enthusiasm.
February 12	Abraham Lincoln's birthday becomes a national holiday.
1894	Nicolay and Hay edit and publish two massive volumes of Lincoln's *Complete Works*.
1919	Robert Todd Lincoln deposits his father's papers with the Library of Congress; later he bequeaths them to the United States but requires that they shall remain sealed until twenty-one years after his own death.
1947	Long-anticipated opening of the Lincoln Papers disappoints scholars who had hoped to find clues concerning his

illegitimacy or involvement of cabinet members in his assassination.

1953–55   Edited by Roy P. Basler, an annotated version of *The Collected Works of Abraham Lincoln* is issued in a nine-volume set.

1976
February 12   Daniel Boorstin, Librarian of Congress, opens a box sealed for 111 years. It contains items from Lincoln's pockets at the time of his assassination and subsequently turned over to Robert Todd Lincoln. Public display of the relics sparks renewed interest in details concerning the life and death of the president.

1990   Wide interest in theories that Lincoln suffered from Marfan syndrome—a malady marked by elongation of arms and legs—leads to a strong but futile cry for DNA analysis of tissue samples from the body of the martyred president.

1992
December   Rare photographs from the famous Meserve collection form the basis of a four-hour biography of Abraham Lincoln, aired by ABC TV.

TOP BRASS: MAJOR LEADERSHIP POSITIONS
IN UNION ARMIES

Throughout his presidency, Abraham Lincoln exercised full authority as commander in chief. Many of his directives were transmitted through the secretary of war, the field commander, or the general in chief—except during periods when one or more of these posts was empty. He promoted, demoted, and transferred top leaders many times. Few weeks passed during which the commander in chief was not faced with personnel decisions at the level of army or military department commanders. Recognizing that official sources often differ by a few days concerning effective dates, some of the myriad of major leadership positions held and lost by Union major generals are listed in chronological order:

1861

March 5 — Brevet Lt. Gen. Winfield Scott has been commander in chief, U.S. Army, since 1841.

April — Robert E. Lee offered field command of all federal forces and declines; becomes commander of Virginia troops on April 23.

April 15 — Scott gives the command of the Department of Pennsylvania to Robert Patterson, a major general in the state's volunteers.

April 18 — Scott gives command of the Department of Pennsylvania to Robert Patterson, a major general in the state's volunteers.

April 27 — Benjamin F. Butler, a brigadier general of the Massachusetts volunteers, assumes command of the Department of Annapolis.

May 13 — George B. McClellan, a major general of the Ohio volunteers, is placed in command of the Army of Occupation in Western Virginia.

May 22 — Butler assumes command of the Department of Virginia.

May 27 — Brig. Gen. Irvin McDowell, U.S.A., is placed in field command of the Army and Department of Northeastern Virginia.

June 11 — Maj. Gen. Nathaniel P. Banks. U.S. Volunteers, is made commander of the Department of Annapolis.

July 23 — Brig. Gen. William S. Rosecrans, U.S.A., heads the Army of Occupation in Western Virginia and commands the Department of the Ohio.

July 25 — Banks becomes commander of the Department of the Shenandoah.

Now a major general, U.S.A., McClellan takes command

of the Division of the Potomac, with McDowell as a subordinate.

Maj. Gen. John Charles Frémont, U.S.A., is given command of the Western Department.

Patterson is relieved of command and will be mustered out of the service on the twenty-seventh.

August 15	McClellan is made commander of the Army and Department of the Potomac.
October 1	Butler is placed in command of the Department of New England.
October 8	Brig. Gen. William T. Sherman, U.S.V., is given command of the Department of the Cumberland for thirty days.
October 11	Rosecrans is named head of the Department of Western Virginia.
November 1	Scott retires after being subjected to much badgering by McClellan.
November 2	Maj. Gen. David Hunter, U.S.V., takes command of the Western Department.
November 3	Brig. Gen. David Hunter, U.S.V., takes command of the Western Department.
November 5	McClellan becomes general in chief.
November 19	Maj. Gen. Henry W. Halleck, U.S.A., commands the Department of the Missouri.
November 21	Brig. Gen. Don Carlos Buell, U.S.V., is placed at the head of the Department and Army of the Ohio.

1862

January 13	Brig. Gen. Ambrose E. Burnside, U.S.V., heads the Department of North Carolina.
March 11	While in the field with the Army of the Potomac, McClellan is relieved; he retains command of the Army and Department of the Potomac.
	Halleck is put at the head of regions soon combined to form the Department of the Mississippi.
	No general in chief is named to replace McClellan; all generals are instructed to report directly to the secretary of war.
March 14	Rosecrans is placed in command of the Mountain Department.
March 15	Hunter is transferred to the Department of the South.
March 20	Butler is placed at the head of the Department of the Gulf.
March 24	Frémont becomes commander of the Mountain Department.
April 4	Banks is again put in charge of the Department of the Shenandoah.

June 10	Buell is demoted and assigned to head a corps.
June 17	Banks is informed that his forces will be absorbed by the Army of Virginia.
June 26	Pope is made head of the Army of Virginia.
	Frémont is demoted to command of the 1st Corps, Army of Virginia.
	Rosecrans takes command of the Army of the Mississippi.
July 11	Halleck is elevated to the post of general in chief.
September 2	Now a bigadier general, U.S.A., Pope is relieved of command.
September 16	Pope is assigned to the Department of the Northwest.
October 11	Rosecrans is transferred to the Department of Western Virginia.
October 16	Maj. Gen. U. S. Grant, U.S.V., is elevated to command of the Army and Department of the Tennessee.
October 24	Rosecrans is again transferred, this time to the Department of the Cumberland.
November 8	Banks becomes commander of the Department of the Gulf.
November 9	McClellan is removed from command of the Army of the Potomac and is replaced by Burnside, now a major general, U.S.V. Having twice refused the post, this time he feels that military obedience requires him to accept.
November 16	Brig. Gen. Joseph Hooker, U.S.A., heads the Department and Army of the Potomac.
November 20	Hunter commands the Department of Kansas.
December 17	Banks becomes commander of the Department of the Gulf.
1863	
January 23	Hooker is dismissed by Burnside.
January 25	Lincoln names Hooker as commander of the Department and Army of the Potomac.
March 25	Having twice offered to resign, Burnside is shifted to command of the Department of the Ohio.
June 27	Hooker is replaced by Maj. Gen. George G. Meade, U.S.V., who takes command of the Army of the Potomac.
October 1	Hooker is sent to head the Northern Department.
October 17	Rosecrans is relieved of command of the Department of the Cumberland.
October 18	Now a major general, U.S.A., Grant becomes head of the Division of the Mississippi.
October 24	Sherman, who became a brigadier general, U.S.A., in July, is named to the command of the Army and Department of the Tennessee.

October 30	Now a major general, U.S.V., Rosecrans takes command of the Army and Department of the Cumberland.
November 11	Butler is transferred to the Department of Virginia and North Carolina.

1864

January 22	Rosecrans assumes command of the Department of the Missouri.
January 30	Rosecrans is named commander of the Department of the Missouri.
March 2	Grant becomes the first full lieutenant general of the U.S. Army since George Washington.
March 10	Maj. Gen. Franz Sigel, U.S.V., is named to head the Department of Western Virginia.
March 12	Grant is named commander in chief, U.S.A., and Halleck becomes chief of staff.
March 18	Sherman is placed in command of the Division of the Mississippi.
April 4	Maj. Gen. Philip H. Sheridan, U.S.V., commands the Cavalry Corps of the Army of the Potomac.
April 9	Butler becomes commander of the Army of the James.
April 16	Halleck heads the Department of Virginia and Army of the James.
	Sigel is superseded by Hunter as head of the Department of Western Virginia.
May 21	Hunter takes over the Department of West Virginia.
July 1	McDowell is assigned to command of the Department of the Pacific.
August 6	Sheridan is placed in command of the Army of the Shenandoah.
December 10	Rosecrans is replaced by Maj. Gen. Grenville M. Dodge, U.S.V.

1865

March	Now a major general, U.S.A., Sheridan is given command of his own troopers—Sheridan's Cavalry.

BIBLIOGRAPHY

PRIMARY SOURCES

Abraham Lincoln's letters, telegrams, speeches, proclamations, legislation, congressional messages, other official documents, and the diaries, letters, and notes of his contemporaries.

Bates, Edward. *Diary.* Edited by Howard K. Beale. Washington, D.C.: Government Printing Office, 1933.

Binney, Horace. "The Privilege of the Writ of Habeas Corpus." Philadelphia, 1862. Pamphlet.*

Browning, Orville H. *The Diary of Orville Hickman Browning.* Edited by Theodore C. Pease, and James G. Randall. Springfield: Illinois State Historical Library, 1925–33.

Bullitt, J. C. "The Privilege of the Writ of Habeas Corpus." Philadelphia, 1862. Pamphlet.*

Chase, Salmon P. *Diary and Correspondence.* 2 vols. Washington, D.C.: Government Printing Office, 1903.

Current, Richard N., ed. *The Political Thought of Abraham Lincoln.* Indianapolis: Bobbs-Merrill, 1967.

Douglass, Frederick. *Oration Delivered on the Occasion of Unveiling the Freedman's Monument in Memory of Abraham Lincoln.* Washington, D.C.: Gibson, 1876.

Edwards, Herbert J., and Albert Fried, eds. *The Essential Lincoln.* Orono: University of Maine Press, 1962.

Grant, Ulysses S. *Personal Memoirs.* 2 vols. London: Low Marston, 1886.

Herndon, William H., and Jesse W. Weik, *Abraham Lincoln.* 3 vols. New York: Appleton, 1892.

Jackson, Tatlow. *Authorities Cited Antagonistic to Horace Binney's "Conclusion on the Writ of Habeas Corpus."* Philadelphia: Campbell, 1862.*

Lincoln, Abraham. *Papers.* Library of Congress, Washington, D.C. Microfilm.

―――. *Abraham Lincoln Papers Index.* Washington, D.C.: U.S. Government Printing Office, 1960.

―――. *Autobiographical Writings.* Edited by Paul M. Angle. Kingsport, Tenn., 1947.

―――. *An Autobiography of Abraham Lincoln.* Compiled by Nathaniel W. Stephenson. Indianapolis: Bobbs-Merrill, 1926.

―――. *Collected Works.* Edited by Roy P. Basler. 9 vols. New Brunswick, N.J.: Rutgers University Press, 1953–55.

―――. *Collected Works, Supplement 1832–45.* Edited by Roy P. Basler. Westport, Conn.: Greenwood, 1974.

―――. *Collected Works, Supplement 1848–65.* Edited by Roy P. Basler. Westport, Conn.: Greenwood, 1990.

―――. *Complete Works.* Edited by John G. Nicolay and John Hay. 2 vols. New York: Century, 1894.

―――. *Complete Works.* Edited by John G. Nicolay and John Hay. Limited ed. 12 vols. New York, 1894.

―――. *Complete Works.* Edited by John G. Nicolay and John Hay. 6 vols. New York: Tandy-Thomas, 1905.

―――. *Lincoln: His Words and His World.* Compiled by Robert L. Polley. New York: Hawthorn, 1965.

―――. *The Lincoln Papers.* Edited by David C. Mearns. 2 vols. Garden City, N.J.: Doubleday, 1948.

―――. *The Lincoln Reader.* Edited by Paul M. Angle. New Brunswick, N.J.: Rutgers University Press, 1947.

―――. *The Living Lincoln.* Edited by Paul M. Angle and Earl S. Miers. New Brunswick, N.J.: Rutgers University Press, 1955.

―――. *New Letters and Papers.* Edited by Paul M. Angle. Boston: Houghton Mifflin, 1930.

―――. *A Shelf of Lincoln Papers.* Edited by Paul M. Angle. Westport, Conn.: Greenwood, 1946.

————. *Speeches and Letters.* Edited by Paul M. Angle. New York: Dutton, 1957.

————. *Speeches and Writings.* Edited by Paul M. Angle. Cleveland: World, 1946.

————. *Uncollected Letters of Abraham Lincoln.* Edited by Gilbert A. Tracy. Boston: Houghton Mifflin, 1917.

————. *Uncollected Works.* Edited by Rufus R. Wilson. 2 vols. Elmira, N.Y.: Primavera, 1947–48.

Montgomery, J. T. *The Writ of Habeas Corpus and Mr. Binney.* Philadelphia: Campbell, 1862.*

Official Records of the Union and Confederate Navies in the War of the Rebellion. 29 vols. Washington, D.C.: Government Printing Office, 1894–1903; General Index, 1927.

Richardson, James, ed. *A Compilation of the Messages and Papers of the Presidents 1789–1897.* 10 vols. Washington, D.C.: Authority of Congress, 1898.

Roche, A. K., ed. *Even the Promise of Freedom—In the Words of Abraham Lincoln.* Englewood Cliffs, N.J.: Prentice-Hall, 1970.

Schurz, Carl. *Intimate Letters.* Edited and translated by Joseph Schafer. Madison: Wisconsin State Historical Society, 1928.

Seward, William. *Diary.* Lincoln, Ill.: Gordon and Fledman, 1930.

Stearn, Gerald W., and Albert Fried, eds. *The Essential Lincoln.* New York: Collier, 1952.

Van Doren, Carl, ed. *The Literary Works of Abraham Lincoln.* Madison: University of Wisconsin Press, 1941.

The War of the Rebellion: A Compilation of the Official Records of the Union and Confederate Armies. 127 vols. Washington, D.C.: Government Printing Office, 1880–1901.
    [Note: The voluminous Lincoln papers reprinted here and in the Naval records are not always identical with those that appear in *Collected Works* edited by Basler and others.]

Welles, Gideon. *Diary.* Edited by Howard K. Beale. 3 vols. New York: Norton, 1960.

*These pamphlets, varying in size, appeared during the Civil War. Perhaps because they were anti-administration, they often lack some traditional publishing data. Some libraries have bound eight to twelve of these together, making a single bound volume, indexed under *habeas corpus.*

SECONDARY SOURCES

Allen, W. C. *Annals of Haywood County.* Privately issued, 1935.

Alley, Felix E. *Random Thoughts and Musings of a Mountaineer.* Salisbury, N.C.: Rowan, 1941.

Anderson, Dwight G. *Abraham Lincoln: The Quest for Immortality.* New York: Knopf, 1982.

Angle, Paul M., ed. *Herndon's Life of Lincoln.* Cleveland: World, 1930.

———. *Lincoln 1854–61.* Springfield, Ill.: Abraham Lincoln Association, 1933.

Annals of the War. Philadelphia: Times, 1879.

Arnold, W. E. *A History of Methodism in Kentucky.* Herald Press, 1935.

Arthur, John P. *Western North Carolina—A History.* Raleigh: Edwards, 1914.

Baker, Jean H. *Mary Todd Lincoln.* New York: Norton, 1987.

Ballard, Colin R. *The Military Genius of Abraham Lincoln.* New York: Oxford, 1926.

Bancroft, Frederick. *The Life of William H. Seward.* New York: Harper, 1900.

Barnes, Thurlow W., ed. *Life of Thurlow Weed.* 2 vols. Boston: Houghton Mifflin, 1884.

Barringer, William E. *The Philosophy of Abraham Lincoln.* Indian Hills, Colo.: Falcon's Wing, 1959.

Barton, William E. *Abraham Lincoln and Walt Whitman.* Indianapolis: Bobbs-Merrill, 1928.

———. *The Life of Abraham Lincoln.* 2 vols. Indianapolis: Bobbs-Merrill, 1925.

———. *The Lineage of Lincoln.* Indianapolis: Bobbs-Merrill, 1929.

———. *The Paternity of Abraham Lincoln.* New York: Doran, 1920.

———. *The Soul of Abraham Lincoln.* New York: Doran, 1920.

Barzun, Jacques. *The Literary Genius of Abraham Lincoln.* Glenview, Ill.: Scori, 1960.

Basler, Roy P. *Lincoln.* New York: Grove, 1961.

———. *The Lincoln Legend.* New York: Houghton Mifflin, 1935.

————. *A Touchstone for Greatness*. Westport, Conn.: Greenwood, 1973.

Bates, David H. *Lincoln in the Telegraph Office*. New York: Century, 1907.

Bernstein, Iver. *The New York City Draft Riots*. New York: Oxford, 1990.

Beveridge, Albert J. *Abraham Lincoln, 1809–58*. 2 vols. Boston: Houghton Mifflin, 1928.

Boller, Paul F. *Presidential Campaigns*. New York: Oxford, 1984.

Borritt, Gabor S., and Adam Borritt. "Lincoln and Marfan Syndrome." In *Civil War History*. 24, no. 3 (1933).

Borritt, Gabor S., and Norman O. Forness, eds. *The Historian's Lincoln*. Urbana: University of Illinois Press, 1988.

Bowman, John S., ed. *The Civil War Day by Day*. Greenwich: Brompton, 1989.

Boyd, Lucinda. *The Sorrows of Nancy*. Richmond, 1899.

Braden, Waldo M. *Abraham Lincoln, Public Speaker*. Baton Rouge: Louisiana State University Press, 1988.

Brogan, Denis W. *Abraham Lincoln*. New York: Schocken, 1963.

Brooks, Noah. *Abraham Lincoln and the Downfall of American Slavery*. New York: Putnam's, 1894.

————. *Washington in Lincoln's Time*. New York: Century, 1895.

Browne, Francis F. *The Everyday Life of Abraham Lincoln*. New York: Thompson, 1886.

Bruce, Robert V. "Lincoln and the Riddle of Death." Paper read at the 4th Annual McMurtry Lecture at Louis A. Warren Lincoln Library and Museum, Fort Wayne, Indiana, 1981.

————. *Lincoln and the Tools of War*. Indianapolis: Bobbs-Merrill, 1940.

Butler, Benjamin F. *Autobiography*. Boston: Thayer, 1892.

Canby, Courtlandt, ed. *Lincoln and the Civil War*. New York: Braziller, 1960.

Carman, Harry J., and R. H. Luthin. *Lincoln and the Patronage*. New York: Columbia University Press, 1943.

Carpenter, Francis B. *The Inner Life of Abraham Lincoln*. Boston: Houghton Mifflin, 1867.

————. *Six Months at the White House.* New York: Hurd, 1866.

Cathey, James H. *The Genesis of Lincoln.* Atlanta: Franklin, 1899.

Catton, Bruce. *Bruce Catton's Civil War.* New York: Fairfax, 1984.

Charnwood, Lord (Godfrey R. Benson). *Abraham Lincoln.* New York: Holt, 1916.

Chase, Salmon P. *Inside Lincoln's Cabinet.* Edited by David Donald. New York: Longman's, 1954.

Clark, Elmer T. *Journals and Letters of Francis Asbury.* 3 vols. Nashville: Abingdon, 1975.

Clark, L. Pierce. *Lincoln: A Psycho-biography.* New York: Scribner's, 1933.

Coggins, James C. *Abraham Lincoln, A North Carolinian.* Asheville: Cook, 1917.

————. *The Eugenics of Abraham Lincoln.* Elizabethtown, Tenn.: Goodwill, 1940.

Coleman, J. Winston. "A Preacher and a Shrine." *Lincoln Herald* 47, no. 4 (1944).

Coleman, William M. *The Evidence That Abraham Lincoln Was Not Born in Lawful Wedlock.* Dallas, 1899.

Current, Richard N. *The Lincoln Nobody Knows.* New York: McGraw, 1958.

————. *Speaking of Abraham Lincoln.* Urbana: University of Illinois Press, 1983.

Curtis, Francis. *The Republican Party, 1854–1904.* New York: Putnam's, 1940.

Curtis, William E. *The True Abraham Lincoln.* Philadelphia: Lippincott, 1903.

Davis, Cullom, and others, eds. *The Public and the Private Lincoln.* Carbondale: Southern Illinois University Press, 1979.

Davis, Michael. *The Image of the South.* Knoxville: University of Tennessee Press, 1971.

Decision of Chief Justice Taney in the Merryman Case. Philadelphia: Campbell, 1862.

Donald, David, gen. ed. *Divided We Fought.* New York: Macmillan, 1952.

————, gen. ed. *Inside Lincoln's Cabinet.* New York: Longman's, 1954.

———. *Lincoln Reconsidered.* New York: Knopf, 1956.

Duff, John J. *Abraham Lincoln, Prairie Lawyer.* New York: Holt, 1960.

Dumond, Dwight L., comp. *Southern Editorials on Secession.* New York: Century, 1931.

Eisenschmiel, Otto, and Ralph Newman. *The Civil War.* Indianapolis: Bobbs-Merrill, 1947.

———. *In the Shadow of Lincoln's Death.* New York: Funk, 1940.

Eliot, Alexander. *Abraham Lincoln.* London: Bison, 1985.

Fehrenbacher, Don E. *The Leadership of Abraham Lincoln.* New York: Wiley, 1970.

———. *Lincoln in Text and Context.* Stanford: Stanford University Press, 1967.

———. *Prelude to Greatness.* Stanford: Stanford University Press, 1962.

Flower, Frank A. *Edwin McMasters Stanton.* 2 vols. New York: Wilson, 1899.

Foner, Eric. *Free Soil, Free Labor, Free Men.* New York: Oxford, 1970.

Foote, Shelby. *The Civil War.* 3 vols. New York: Random, 1958.

Forgie, George B. *Patricide in the House Divided.* New York: Norton, 1979.

Fox, Gustavus V. *Confidential Correspondence.* 2 vols. New York: Privately issued, 1981.

Frank, John P. *Lincoln As a Lawyer.* Urbana: University of Illinois Press, 1961.

Hamilton, Charles, and Lloyd Ostendorf, eds. *Lincoln in Photographs.* Norman: University of Oklahoma Press, 1963.

Hamlin, Charles E. *Life and Times of Hannibal Hamlin.* Cambridge: Riverside, 1899.

Handlin, Oscar, and Lilian Handlin. *Abraham Lincoln and the Union.* Boston: Little, Brown, 1980.

Harper, Robert S. *Lincoln and the Press.* New York: McGraw-Hill, 1951.

Headley, J. T. *Pen and Pencil Sketches of the Great Riot.* New York: Treat, 1882.

Hertz, Emanuel. *Abraham Lincoln: A New Portrait*. 2 vols. New York: Liveright, 1931.

————. *The Hidden Lincoln*. New York: Viking, 1928.

————, ed. *Lincoln Talks*. New York: Viking, 1939.

Hill, Frederick T. *Lincoln the Lawyer*. New York: Century, 1906.

History of Warrick, Perry and Spencer Counties, Indiana. Chicago: Goodspeed, 1885.

Hitchcock, Caroline Hanks. *Nancy Hanks*. New York: Doubleday, 1899.

Horner, Harlan H. *Lincoln and Greeley*. Urbana: University of Illinois Press, 1953.

Holland, Josiah G. *Life of Abraham Lincoln*. Springfield, Mass.: Bill, 1866.

Holzer, Harold, and others. *The Lincoln Image*. New York: Scribner's, 1984.

Houser, Martin L. *Lincoln's Education*. New York: Bookman, 1957.

Howe, M. A. de Wolfe. *Life and Letters of George Bancroft*. New York: Scribner's, 1908.

Howell, William Dean. *Life of Abraham Lincoln*. Bloomington: Indiana University Press, 1960.

Hyman, Harold M. *The Impact of the Civil War*. New York: Knopf, 1973.

The Image of War. 5 vols. New York: Doubleday, 1981–83.

Jefferson, Thomas. *The Writings of Thomas Jefferson*. Edited by Andrew A. Lipscomb, and Albert E. Bergh. 20 vols. Washington, D.C.: Jefferson Memorial Association, 1904.

Jennison, Keith W. *The Humorous Mr. Lincoln*. New York: Crowell, 1963.

Johannsen, Robert W. *Stephen A. Douglas*. New York: Oxford, 1973.

Kane, Joseph. *Facts About the Presidents*. New York: Wilson, 1988.

Kimmel, Stanley P. *Mr. Lincoln's Washington*. New York: Coward-McCann, 1957.

King, Willard L. *Lincoln's Manager, David Davis*. Cambridge: Harvard University Press, 1960.

Kirkland, Edward C. *The Peacemakers of 1864*. New York: Macmillan, 1927.

Kranz, Henry L. *Abraham Lincoln.* New York: Putnam's, 1959.

Kunhardt, Dorothy M. *Twenty Days.* New York: Castle, 1965.

Lamon, Ward H. *The Life of Abraham Lincoln.* Boston: Osgood, 1872.

Lanier, Robert S. managing ed. *The Photographic History of the Civil War.* 10 vols. New York: Review of Reviews, 1912.

Leech, Margaret. *Reveille in Washington.* New York: Harper, 1941.

Life of Abraham Lincoln. Chicago: Press and Tribune, 1860.

Life of Abraham Lincoln. New York: Tribune Tract #60, 1860.

Lorant, Stefan. *The Glorious Burden.* New York: Harper, 1968.

———. *Life of Abraham Lincoln.* New York: Harper, 1952.

———. *Lincoln: A Picture Story of His Life.* New York: Harper, 1952.

———. *The Presidency.* New York: Macmillan, 1951.

Lossing, Benjamin J. *Lossing's Pictorial Field Guide to the Great Civil War.* Boston: Nagle, 1889.

———. *Pictorial Field Guide to the Civil War.* Hartford: Belknap, n.d.

Ludwig, Emil. *Lincoln.* New York: Little, Brown, 1929.

Luthin, Reinhard H. *The First Lincoln Campaign.* Gloucester: Smith, 1964.

———. *The Real Abraham Lincoln.* Englewood Cliffs, N.J.: Prentice-Hall, 1960.

McChord, W. C. 1909 letter to Ben Johnson. Springfield, Ky.: Sun, March 1934.

McClure, Alexander K. *Lincoln As a Politician.* Putnam, Conn.: Tracy, 1916.

McHenry, Robert, ed. *Webster's Military Biographies.* New York: Dover, 1978.

McMurtry, Gerald R. "My Lifelong Pursuit of Abraham Lincoln." Fort Wayne, Ind.: Warren Library, 1971. Booklet.

McPherson, James M. *Battle Cry of Freedom.* New York: Oxford, 1988.

———. "Lincoln and the Strategy of Unconditional Surrender." Fortenbaugh Lecture, Gettysburg College, 1984. Booklet.

Miers, Earl S. *The American Civil War.* New York: Golden, 1961.

Minor, Charles L. C. *The Real Lincoln*. Richmond: Waddey, 1901.

Mitgang, Herbert. *Lincoln As They Saw Him*. New York: Rinehart, 1956.

Neely, Mark E. *The Abraham Lincoln Encyclopedia*. New York: McGraw-Hill, 1982.

———. *The Fate of Liberty*. New York: Oxford, 1991.

Nevins, Allan. *The Emergence of Lincoln*. 2 vols. New York: Scribner's, 1950, 1954.

———. *Ordeal of the Union*. 2 vols. New York: Scribner's, 1947.

———. *The War for the Union*. 2 vols. New York: Scribner's, 1959.

Nichols, S. S. *Martial Law*. Philadelphia: Campbell, 1862.

Nicolay, John G., and John Hay. *Abraham Lincoln, A History*. 10 vols. New York: Century, 1890.

Oates, Stephen. *Abraham Lincoln: The Man Behind the Myths*. New York: Harper, 1984.

———. *With Malice Toward None*. New York: Harper, 1977.

Paludin, Phillip S. *A Covenant with Death*. Urbana: University of Illinois Press, 1975.

Parker, Joel. *Habeas Corpus and Martial Law*. Philadelphia: Campbell, 1862.

Perkins, Howard C., ed. *Northern Editorials on Secession*. 2 vols. New York: Appleton, 1942.

Phillips, Christopher. *Damned Yankee—Life of Nathanael Lyon*. Columbia: University of Missouri Press, 1990.

Plowden, David, ed. *Lincoln and His America*. New York: Viking, 1970.

Pratt, Harry E. *Abraham Lincoln Chronology*. Springfield: Illinois State Historical Library, 1953.

Pratt, Harry E. *The Personal Finances of Abraham Lincoln*. Springfield: Abraham Lincoln Association, 1943.

Randall, James G. *Constitutional Problems Under Lincoln*. New York: Appleton, 1926.

———. *Lincoln, the Liberal Statesman*. New York: Dodd, 1947.

———. *Lincoln, the President*. 4 vols. New York: Dodd, 1945–55.

Rankin, Henry B. *Intimate Character Sketches of Abraham Lincoln*. Philadelphia: Lippincott, 1924.

Rice, Allen T. *Reminiscences of Abraham Lincoln by Distinguished Men of His Time.* 5th ed. New York: North American Review, 1888.

Riddle, Donald W. *Congressman Abraham Lincoln.* Urbana: University of Illinois Press, 1957.

————. *Lincoln Runs for Congress.* New Brunswick, N.J.: Rutgers University Press, 1948.

Ross, Ishbel. *The President's Wife.* New York: Putnam's, 1973.

Rossiter, Clinton. *The American Presidency.* New York: Harcourt, 1956.

Sandburg, Carl. *The Prairie Years.* 2 vols. New York: Harcourt, 1926.

————. *The War Years.* 4 vols. New York: Harcourt, 1939.

Schurz, Carl. *Abraham Lincoln.* 2 vols. Boston: Houghton Mifflin, 1891.

Schwartz, Bernard. *The Reins of Power.* New York: Hill and Wang, 1963.

Scripps, John W. *Life of Abraham Lincoln.* New York: New York *Tribune,* 1860.

Seale, William. *The President's House.* 2 vols. Washington, D.C.: White House Historical Association, 1986.

Searcher, Victor. *Lincoln Today.* New York: Yoseloff, 1969.

Semmes, Raphael. *Memoirs of Service Afloat.* Secaucus, N.Y.: Blue and Gray, 1987.

Shackleford, George C. *George Wythe Randolph and the Confederate Elite.* Athens: University of Georgia Press, 1988.

Shaw, Archer H. *The Lincoln Encyclopedia.* New York: Macmillan, 1950.

Shannon, Fred A. *The Organization and Administration of the Union Army, 1861–65.* Cleveland: Clark, 1928.

Short, Roy H. *Methodism in Kentucky.* Rutland, Vt.: Academy, 1964.

Shutes, Milton. *Lincoln and the Doctors.* New York: Pioneer, 1933.

————. *Lincoln's Emotional Life.* Philadelphia: Dorrance, 1957.

Simon, John Y. "House Divided: Lincoln and His Father." Paper read at the 10th Annual McMurtry Lecture at the Louis A. Warren Lincoln Library and Museum, 1987.

Stampp, Kenneth M. *America in 1857.* New York: Oxford, 1990.

Starr, John W. *Lincoln and the Railroads.* New York: Dodd, 1927.

Stephens, Alexander H. *Constitutional View of the Late War Between the States.* 2 vols. Philadelphia: National, 1868–70.

Stephenson, Nathaniel W. *Lincoln.* Indianapolis: Bobbs-Merrill, 1922.

Strode, Hudson. *Jefferson Davis.* 3 vols. New York: Harcourt, 1955.

Strozier, Charles B. *Lincoln's Quest for Union.* New York: Basic Books, 1982.

Suppinger, Joseph. *The Intimate Lincoln.* Lanham, Md.: University Press of America, n.d.

Swandberg, W. A. *First Blood: The Story of Fort Sumter.* New York: Scribner's, 1957.

Swisher, Carl B. *The Taney Period.* New York: Macmillan, 1974.

Tarbell, Ida M. *The Life of Abraham Lincoln.* 4 vols. New York: McClure, 1885–89.

Temple, Wayne. *Lincoln, the Railsplitter.* La Crosse, Wis.: Willow, 1961.

Thayer, William R. *Life and Letters of John Hay.* 2 vols. Boston: Houghton Mifflin, 1915.

Thomas, Benjamin P. *Abraham Lincoln.* New York: Knopf, 1952.

Thomas, Benjamin, and Harold P. Hyman. *Stanton: The Life and Times of Lincoln's Secretary of War.* New York: Knopf, 1962.

Turner, Justin. *Mary Todd Lincoln.* New York: Knopf, 1972.

Tyrner-Tyrnauer, A. R. *Lincoln and the Emperors.* New York: Harcourt, 1962.

Ulrich, Bartow A. *Abraham Lincoln and Constitutional Government.* Chicago: Legal News, 1916.

U.S. National Park Service. *Abraham Lincoln.* Washington, D.C.: Government Printing Office, n.d.

Van Deusen, Glyndon. *William Henry Seward.* New York: Oxford, 1967.

Ward, Geoffrey C.; Burns, Ric; and Ken Burns. *The Civil War.* New York: Knopf, 1990.

Warren, Louis A. *Lincoln's Youth: Indiana Years, Seven to Twenty-one, 1816–30.* New York: Appleton-Century, 1959.

————. *Lincoln's Youth, Indiana Years.* Indianapolis: Indiana Historical Society, 1959.

Webb, Willard. *Crucial Moments of the Civil War.* New York: Bonanza, 1941.

Weems, Mason. *A History of the Life and Death, Virtues and Exploits of Gen. George Washington.* Edited by Mark Van Doren. Macy-Masius, 1927.

Wheeler, Richard. *Voices of the Civil War.* New York: Crowell, 1976.

Whiting, William. *Military Arrests in Time of War.* Washington, D.C.: Government Printing Office, 1863.

Whitney, Henry C. *Life on the Circuit with Lincoln.* Boston: Estes, 1892.

Williams, Kenneth P. *Lincoln Finds a General.* 2 vols. New York: Macmillan, 1949.

Williams, T. Harry. *Lincoln and His Generals.* New York: Knopf, 1952.

————. *Lincoln and the Radicals.* Madison: University of Wisconsin Press, 1941.

Woldman, Albert A. *Lawyer Lincoln.* New York: Houghton Mifflin, 1936.

Wright, John S. *Lincoln and the Politics of Slavery.* Reno: University of Nevada Press, 1970.

Zoronow, William. *Lincoln and the Party Divided.* Norman: University of Oklahoma Press, 1954.

INDEX

■

Illustrations listed in **boldface**